Michael Dickson is an entrepreneur who set up and ran a retail chain in the 80s. In 1990 he established and became a founding director of the children's charity Whizz-Kidz, which is now a major force in the supply of mobility aids to disabled children. As such, Whizz-Kidz co-operates with a wide variety of specialist disability charities, such as The Muscular Dystrophy Group and Spinal Injuries Association.

PROPERTY OF:

**COMPASSION IN WORLD FARMING
INFORMATION LIBRARY**

PETERSFIELD GU32 3EH

PLEASE BOOK OUT BEFORE BORROWING

WHICH CHARITY?

Michael Dickson

WARNER BOOKS

A *Warner* Book

First published in Great Britain by Warner Books in 1996

Copyright © 1996 The Marketing Department

The moral right of the author has been asserted.

All rights reserved.
No part of this publication may be reproduced, stored in a retrieval system, or transmitted, in any form or by any means, without the prior permission in writing of the publisher, nor be otherwise circulated in any form of binding or cover other than that in which it is published and without a similar condition including this condition being imposed on the subsequent purchaser.

A CIP catalogue record for this book is available from the British Library.

ISBN 0 7515 1413 6

Typeset in Perpetua by M Rules
Printed and bound in Great Britain by Clays Ltd, St Ives plc

UK companies, institutions and other organisations wishing to make bulk purchases of this or any other book published by Little, Brown should contact their local bookshop or the special sales department at the address below. Tel 0171 911 8000. Fax 0171 911 8100.

Warner Books
A Division of
Little, Brown and Company (UK)
Brettenham House
Lancaster Place
London WC2E 7EN

'It is the little things we do each day that shape our lives.'

Dedicated to everyone who gives what they can, when they can, to others less fortunate without any thought of personal gain. They already know that, by giving, they enormously enrich their own lives. May their example encourage others to do the same.

ACKNOWLEDGEMENTS

I would like to acknowledge the help of numerous people from every area of the charity business who supported the aims of this book and provided encouragement, contacts and wise advice.

Contents

1	INTRODUCTION: Britain's second biggest industry	1
2	FINANCES: how the money comes and goes	13
3	THE NATIONAL LOTTERY: friend or foe?	28
4	VOLUNTEERING: a commitment through choice	35
5	TRUSTEES: the role and responsibilities	50
6	FUNDRAISING: a conflict in expectations	59
7	INSPIRATIONAL STORIES AND QUOTES: from founders, volunteers, workers and beneficiaries	76
8	Tax-efficient ways of giving	135
9	Useful organisations	138
10	Charity profiles	145
11	Charities mentioned in the editorial	347
12	Index of Charities	354

1
INTRODUCTION: BRITAIN'S SECOND BIGGEST INDUSTRY

Where are today's visionaries and entrepreneurs? Quite possibly working for charities, now Britain's second largest industry after manufacturing, one of the few areas which grew during the recession. Created by ordinary people, governed by volunteers, employing six times as many as major manufacturing companies, they are growing apace. The 'not-for-profit' sector is a unique part of our national heritage, and when we look at the energy and commitment involved, and the advances that charities have made – breaking new ground which others follow – we can be justifiably proud of what we, the people of Britain, have created.

In the beginning

Five years ago, I started a charity. It wasn't something I'd planned but a series of events which seemed to happen to me. As I put *Which Charity?* together, I discovered that what I believed to be unusual is commonplace when people become involved in helping others. Somehow, life takes on a momentum of its own.

Having become involved, I then realised how misinformed I'd

been in the past and how difficult it is for the average person to get straightforward information to help find out about how charities work. Particularly if the wish is to fundraise or volunteer. Every charity will send information to encourage you, but how do you know you're supporting a genuine, well-run cause? How can you find smaller charities who desperately need your support, but can't afford to publicise themselves?

Which Charity? is a compilation of charities, explaining how they work, with first-hand experiences from people who've been involved at all sorts of levels. It's been written to inspire as well as inform! It's about people who've seen an injustice and decided to put it right, or been prompted to do something to help someone less fortunate. It's about people who never give up and never take 'No' for an answer, and others who know they can do something to make a difference, and do it. It's the story of what one person can do, and the importance of the little things in life. It illustrates how, when people step out to volunteer, they nearly always get back more than they give.

I have been amazed by the number of well-known charities that were started in a small way by one person. Some are legendary: Chad Varah of the Samaritans, William Booth of The Salvation Army, Eglantyne Jebb of Save the Children, Dr Barnardo of Barnardo's; all of them great entrepreneurs and visionaries. Other charities have been set up by groups of parents determined to get a better deal for those they care for, or by members of a community wishing to improve local services.

Charities change lives

Lives change in totally unexpected ways. It doesn't matter whether you're a volunteer, someone who needs help, or employed by a charity. It's the involvement that counts. We've talked to hundreds of people and, in doing so, a clear pattern emerges.

INTRODUCTION

- Ordinary people who go out of their way to help a cause often find their lives take off in quite extraordinarily fulfilling and unimagined directions.

- Tragedy may be the catalyst, but out of life-shattering disasters great good emerges.

- Seeds sown often take many years to germinate. It's only by looking back that we can see how often something that happened years before was the real motivating factor.

- Where there's a will there is a way. Charities are the very spirit of entrepreneurialism. They reflect our determination to put people before doctrines and budgets. They experiment when the system doesn't allow for experimentation. They challenge accepted truths until a better way can be found. They show what can be achieved against all the odds and place small acts of kindness where they should be: at the very centre of our lives. Most of all they are generous in helping people to help themselves.

- Without them, this country would be a poorer place. They enrich us in an enormous variety of ways – even though many of us don't quite understand the breadth and depth of their impact.

Charity Facts

- **Britain has more charities per head than anywhere else in the world: 178,609 in 1994.**

- **Of these, only 37,500 have an income of over £10,000 a year.**

- **After manufacturing, charities represent the second largest 'industry' in the UK, generating an estimated £12.8 billion a year.**

- **New charities registered currently average 22 a day: 8,000 a year.**

- **Charities are run by governing trustees, who are accountable to the Charity Commissioners.**

The first charity to be founded that still exists today was established by Royal Charter in 1282: to maintain and support London Bridge, Blackfriars Bridge, Southwark and Tower Bridges and towards the provision of transport and access to it for elderly or disabled people in the Greater London area. London Bridge is now somewhere in the USA, but Bridge House Estates is still active!

Britain has more charities per head than anywhere else in the world – 178,609 at the last count. As an industry the voluntary sector is second only to manufacturing . . . and growing faster. We have charities which are so much the fabric of everyday life that we don't even think of them as charities. Disused buildings have been converted into community centres, redundant train tracks into cycle paths, telephone helplines set up, information provided . . . where a need has been seen, people have leapt at the opportunity to fill it. And as voluntary organisations are being asked to do more and more – particularly in the field of support and care – they need to be seen to do it properly, and are becoming increasingly professional and accountable.

Charities in England and Wales are regulated by the Charity Commissioners. Anyone thinking of starting a charity should make them their first port of call. All charities with an income over £1,000 a year are required to register with the Commissioners (unless operating from the Channel Islands, the Isle of Man, Scotland or Northern Ireland where local registration bodies exist), although some organisations are exempt and some which are not registered charities are treated as such by the Inland Revenue. Numbers are increasing. An additional 8,000-plus are expected to register every year for the next few years – which inevitably leads to a much more competitive environment. In addition to charities there are an estimated 300,000 voluntary organisations – it's often the way organisations start, becoming charities as they become more established.

There's much debate about charities picking up work which should rightly be a statutory responsibility, and there's no doubt they do. But whilst there's a need, charities will act to try to ensure it is met, and to develop a level of knowledge on the subject to use as ammunition to lobby the Government of the day.

The advantages of being a charity

To be a charity you have to have charitable aims: broadly speaking, the relief of the poor, handicapped and aged; the advancement of education, religion or other purpose 'beneficial to the community'.

You can't set up a charity to benefit specific individuals; for those who used to work for you, or friends who are down on their luck! The public – or at least a reasonable section of them – have to be seen to benefit. Having said this, some older established charities are so specific in their aims (quite often defined by a very limited geographic area) that they find it difficult to find enough suitable people to give their money to.

You can't set up a charity for political ends or to spread propaganda. So whilst political parties are non-profit-making organisations, they can never be charities. Neither can Amnesty International or Greenpeace.

The advantages that come with charitable status include no tax on 'profits' and relief on a proportion of property rates. Registered charities also find it easier to get funds from grant-making trusts and local government and can claim tax back on some donations from the public. Companies get tax breaks on charitable donations and since most people know charities are monitored there's more confidence in an organisation which is a registered charity.

One of the most common reasons for contacting the Charity Commissioners is to establish that a charity is genuine, or that a fundraiser is acting with a particular charity's authority. The Charity Commissioners are happy to take your call. They estimate that in 1994 their intervention saved the public from being defrauded of some £21.5 million.

How charities are organised and what they do

Charities are as diverse as any field of business. The vast majority are tiny. Whilst the top six per cent raise 98 per cent of the total income, four out of every five have an income of less than £10,000 a year.

The big are expanding at the expense of the small. Between 1993 and 1994 the major charities (the 11,000 which raise nearly all the money) saw their income grow by an average 13 per cent. Over the same period eight out of ten showed no change or a decrease in income.

There is, however, an enormous role for the smaller charities. We tend to think of many charities as national organisations, when they are often registered as hundreds of small, totally independent regional charities, under a campaigning, co-ordinating HQ. **MENCAP, Riding for the Disabled** and **The Abbeyfield Society** are three examples of groups of regional charities that, despite well-known national names, consist of hundreds of independent local entities entirely dependent on local fundraising efforts for their income. The head office role is in part to encourage, set policy and standards and advise – but not necessarily to fundraise for local projects.

INTRODUCTION

Tools for Self Reliance is a small, overseas-aid charity set up by a group of volunteers who'd spent time working on a variety of different overseas projects with major charities. They recognised the value of large programmes but also saw that there is another way. They now refurbish and supply tools – from sewing machines to saws and hammers – because they recognise that basic implements can make a huge difference at local level, even changing the economy of a village.

Local charities often develop a deep understanding of their community, so they can make progress with more sensitivity than their national counterparts. They know the social workers and the social fabric of the area in a way no outside organisation can.

Charities may be set up as trusts, limited companies, associations or societies. Some give money away, some fundraise for others. All will operate to a governing document approved by the Charity Commissioners which sets out what they aim to do. The governing document can be – and quite often is – changed to meet needs as they develop over the years. All will be governed by unpaid volunteers, the charity trustees.

In 1962/63 the Charity Commissioners' actuaries said there would be a declining need for the service we offered, so we stopped fundraising. In fact our constitution has changed at various stages and fundraising is now definitely needed again.

Originally, we were to help servicemen who were blinded serving the country in war. Our constitution has been amended over the years to include women, then service personnel in peacetime, then other services including police, fire and ambulance.

St Dunstan's

Charities in the 1990s

The word charity smacks of paternalism and patronage. Voluntary organisation is better. A voluntary organisation is people coming together to work for a cause, to alleviate problems. They're a strength because they allow the spontaneity to come together and create; they allow people to identify and do; they provide direct action.

National Autistic Society

We can be flexible, fill gaps, create new models of working, test them and hopefully influence Government policy. The Government is caught in a cycle which makes it very hard to work on a small scale and then go bigger.

What we do we do well and better than others. We do things that other organisations don't do. There's very good co-operation in this area. We look at who's addressing what and make sure we let everyone build on their area of expertise. When smaller organisations start operating, they benefit enormously from the infrastructure we've already set up.

Oxfam

It wasn't so very long ago that charities were regarded with some justification as organisations run by well-intentioned amateurs. Whilst a little of this attitude may linger, successful charities today are run very much as businesses – with the added advantage of volunteers to help them on their way.

I've been involved for over 15 years, first as a volunteer then as a member of the paid team.

Society's views have changed as people realised charity work is about the only sector not in recession, and service industries have started to look to charities for good business – direct mail, PR and publicity fits in with the changing attitude of people towards charity. It was a heinous crime to be paid, now it's widely acknowledged that in order to get the right quality of administrators charities need to at least approach the market rates of pay.

Now as a nation we must readdress what we really want – we expect charities to run as successful businesses, to keep to employment law, not to steer clear of convention. There are benefits; they are tax free and people might work for them for nothing. Charities have always acted in a very democratic and professional way, but are different because of the balance of commercial aspects with the attitudes of carers. Charity care has time and gives time. In the commercial part there is never enough time and we have to learn to say no. From the care side our commitment is open-ended, there is always more we can do.

Acorn Children's Hospice

Aren't there too many charities?

From the public's point of view the answer has to be 'yes'. We face a confusing array of causes and often several different charities working for what appears to be the same cause. More and more hospitals are becoming trusts with charitable status, as are schools. But at the same time the challenges charities face are on the increase rather than fading away. It's true to say, with only a few notable exceptions, today's charities could make use of funds far in excess of those they have. Despite the advances of technology and medicine, there are as many vulnerable people as there ever were, and today we recognise needs which we may have been unaware of before. *Overall demand is far greater than charities can meet, and expanding rapidly.*

Despite the ongoing debate about the role of charities, with most people believing it's the Government's responsibility to provide certain levels of care, charities continue to tackle problems which others only talk about.

Homelessness is just one example of a problem that hasn't gone away. Between 1904 and 1921, homelessness in London reduced from an estimated 2,000-plus to 76. In 1991, The Salvation Army estimated London was back to the 1904 total – over 2,000 men and women sleeping rough on the streets.

WHICH CHARITY?

I suppose amongst the problems of a great city there will always be a fresh daily crop of unfortunates, who for one reason or another find themselves homeless, destitute and friendless. But . . . it required years of agitation in public and private to bring into existence the machinery necessary to reduce this blot to a reasonable minimum with a hope of its complete elimination.

I venture to predict that London will never see a return of its homeless poor to be huddled in doorways, stairways and arches, in the cold, bleak, miserable weather, with the biting, cutting winds which mark our English winters. The next generation will never know what London knew 50 years ago.

The Salvation Army, 1921

Local homelessness problems are severe, but fairly unseen. There are no cardboard cities as in London, yet we can only house 35 per cent of the applicants we see. With salary costs of £1,800 a month, revenue is vital. Unfortunately, the vast majority of charitable trusts and organisations prefer to donate towards a specific capital item. You can only purchase so many capital items. The trusts are in general only keen to support once or possibly twice and expect you to increase Governmental support. The problem with that theory is that the relevant agencies are themselves keen to cut back their grants.

HYPED (Homeless Young People in Eastern Dorset)

All too often we have to rely on charities to get to the root cause of problems which seem too large and politically difficult to handle. It is estimated that a third of today's homeless are mentally ill and 35 to 40 per cent of the prison population are dyslexic against a national incidence of 6 to 10 per cent. These enormous injustices reflect wasted lives at a huge cost to the nation.

The cancer charities are always being asked why they don't link up, but some deal with care whilst others are primarily carrying out research, and they know that they attract more money into the sector by being in competition.

INTRODUCTION

You might be forgiven for thinking that medical advances have wiped out or reduced problems. However, it seems – even without the advent of new diseases such as AIDS – that no sooner has a cure been found for one disease than something else takes its place. More premature babies are surviving than ever before, but often blind and with multiple handicaps. Problems of dislocated families and an alienated society take their toll on the old, the young and the vulnerable.

Overseas, the story is repeated. Charities which were primarily development organisations are now ever more frequently having to divert their resources to help out in areas of conflict. Where society totally breaks down, development projects inevitably get postponed.

> *The world was defined by the Cold War. Now it is defined by strategic interest, which is more dangerous. Western interests have become totally disengaged from parts of the world, and emergencies are becoming more and more complex . . . civil strife, mass movements of people, famine . . . through lack of cash education collapses, health collapses, there are huge power plays in government with very weak accountability to the electorate. It seems an absolute crime that UN governments did nothing to prevent the genocide in Rwanda.*
>
> *But we have only one planet. We can't ignore whole areas of it. What happened in Rwanda could well happen in Burundi, yet nothing is done.*
>
> ***Oxfam***

However, there's much to encourage us. Charities focus on individuals. They may be idealistic, but this helps set standards in care. They often develop an enormous knowledge about a particular subject which they can use to influence and change Government policy. Some work as global networks passing information effectively round the world. (For instance, British projects for **Save the Children** have benefited from knowledge gained from projects in the Third World.)

Many smaller charities are worried by increasing competition; some are already suffering and not all will survive. Those that do will carry on because of the extraordinary energy and dedication of the band of people who run them. It is the people who make charities different. As the founder of **Voluntary Service Overseas**, Alec Dickson, said:

> *Even today, the ultimate step, the final thing that counts, is not what the great national or global organisations do – but the individual act and personal courage of a single volunteer.*

2
FINANCES: HOW THE MONEY COMES AND GOES

Financial Facts

- Charities rely on a wide variety of sources of income. Some never appeal to the public for funds. Individuals donate an estimated 18 per cent of charity income.

- Low overheads don't necessarily mean an efficiently run charity. Overheads levels vary according to size, aims and the service provided.

- The Charity Commissioners recommend reserves be kept at a level which can keep the charity running for between three months and two years, should income dry up.

- 'National' charities are often groups of independent and separately registered charities, with completely separate incomes.

WHERE DOES THE MONEY COME FROM?

Charities we've heard about will almost certainly raise some of their money from the public, but this is by no means the norm. Public fundraising is expensive, and everyone knows some causes capture the imagination far more than others. A Charities' Aid Foundation survey showed that whilst only one person in 60 gives to the arts, one person in four supports medical charities, with support for other categories slotting in between.

So where do charities get their money from?

Almost Invisible Sources

Grant-giving trusts, such as the Joseph Rowntree Foundation, and not forgetting the National Lottery Charities Board, exist to give money away. The vast majority have specific criteria regarding the type of work they will support. They have often been established by wealthy individuals or companies and don't raise money from the public. With the growth in charities registered, the requests that land on their desks are on the increase and they are having to become ever more selective. This is a source of money under pressure!

The Government. Charities can apply to the Government for help with research, overheads and projects. Another source of funds under pressure . . .

Local Authority and Health Authority Fees pay for accommodation, education or medical care supplied by charities which meet recognised needs. This secures regular levels of income which can make the charities seem affluent. They are at pains to point out this is not the case! Nearly every charity operating on this basis will rely on volunteers and subsidise the quality of care provided through extra charitable funds.

On the plus side, income is relatively secure. However, additional fundraising from the public can be difficult when few have heard of you. **The Shaftesbury Society**, for example, has been providing residential care for children for many years. Its annual income is over £15 million, but 90 per cent of this is in fees paid by local authorities. Despite the amount of good work it does, their own survey shows only five people in a hundred have heard of them – which makes fundraising from the public an uphill struggle.

Overseas Development Agencies, overseas governments and the **European Union** support the work of overseas projects. The problem here is to ensure they don't fund too much, or political compromises may be inevitable.

Membership income. An association may charge fees to all its members in return for which it supplies information and advice. The **Downs Syndrome Association**, for example, is a membership association run by parents and those with Downs Syndrome who have grown up. It has 45,000 members across the age bands and relies on them for fundraising without a public profile. Provided you have enough members they are likely to be your best fundraisers. However, smaller groups, or charities helping those under severe pressure can't rely on family support for fundraising.

Investment income is often a significant source of money, but relies on the charity being able to limit its spending to the income not the capital, as well as making consistently sound investment decisions. Charities with significant investment income may find the public less eager to fundraise for them.

> *Charities should not look to the Charity Commissioners as investment experts. Trustees need to adopt a clear policy and there's*

a need for proper advice. It's surprising how often it needs to be emphasised that charities must start evolving their investment strategy by considering what the point of the charity is. Risk cannot be eliminated, but must be prudently managed.

Richard Fries, Chief Charity Commissioner

Public Fundraising

Most charities spread their fundraising efforts as wide as possible, so whilst they may raise part of their income from the less visible sources, they also actively work with the public, generating money in a variety of different ways.

Fundraising charities. Some charities, such as **Children in Need** and **The King George's Fund for Sailors**, exist purely to fundraise and redistribute the money. They carefully evaluate requests from smaller charities and try to make sure the cash is distributed to the most needy, rather than those with large reserves in the bank. The advantages of providing this sort of service are that it gives them the low overheads much beloved by the public as well as a wide range of charities they can support: children on the one hand; all seafaring charities on the other.

Products. Christmas cards, gift catalogues, training courses and T-shirts are just some of the products on offer. Such products are increasingly popular with charities which then have total control over the way the profits are spent.

Shops, selling second-hand as well as new merchandise. Along with house-to-house collections, the charity shop is one of the biggest users of volunteers.

Entry fees and memberships. Museums, for example, are able to charge entrance fees. Unfortunately, many people feel that once they've paid to get in, the museums should be able to support themselves! **The National Trust** is a hugely successful charity, where a membership of over two million makes a significant contribution to the overall income. **London Zoo** fares less well: it's such an established part of London that half of the zoo visitors still don't think of it as a charity.

Legacies. These can prove invaluable, if rather unpredictable, for well-established charities. The **RNLI** receives over half its income from this one source. All charities are particularly keen to be left the residue of an estate, knowing how investments and inflation can alter personal wealth over the last few years of life. A lifelong supporter of **The Royal Society for the Protection of Birds** left her favourite charity £7,500 (in response to an old appeal to fund the cost of a new aviary) and the residue of her estate (which was several hundreds of thousands of pounds) to **Birthright** (now Wellbeing), a charity she'd never supported during her lifetime. **Birthright** were naturally surprised and thrilled! However, legacy income is at best unpredictable, and under threat as people are expected to live longer and spend more on staying alive!

Voluntary income. This is when the public are asked to dip into their pockets. If you've heard of a charity, it will almost certainly be trying to raise money through what is known as 'voluntary income'. Charities approach businesses and schools as well as wealthy and not so wealthy individuals with ideas to encourage us to part with our cash. It's an expensive form of fundraising, and in return the public wants to make sure the money raised is being used in ways of which they approve.

How Is The Money Spent?

First, understand how and why the charity functions

Unrealistic expectations from the public cause serious headaches! So much so that some charities decide against exposing themselves to the public's gaze, because it's too difficult to explain the detail of the charity in a motivating advertisement or direct mail shot that will generate funds.

Overheads levels pose potentially the biggest dilemma. It costs money to fundraise, yet in an ideal world everyone would like all the money they give to go straight through to the cause. We tend to have unrealistic expectations. We'd be horrified if a charity's accounts were out of order, or if staff looking after vulnerable groups were not properly qualified. Yet, there's an unrealistic aspect of human nature that wants the best, provided we don't have to pay for it!

Charities that have low overheads know this appeals to the public and make the most of it, but that doesn't mean others are inefficient. It's a question of understanding how they operate.

Service providers

These charities sell the service they provide, often to statutory authorities. Charitable status allows them to attract volunteers and deliver a level of care far above that which is paid for, but when you look at the finances income seems high. Ironically, the higher the overheads the better service they may be providing. One-to-one care isn't cheap.

Trading subsidiaries

Other charities deliberately develop products. They may sell training, develop mail-order catalogues or open shops to try to ensure some level of guaranteed income year on year. All have the same advantages – shops, for example, can use volunteers, and profits aren't taxed – so making that profit is less of a risk than a normal commercial venture. All products create income which we give freely in return for whatever we've bought; which means the charities can allocate the funds as they think fit, without having to explain their actions further.

Information providers

The need for information has never been greater, but telephone helplines use up more cash as their success grows and the ethos of charities is to be there for those in need, not restrained by the budget.

We can illustrate this with just two examples. **Contact a Family** has a database of rare medical conditions and those who suffer from them. Its principal service is giving information over the phone and the more spent on this the more people the charity will help. One of its main problems is fundraising from the public, who see no instant result for their efforts.

Look is primarily a parents' organisation which exists to cut through the maze of regulations in order to assist families to obtain all the benefits and help they should have when caring for a visually impaired person. The more time spent sorting people out, the better job the charity is doing.

Overheads

Understanding overheads means understanding in depth the kind of business the charity is and how it operates. In the following example an audit was required to set everyone's minds at rest!

'Inter-Action is based on a ship in the City of London? But you're a charity. The costs must be overwhelming!'

WHICH CHARITY?

I have heard this so often that I feel like wearing a pirate's patch and reaching for my pistol and cutlass. But, alas, I have none of these things; only facts and sweet reason.

Many people have the misguided impression that charities should have no overheads. I wish they could convince landlords, gas, electricity, water and telephone companies, the Royal Mail, etc.

In Inter-Action's particular case the charity owns HMS President (1918), moored on the Thames near Blackfriars Bridge. Known as the Ship-in-the-City, the President was built as a 'Q Class' or 'Mystery' ship. Disguised as a merchant vessel to sail in convoys she would act as a decoy to lure U-boats to the surface and then attempt to sink them. The Royal Navy brought her to her current mooring in 1923, removed the engines, added an upper deck and transformed her into a training ship until she was bought by Inter-Action in 1988.

The question of reasonable overheads was the subject of a recent study (also vetted by our auditors KPMG, helping out on a very generous basis) to convince everyone once and for all we were being sensible rather than profligate. The facts were stark and clear: any likely alternative — for example a move to the least expensive space on an industrial estate in any inner London borough — would double our overheads and plunge our earning capacity to zero.

To explain the last point: Inter-Action has a wholly owned trading company which earns a third of our income every year by hiring out space for private and corporate hospitality and training. This is space on board which isn't required for our charity work.

My surprise is not that people might think that we have high overheads. My real surprise is that many more charities aren't using ships as their base, when virtually all the major cities in the world have grown up around bodies of water.

ED Berman MBE, Inter-Action Trust

FINANCES

It's amazing how overheads grow. At the outset it seems easy – a new charity can set itself up in a front room with a volunteer or two. The telephone bill will need to be paid, plus stamps, stationery, maybe a computer . . . or two. With an eye to future efficiency it's easy to see how the organisation can quickly become more complex. It's unlikely that all the people helping out will be volunteers, so the next cost is wages. Then, if you continue to expand, the front room becomes a bit cramped and offices need to be found. Even if someone has space to spare, they may expect you to pay the rates. There are not only statutory regulations, but the Charity Commissioners' code of practice to adhere to:

We are running a medium-size business. We have to abide by statutory accountancy practices, health and safety and employment laws. We provide the service we do because in addition to 120 on the payroll we have 300 volunteers. We give time – as much as the families want – and very specialist support with experts. We don't knock off at 5 o'clock on Friday. We co-ordinate what is there and then add a bit more. We evaluate whether we're doing a good job or not by listening to families, GPs and consultants. The administration we have to run to business disciplines, the delivery of care is infinitely expandable.

Acorn Children's Hospice

So, what constitutes the 'right ' level of overheads?

I'd like people to understand that small charities can't give 95p in the pound to the cause. Someone gives us a pound and 40p is used because although we only have three staff our income as a new charity is tiny. It's a dilemma for small organisations who don't have retail outlets, insurance commissions etc, generating extra cash.

We are a resource centre and we're developing knowledge and counselling services. The staff are our overheads.

Action on Elder Abuse

> *Comic Relief have the huge luxury of saying they spend nothing on admin. That every penny of income goes to the cause. No one else can do that.*
>
> **Recipient of Comic Relief Funds**

> *Often our programme is our staff. They may be dealing with 12 communities and can see tension building and try to diffuse it – the costs come in as admin. but are essential. Our philosophy is to set up projects which local people run themselves and our overall project costs are usually quite low.*
>
> **Oxfam**

The Charity Commissioners will certainly investigate charities which appear to be inefficiently run, but low overheads may be equally misleading. Understand, first, how the charity is operating and listen to the reasons for the overheads, which are often in the region of 30 to 40 per cent.

Reserves

Once a charity has established itself, there are likely to be beneficiaries who depend on the services provided, and employees who are entitled to benefits and redundancy payments, so how can anyone ensure the income keeps rolling in? There is some security in providing a service which is bought by one of the statutory authorities because you have a relatively captive market, but even these face cutbacks, and as has been pointed out most sources of funds are under pressure. To make sure the service doesn't collapse when income dives, most charities try to operate with a reasonable level of reserves.

> *On site we have 120 folk dependent on us. We are their home. If income dries up, we close down. We've been to trusts and been*

turned down because we have healthy reserves. We hold in reserve enough to keep us going for just under six months — against costs of £4 million a year.

Seeability

We are adamant we need a year's running costs in reserve. At the moment we don't have them. Yet if we were to close it would cost us £500,000. We also have a responsibility not to let the 6,000 young people in the programme down — to finish their counselling and courses would cost £1 million. We follow through and monitor progress for up to two years.

One of our Council says he wouldn't give if he saw reserves like that. So I say he's likely to support a charity that will go bust.

Fairbridge

A total lack of reserves can be very damaging. One fundraising charity, governed by trustees from the charities that take its funds, is constitutionally required to give all its money away on a very regular basis. The result is a catch-22 situation. Without cash reserves, it is dependent on short-term fundraising programmes which are cheap to set up and run. Experience shows these are one of the least efficient ways of raising money. The charity's accounts therefore show high overall costs which, in turn, deter grant-giving trusts and major companies that should be approached for support.

Reserves allow forward planning to be done with some confidence. They keep everything going should income fall; give a breathing space to refund the organisation and balance the needs of the present with the demands of the future. If a charity can't explain what its reserves are needed for, the reserves are probably too high. And whilst not everyone gets as close to closure as the Zoological Society of London, it's probably one of the best known stories of a charity that was largely reliant on the public for income, and when that income fell had to restructure completely in order to survive.

> *In the fifties and sixties there were two to three million visitors a year. The zoo was 'a good thing'; animals in captivity weren't a public concern. We also had a very influential president who was good at getting money when funds ran short.*
>
> *In the seventies and eighties the cause was less popular, there was more choice for the public, and our visitors went down to 700,000 with no funds at all available for capital investment. Eventually a buy-out was organised under the Tories. The Society was given a once-only payment of £10 million. By 1991/2 we were near closure and placed in the hands of a receiver who pushed us through a season. The Emir of Kuwait saved us by giving £1 million to keep the zoo open.*
>
> *Since then we have restructured with the emphasis on conservation, and visitors are now up to one million a year and rising. We still don't have enough for capital investment and are having to launch an appeal to repair and refurbish the aquarium. We have four or five Grade I listed buildings and more that are listed Grade II, which means repair and refurbishment can be expensive. A lot of the work we do isn't visible to visitors — breeding programmes for endangered species that have to include the cost of air flights back to the country the animals came from. Our major problem is making the public aware that we aren't just a zoo, but a conservation charity.*
>
> **Zoological Society of London**

So what is the right level of reserves? It seems to depend on faith and confidence as much as prudent financial management. The Charity Commissioners recommend three months to two years, but stress that reserves can only be justified when there are realistic future forecasts for income and expenditure, and that the reserves policy should be explained clearly in the annual report.

Hoarding cash does nothing if the charity has no vision. I arrived to find £6 million doing nothing. Now we carry two months' running expenses.

We've found since we've cut back on reserves we're being much more successful in getting money from trusts and companies.

National Autistic Society

Our reserves have been reduced. Supporters don't give you money to buy stocks and shares.

Wellbeing

Why do charities carry on fundraising when they have lots of money in the bank? Shouldn't legacies ideally be left to those that don't have these types of reserves? Our task is to create such a reserve. we now have 4,000 homes to manage each year.

MENCAP

Reserves? Small charities don't have reserves. We are struggling to survive.

Camden Housebound Link

One point the Charity Commissioners are quite clear about: charities aren't allowed to mislead you into thinking you're giving to help the cause when they are intending to build up their general reserve fund.

Which organisation is the money going to?

Age Concern seems like a huge charity, but is in fact over a thousand regional charities. Many charities we imagine to be huge national organisations are in fact hundreds of much smaller, local ones. The regional branches may get advice and information but little or no funding from their head office. In fact, quite the opposite; they often pay a subscription for the support they receive.

WHICH CHARITY?

There's a perpetual conflict between money for the Association or for the local groups. Some are registered as separate charities: all have central back-up. The new accountancy regulations (SORPS) mean that our overall income will look huge, because we will have to show all the income from each local group – and it may well be that more of the local groups will split into separate charities so they don't need to send their accounts through for consolidation. Local groups fundraise for themselves and benefit so much from local commitment and enthusiasm that each develops its own style. Our aim is to have a corporate entity with regular conference and training days . . . to maintain a structure of associations of local groups who send money into HQ.

Riding for the Disabled

Many charities were started by groups of people who'd been moved to do something to support disadvantaged people they knew. Their whole purpose was to help out at a local level. National associations developed to enable everyone to learn from each other, build national awareness for better fundraising and powerfully lobby for change.

At the same time it's quite possible for central and local organisations to be in conflict. They may have different aims and objectives. Money donated to a central charity can end up in a reserve fund rather than redistributed to a local member. The central charity may wish to distance itself financially from organisations over which it has little control. The regions may find themselves too busy to give information to head office – which ends up spending resources chasing the paperwork!

Many local charities also have far greater financial commitments than their national parent: for example, when they run schools or homes, with the capital and maintenance costs these involve.

FINANCES

SORPS 2: the new financial control system

The public are quite sceptical about how their donations will be used and, because charities often like to hide their assets rather than reveal them, and disguise their overheads should they seem to be getting beyond acceptable levels, new accountancy practices came into force from March 1996 to ensure accounts are set out in a standard way. The objective is to make reading the accounts easier. SORPS, which stands for Statement of Recommended Practice, also requires directors' salaries to be revealed.

There's obvious nervousness about this as directors of major charities earn good salaries. It's a stance they feel needs defending in view of media reports of top earnings. One of the more recent surveys shows charity chief executives receive 18 per cent less than their commercial counterparts; a gap that's widened over the past few years. Given the importance of the industry to our national wellbeing we should be grateful it still attracts such a high calibre of people.

SORPS is intended to make financial information more accessible. While no one objects in principle, small branches of national charities, which under SORPS are now required to set out their accounts in a standard format, may decide they will break away.

Before SORPS it was possible to share a charity registration and keep the money and accounts separate. Now all charities registered under the same number must include their income and expenditure in a single 'consolidated' set of accounts with the 'parent' charity.

As a result charities with a large number of regional branches will suddenly reveal a much higher income from their consolidated accounts. If the smaller charities decide to break away and operate financially independently the parent charity won't reflect any sudden rise – so we may still not be comparing like with like.

3
THE NATIONAL LOTTERY:
FRIEND OR FOE?

Lottery Facts

- **Of the money spent on the lottery approximately 28p in the pound goes to good causes. Of this, about 5½p is distributed through the National Lottery Charities Board to registered charities and voluntary organisations.**

- **Sixteen thousand charities applied for the first tranche of Lottery money, and 2,460 received grants, totalling £159 million.**

- **Small charities believe they are losing out to the Lottery, and have the evidence to prove it.**

- **Ninety per cent of adults in the UK have played the Lottery, 65 per cent play regularly.**

Our National Lottery took off from Day One. In a mere 12 months it had become the largest lottery in the world. We had spent £4.4 billion. We read about the winners and the huge amounts of cash going to good causes (£1,220 million in the first year), and we know we can't resist buying a ticket, so surely there's nothing wrong with it?

Alexandra Rose Day is a charity which fundraises for over a thousand smaller charities each year. Their survey of these charities paints a rather less rosy picture:

We've been absolutely hit. It has caused devastation. The Flag Day is down 12 per cent on the previous year – when it poured with rain. Income from the Draw is down 38 per cent and now finding it difficult to break even.

We have carried out a survey of the charities taking part in our Flag Day. About one in three have lost money. Only one of the charities in our survey had received any Lottery cash and that was for £5,000 over three years.

These are small charities, without reserves. What's more they don't have the time it may take for Lottery cash to get through.

The pound in people's pocket has gone to the Lottery or the parking meters. It's a David and Goliath battle, where the small charities are losing out. The effect the Lottery's having will not be accepted as real by the Government until many smaller charities have failed to survive. They do enormous amounts of grass-roots work. They are vital to so many people around the country and I fear for the future. For the Government to refer to charities as 'whingeing' is grossly unfair. It is a matter of survival.

Alexandra Rose Day

The reference to David and Goliath is probably inappropriate only because David looks set to lose! The bigger charities have been able to cast their fundraising nets wide enough not to be affected by the Lottery. Smaller charities, who rely much more on collecting boxes, local house-to-house collections, coffee mornings and the like have lost out.

Their tale of woe is widespread:

People feel good about buying a ticket because charities will benefit, but it's not like that — we depend on disposable income from the public, and that disposable income is heading for the Lottery.
PHAB – Physically Handicapped and Able-Bodied

We're a very small charity so we don't get cash from the public. We depend on other charities that know us. We're finding they can no longer support us because their figures are down from the Lottery. And it's all very well saying Lottery cash may be coming, but if I make an application today, when will I see it? We can't wait six or nine months. The money's needed now.

Camden Housebound Link

It's not only the small charities that have been affected by the National Lottery. **Tenovus** is a cancer research and counselling charity which ran its own nationwide lottery for nearly 20 years until the bubble burst in 1995. By 1994 about 50 per cent of Tenovus's £3 million total annual income came from their lottery. It was widely regarded as a brilliant success.

In March 1995, with the launch of National Lottery scratch cards in direct competition and sold through the same retail outlets, Tenovus made the painful decision to close a large part of its lottery down, blatantly pointing the finger at the National Lottery as the reason why:

Since the launch of the National Lottery, we have lost the majority of our retail sites and seen a 25 per cent fall in sales at our few remaining outlets, and although we had taken steps to counter this the launch of the scratch cards is the final straw. We simply cannot compete against the massive prizes and advertising budgets that the National Lottery has at its disposal.

Ultimately this will result in a reduction of almost half of all income into Tenovus Charity and is a direct consequence of the overwhelming competition from the National Lottery.

Tenovus

Less than a year on, urgently needing to boost their fundraising, the Tenovus lottery is rolling again, but on a much smaller scale. They point out that despite the devastating effect on their income, medical research charities haven't received a penny of National Lottery money so far, and they're lobbying for a Research Fund to replace the Millennium Fund when it closes in six years' time.

With the arrival of the National Lottery other lotteries believe they can benefit from the fact that 'everyone's doing it'. The UK Charity Lotteries (owned by three major charities) announced plans for their first-ever TV advertising in 1996. Their lottery has been around since 1992, and is doing rather nicely, thank you.

David Seiff, Chairman of the National Lottery Charities Board, says he wants those least able to fundraise to benefit from the Lottery. The Board will be looking at the quality of the work being done rather than the brilliance of the presentation. As yet, it's an argument the small charities find hard to believe.

Everyone believed that largesse was about to be provided. Well, once you've heard about Covent Garden receiving £55 million, it seems as though a request for a few thousand must be easy to meet. Sixteen thousand applications were received for the first tranche of £40 million and the requests were for a total £2.4 billion. Although the criterion was poverty, this was liberally interpreted by those who applied.

Income from volunteers is the lowest for five years with the Lottery. It's hit regional fundraisers who organise local village events. The accountants estimate the revenue we've lost because of the Lottery at £50,000, so that's what we're applying for.

British Kidney Patients' Association

> *We need to invest in a major capital programme to update the houses in the village, all of which are occupied by poorer people. We've applied to the Lottery to make up the loss of interest on the money we'll be using from our reserve.*
>
> **Whiteley Homes**

The criterion was not so liberally interpreted by the official Lottery Assessors, who seemed particularly interested in ethnic minorities within charities – no matter where based or how small the staff numbers.

It's very easy to blame the Lottery for fundraising problems, but it's never quite that black and white:

> *There's massively growing competition. Every school, every health trust is becoming a charity. And people are cautious about spending and committing themselves to covenants.*
>
> **The Children's Society**

So, perhaps the Lottery isn't to blame. **The Zoological Society of London** (of which London Zoo is a part) hit the headlines last year with a grant of £2.2 million for a major redevelopment project. But, as their Fundraising Director points out, such a grant doesn't necessarily solve their problems. The Lottery money they've been awarded is conditional on matched giving – it can only be used if it is matched with an equal amount which the charity must raise:

> *The public think the contribution from the Lottery is greater than it is. They think once Lottery cash has been given that's it. We have received £2.2 million against a target of £28 million and it's conditional on matched giving. While it's a great start, everyone with Lottery money on this basis is out there looking for the other half. The amounts of money mean most of us are approaching the same companies and wealthy benefactors.*
>
> **Zoological Society of London**

There *are* good-news stories. Although not successful, The National Autistic Society are enthusiastic about the opportunities the Lottery has opened up.

> *We made an application to fund family support workers across the country. It doesn't neatly fall into any category, but our aim is to get one family support worker for each society. There is nowhere else we could go to get this sort of money in one go – we applied for £4 million and hope to get at least £2 million. We hope to convert this short-term grant into long-term posts. We'll help local authorities work out where their priorities lie. Local authorities aren't nearly as ignorant as they're painted, but they are short of cash. Where there is a knowledgeable professional they can make better use of resources.*
>
> **National Autistic Society. No grant received**

> *The Lottery people were incredibly professional. They cross referenced everything. They really did their homework.*
> **Kensington Tabernacle (Inner City Community Centre),**
> **grant received £1 million**

In a single day I saw two oversized cheques sitting in different charities' directors' offices. Seeing the cash in accessible form has a certain impact: one cheque was for £2.6 million and the other for £3 million. And whatever the down side, the charities admit that to receive that amount of cash in one day in one cheque – albeit conditional on raising an equal amount – is an enormous boost to the cause.

Since only about 5½p of each pound we spend on the Lottery gets through to the charities, it shouldn't come as a surprise that these same causes are feeling the pinch. And while Camelot isn't responsible for selecting the beneficiaries, the five organisations doing this work clearly have overheads which need to be met before the cash can be handed out.

The National Autistic Society managed to find a national project it could apply for to benefit all its regional societies. At the other end of the scale Age Concern branches submitted 1,400 separate applications for funds locally because there was no overall national project they could put forward. They argue it would be much more efficient to allow their head office to receive and distribute funds.

So, what's the conclusion? Fundraising is getting harder, and the National Lottery really hasn't helped at all.

The Salvation Army, now the largest provider of social welfare after the Government, does not apply to the Lottery for funds,

Gambling is wrong. We will never apply.
                                                               Salvation Army

and Christian Aid echoes this sentiment. The Lottery is, without doubt, part of the nineties culture. Charities worry that with all these 'extra' grants being made, Government grants, which are already under pressure, will be cut even further. Meanwhile the Home Office has commissioned independent research to establish the impact of the Lottery on charities as a whole – with final results being published in spring 1997. By then, many smaller charities may not be around to benefit.

4
VOLUNTEERING:
A COMMITMENT THROUGH CHOICE

Facts

- There are 23 million volunteers in the UK supported by over 300 Volunteer Bureaux.

- For many charities, volunteers make the difference between an ordinary level of support and care and an exceptional one.

- Such is the importance of volunteers that the Government launched the 'Making a Difference' campaign in 1994 specifically to encourage volunteering.

- Volunteering requires commitment, but this can be as little as a few hours a year.

We'd like to put people in touch with charities who need volunteers, and vice versa. Simple, you might think. There are notice boards in the local library; there are Volunteer Bureaux all over the country – just pop along and they'll help.

Not quite so simple. The Volunteer Bureaux themselves are often staffed by volunteers, not open at the expected times and tucked away in backstreets. They may be trying to find volunteers for over a hundred organisations at any one time and are certainly in competition with other, more specialist organisations. However, their role – the role of volunteers as a whole – is so important that the Government is doing all it can to encourage volunteering.

The 'Making a Difference' Initiative was launched by the Government in early 1994 to develop a slightly more structured approach and try to encourage volunteering across the country. Make no mistake about it, volunteers are in great demand. So if you wish to volunteer you should be able to find something which fits you to a 'T'.

If all the volunteers in the country went on holiday for a week at the same time, the whole country would grind to a halt. They are enormously important.

Methodist Homes

Volunteering isn't ageist or sexist. It can be part-time or full-time. It can use your skills or give you training. It can act as a social life, getting you out and about when you might otherwise be stuck at home. And people who volunteer to help charities are often given an enormous amount of freedom to work within the organisation – particularly where the organisation is small, or understaffed, and needs all the help it can get!

As a volunteer you are committed through choice. You may wish to volunteer because you're lonely, need the work experience, or hope for training which will be useful later. All of these are valid reasons, but organisations don't want 'do-gooders'. They want you to understand that, whatever you do or don't get paid, they will be committed to supporting you and this has a cost to themselves.

VOLUNTEERING

Sue Clements has recently been recruited as a paid member of staff to set up a Mental Health Volunteers Scheme in Ipswich, having previously been a training manager with an insurance company.

We are responsible for recruiting, training and supporting all the volunteers. We have two initial interviews and then offer a seven-week training course. If at any stage during that training you feel it's not for you, you can opt out. There's no pressure to complete. The training itself covers a great deal. It's what we call 'core-based training' and includes areas such as self-awareness and confidentiality. Once the training's over we do need commitment. If you say you're going to turn up, then you must do it. No one's forcing you, it's simply a question of responsibility. We place volunteers with four different mental health charities.

I'd say it does help unemployed people get jobs long-term. Some go on to do an NVQ in Care on a voluntary basis. They may well get to hear about jobs on the grapevine before they are advertised. They work alongside people who've been there and done it before. Having been working on this project just three months, one volunteer is already in full-time work.

Mental Health Volunteers Scheme, Ipswich

Lillian is someone who walked into a volunteering job without thinking about it, and is still there, 11 years later, working three days a week for an 'honorarium' of £50!

How did it start? I'd had a nervous breakdown and wouldn't give in to it. One day I passed the shop and saw this man struggling to put a wedding dress on a display model and I just laughed. Someone had made me laugh when I hadn't laughed for 18 months. I went in – I hadn't noticed the ad in the window for volunteers – and joined up that day.

I know what I'm doing it for, but in my heart it's my shop.

WHICH CHARITY?

Three-quarters of the shop is run by the over-seventies here for the company. It's our Oxfam family. If you're down in the dumps, have a good cry and a good laugh. When I came I cried and was told, 'If you want to cry, you cry.' I just felt someone cared and it lifted me. I love the people here. We never have enough volunteers, and we welcome young and old. As long as they can laugh and lift. Of course, once your friends know you're working they give you carrier bags. I'd say to anyone, 'Give it a try, give it a chance.' You have to be mad to work here, but it's fun! Once a year we go out on a day trip by car and spend all day laughing. Every time we pass another Oxfam shop, there's a yell, 'Oxfam', and the car stops and we all pour out and see what's going on there.

The age of the Oxfam lady is slowly dying, and though the youngsters come and love it here they can't afford to do voluntary work for long, so they're a bit like ships that pass in the night. The rest of us never leave, though the other day we went to the funeral of one of our helpers who was 91. What we want is a mix of religions and races so that we can learn from one another.

We all believe in Oxfam. It's the children I'm doing it for. Adults can understand what's going on but the children can't. Vera came after the first Ethiopian famine. Being a pensioner with no spare money to send she saw the ad in the window and felt she could help another way.

I've been here for 11 years. I say it's hard on the feet and good on the head!

Lillian Smee, Oxfam shop leader

Like Lillian, Victor became committed by doing it:

I confess I was moved to become a volunteer as much by curiosity as by any sense of social responsibility. I have lived abroad for most of my life, went to fee-paying schools and did not go through the British state school system. I wanted to see what a London state school was like.

I suppose I half expected to be shocked by nightmarish scenes of educational mayhem, but of course I wasn't. The pupils were happy and the teachers busy. And the reading ability of the children – at least the ones I saw – was better than I expected.

What do volunteers gain from the process? The satisfaction of helping someone to enjoy reading, certainly; but the contact between two people from different backgrounds who would not normally meet each other is equally important.

The children at the school I went to are just as bright and have just as much potential as anyone else I know, but I suspect – such is British society – that their expectations of what they will be able to do in later life are not as high as they might be. If we – families, teachers, volunteers – can show what is possible, perhaps raise those expectations and thereby allow people to fulfil their potential, then we would certainly have achieved something.

Victor Mallett is Deputy Features Editor at the Financial Times and one of 20 FT staff who volunteer at the Cathedral Primary School in Southwark via CSV.

Volunteers aren't free!

You may think you'll be welcomed with open arms, but this isn't always the case. No one can walk into a charity and work efficiently without someone around to tell them what to do. Working in a shop means learning how to operate the till and credit card machines. Answering the phone needs knowledge as much as a sympathetic ear. For small charities, explaining the systems and the photocopier to volunteers can be a time-consuming diversion. So, ideally, charities want people who are prepared to give some minimum time commitment on a regular basis.

Volunteers should be treated like permanent staff. They should clearly understand there is a commitment to time, and reliability is

WHICH CHARITY?

a key factor. Sometimes it's better to start in a small way, even if it is volunteering once a year to hold a tin. Volunteers can become unmanageable very easily and if they do they could and should be asked to leave. There can also be a problem of volunteers jumping on a bandwagon because it's trendy or sociably good news, but then not doing anything.

Red Cross

Yes, we need volunteers, but I am running the whole department here and if too many rang up I wouldn't be able to deal with them all, so we tend to keep a low profile.

Help the Hospices

Expenses will be paid

You should always be offered expenses, which are quite often supplemented by a lunch allowance if this is appropriate.

Volunteers should claim expenses; it prevents the skew towards ladies of a certain age or the early retired. It should be every volunteer's right to claim expenses – even if they wish later to give them back to the charity. Everyone can then afford to volunteer. It's often something they want to do for themselves. People come to us with no skills and gain confidence and after a while get a paid job.

The most successful are doing it for the rewards they get and the more discerning don't just choose upmarket, sexy projects.

Methodist Homes

We work with volunteers, give them guidelines, interview them properly and don't promise a job unless there really is one. We want daytime commitments for 'x' days and a proper job done. We offer a training course and residential weekends. It's not free to the charity. We always pay travel costs and lunch. We must get rid of

this stigma that volunteers are the amateurs versus the paid professionals. The volunteers are skilled in other areas.
National Deaf Children's Society

If you haven't volunteered before, wait to be amazed by the enormous variety of things you can do. You might still be at school or in your eighties – there will be a role for you. Many charities want the help of ordinary people, particularly when the role involves spending time and befriending. The shape of volunteering is changing with youth unemployment, gap years, student placements and work experience bringing in many younger people.

Working as a volunteer gave me the opportunity to develop my own ideas and use my determination to get them done. Five months ago I couldn't have imagined I would be up on stage in front of 600 people pretending to be Naomi Campbell modelling an exclusive Evergreen Trust T-shirt – I even enjoyed it! What could have been a frustrating time being unemployed became an opportunity which may lead to a new and exciting career.
Gina Borbas, Graduate in European Business Administration, Volunteer with Evergreen Trust

Volunteers are local people who know the families we help. They're an essential back-up to social workers who can't concentrate on one job, because at any moment a court case can take over, and then they have to disappear for weeks. Our volunteers are always there when they're needed.

The Children's Society

You may also be paid

When is a volunteer not a volunteer? If we go back to the principle that a volunteer gives a commitment through choice, many

WHICH CHARITY?

charities support that commitment by giving low wages – usually somewhere in the region of £2.50 an hour. However, the whole area is full of difficulties. No one wants to start attracting tax by earning too much. If you're unemployed you need to make sure you're free to take on another job, if a suitable one is offered.

> *Our Age Resource desks are manned by 2,000 volunteers. We want to use older people to give advice on health, diet etc, and to combat age discrimination in the workplace. It's difficult to pay them as they do in the US as it would cause grief taxwise.*
>
> **Age Concern**

> *We give low pay to full-time workers – the brisk retired. They visit people in rough areas, shop for them, read with them, act as drivers and get enormous satisfaction from it.*
>
> **Metropolitan Society for the Blind**

> *We operate a ticket scheme for people who can't get out and about. Volunteers help with transport and accompany people who are disabled or elderly. The volunteers get practical training at the start, all expenses and a free ticket to the theatre, concert or whatever – but we never have enough.*
>
> **Shape**

> *Voluntary organisations thrive on contact. We can't afford to send people off round the country, so we need people who can talk to people without running up huge expenses.*
>
> **Alexandra Rose Day**

The majority of larger charities couldn't function without their volunteers, but it's worth remembering that if you want responsibility, and arrive at the right time, some of the smaller charities will be so grateful for your help that you'll have a demanding job with responsibility before you can blink.

VOLUNTEERING

The Samaritans have 23,500 active volunteers who usually stay with them between three and five years. This means a continuous recruitment and training programme to meet an increasing need.

Three hundred thousand people turn out once a year to rattle tins and sell poppies for the **Royal British Legion**. This one event raises about £15 million – the vast majority of their annual income of £22 million.

The Abbeyfield Society is supported by over 12,000 volunteers – from the committees that set up and run the local societies to those who visit the elderly in Abbeyfield houses and organise social events and outings. Nine thousand of their own elderly residents themselves volunteer.

Community Service Volunteers is a charity whose purpose is to promote volunteering opportunities. They will accept the challenge of finding the right role for everyone who contacts them.

There's fierce competition for the right sort of volunteers

Take the retail side of charities as an example. Oxfam has 850 shops, Save the Children over 600. Many are in the same cities. Retailing is becoming increasingly competitive. And why not? Charities can take advantage of volunteers to keep the overheads low and quite often sell a range of produce not available anywhere else.

> *Our shop has a paid retail manager but is staffed by volunteers. The manager is involved at the beginning to set it up and set the standards, then moves on.*
>
> **Action for Blind People**

WHICH CHARITY?

Volunteering can be enormously rewarding. It can also lead lives in directions which were never anticipated, when the volunteer first started.

My Voluntary Associate is the first real friend I have ever had in my whole life. My parents never had time to listen to me, now I have someone who does. Thank you.

Beneficiary, New Bridge

Lesley Clarke began by volunteering in a shop with **Oxfam** and is now on their main board of trustees. Jessica Hills helped out by taking typing home when **Sense** had few helpers and no office and is now chair of their council. It is amazing how life can develop from the seemingly small initial steps we take.

I was a teacher of deaf children in London a very long time ago — in the early sixties, when there was a massive rubella epidemic in the US and Europe. Children with rubella were deaf with visual impairment, and because I wanted to find out more about deaf/blind children I was put in touch with Peggy Freeman, one of the founders of Sense. She needed someone to help her because of the flood of families getting in touch. I became her secretary, on an entirely voluntary basis in my spare time, working from home. I'd see her a couple of times a week, pick up what needed to be done, and take it home.

Later, when I had time off from teaching with my family, I took over. I did everything on my own for the next 11 years, until we finally raised enough cash in 1976 to employ someone. I went back to work and became a council member.

You have a changed perspective as a council member. It's a very different type of job. We had to hand over the actual 'doing' to other people. Through the secretary, members of the council are allocated jobs. There's such a lot to do, whether showing films, talking to politicians, it's very much an 'all together' thing.

VOLUNTEERING

What have I got out of it? A huge amount of enjoyment seeing something develop as this has developed. Recently we had a party to celebrate the 10th anniversary of one of the regions and our 40th anniversary. There were 200 children, families, staff, trustees, all together having a party. In a way the pleasure of Sense is seeing what it was and realising that we have parents, professionals, volunteers all together enjoying each other. Seeing that 'family' is enormously satisfying. Two new families turned up who hadn't even been visited yet. They'd contacted us, been invited to the party and came into this wonderful atmosphere. They were completely overcome. We have no feeling that parents are different from the professionals – we are all involved in a partnership – and want to retain that atmosphere of fun.

Now I've retired from my official job I travel all over the country talking to staff and going to the branches. Before I retired we had to have evening meetings – which meant the staff had to come in the evenings – and I think I had about 15 days out of school in addition to weekends and work in the holidays.

Yes, there have been times when we've had to make nasty decisions. Like closing a school unit because it was economically unviable. It had been a dream for many involved. And when we were in a severe financial situation – how were we going to survive? There was difficulty in handing over pet involvements to management as we grew. It seemed that men in dark suits were taking over from parents and how could they possibly know . . .? I think perhaps because I've been so involved all the time I didn't have quite such a problem.

We are now hugely professional, but it doesn't detract from the family atmosphere. It's part of the feeling of the whole organisation. I think more of our council are family members than not. We still have a vast amount to do. Recently council members have been linked with professionals and made responsible for a region. They discuss policy and plans and have a responsibility to report back. It stops the council from being a rubber-stamping group who meet every quarter and nod through what has already been done. Now they're linked in, they have become much more involved and the quality of council meetings has improved a lot.

Being involved with Sense has got me involved in other things: the Council for Advancement of Communication with Deaf People, a working party on Signed English Teaching . . . everything gives an enormous satisfaction.

Jessica Hills, Chairman of Trustees of Sense, where she became involved originally as a part-time secretarial volunteer

Expect to be vetted

When you're offering to work with any vulnerable group, expect to provide references. The Home Office guidelines suggest that checking criminal records is a less effective screening process than proper management, training and supervision. So although you've been to an interview and provided references, there may also be a probationary period.

The vast majority of people honestly want to do something to help but charities can't be too careful. They know that one story in the press can spread worry like wildfire, so it's better to play safe.

Volunteering overseas

To be a useful and vital part of an emergencies team, you have to think above yourself. Working in emergencies requires commitment, dedication, and the will to be unaffected by the conditions you are working in. You should be ready to work in difficult and sometimes frustrating environments. While assessing others' problems, put yourself in their shoes, ie don't judge them from your point of view, but from the aspect of those who are suffering. If you have these qualities, we would be more than happy to welcome you aboard.

Arif Jabbar Khan, Oxfam, Pakistan

It's not necessarily the best plot to take the vanload of goodies to Bosnia when a Red Cross plane can get it there in half the time at half the cost in an ordered fashion. My advice is to work with the current agencies in the field rather than pathfind. Also you can't just go out there and teach in a nursery, there's much more to learn.

British Red Cross

Some charities need very specialist and qualified volunteers, and people like Greg McAnulty, who is a qualified anaesthetist, find they still get an enormous amount of satisfaction from the work they do when they volunteer.

When Greg's six month contract with the NHS expired in early 1995, he decided to go and help to treat the wounded in war-torn Bosnia-Herzegovina. He approached Médécins sans Frontières, a medical charity that works in war zones and in refugee camps, and which needs specialists to help with its efforts. 'The work it does is important. And, if you feel that way, you should help,' says Greg.

He was sent to Gorazde with medical supplies. Nine months earlier MSF had pulled out its operations because fighting in the town had got too intense. After getting clearance from the Bosnian Serb headquarters in Pale, Greg set off by road from Belgrade, passing many checkpoints along the way. As he recalled, 'Once you are in, it is difficult to get out.'

One town was still coming under sniper attack, and a lot of the victims were war wounded. MSF had turned the strongroom in the bank into an operating theatre. 'There were two very good local surgeons there, but no anaesthetist.' Despite the logistics problems of shortages of medical equipment and blood services, Greg found that the survival rates were extraordinary. Some days, the hospital, too, was targeted by the gunmen. 'That is when I thought, "What am I doing here?", but that feeling passed. After all, there were patients to look after, and more beds were being made to accommodate about 200 wounded. When the fighting intensified, we all moved into the cellar.'

Besides assisting with operations, Greg also helped to train the local staff. He has come away amazed at the fortitude of the people. *'The local staff were incredibly brave and an inspiration for expatriates like us, even when they were short of food, suffering from ongoing malnutrition, and resenting the fact that the world was doing nothing to stop this carnage. They are a very tough people. Even though painkillers were being rationed, patients would reject them, saying, "Give it to others more in need."'*

Greg will certainly volunteer again. Of his Gorazde experience, he says: *'It was a challenge. You are used to doing things in a structural way, but the war zone takes you out of your comfortable world. In my old age, I can look back and say I did something. I don't have any illusions about changing the world. But it's nice to put something back into the world instead of living by the pandering self-interest philosophy of the West. What's more, you meet nice people, and see aspects of life that you would not see in any other way.'*

Greg McAnulty, Volunteer with Médécins sans Frontières

Essential Questions To Ask Before You Volunteer

1. **What commitment is required? Is it a couple of hours for a single flag day or a commitment per week and for how many weeks?**

2. **Is there a job description?**

3. **Will any training be given?**

4. **Are expenses/lunch allowance included?**

5. What support is given to volunteers?

6. Will your own transport be needed?

7. What range of volunteering jobs are there?

8. Could volunteering lead to a job and/or a vocational training?

9. Do you need any experience or qualifications?

10. Can you visit to see how the charity works?

5
CHARITY TRUSTEES:
THE ROLE AND RESPONSIBILITIES

Key Facts

- **There are over one million trustees of UK charities.**

- **Trustees take ultimate responsibility for the overall management of a charity which can include financial responsibility should debts be incurred.**

- **Trustees themselves are volunteers. They are not allowed to be paid or receive benefits in kind.**

- **Trustees have a legal requirement to know how the charity runs and should be able to demonstrate how they can make a contribution and attend trustees' meetings.**

Trustee? Committee of management? Council? The words 'Could you help us?' have led over a million people to become responsible

CHARITY TRUSTEES

for governing our nation's charities. It doesn't really matter what you're called (you may even end up being a company director), the position is a voluntary one and the responsibilities are identical.

Trustees set charities apart. It is a legal requirement of all charities to have them, yet it's been said that 'if trustees knew the full extent of the responsibilities they were taking on, no one would put their hand up!' Research[*] confirmed that many actually don't know! Fifty-one per cent of trustees had never read or did not know of their charity's written constitution!

Don't let that put you off! Trustees are there to make sure the charity runs properly, to set the overall direction and to check the finances. Legally, trustees are responsible for the actions of the staff and the volunteers. They are personally accountable for the management of the charity and its assets, and must act 'prudently' in the best interests of the charity and its beneficiaries at all times. The time, work and responsibility is given freely. Trustees are not allowed to be paid – with the exception of legitimate expenses – nor may they benefit in kind. And although it may be quite a responsibility, it's normal to be voted in as a trustee for a limited period – maybe one or two years.

Trustees are often regarded as a mixed blessing. As one senior chief executive put it:

Who are trustees accountable to? They are less publicly accountable than anyone. And the way in which they become trustees is so variable – it may just be the old boy network. Some charities have their trustees for life. It's very difficult asking someone in their eighties to step down, even if they're no longer active at all.

Imagine the frustration! You are running a charity, up to your ears in muck and bullets, dealing with sensitive issues and

---

[*]NCVO and Charity Commission Working Party Report 1992: 'On Trust'.

beleaguered groups of people. You work long hours, desperately try to find the funds to keep a vital service going, and go home with the weight of the world on your shoulders. A pause in the schedule for an essential trustees' meeting. The cool eyes of the outsider, detached but interested, asking questions, making policy and saying 'No' to your latest request before disappearing for several more months . . . it's no wonder the organisation for charity chief executives (known as ACENVO) teams its members together so that they can discuss 'How to deal with the Trustees'.

The frequency with which the trustees meet is also important for the smooth running of the charity. Some charities require their trustees to sign off most expenditure, and if the trustees can't be brought together to make decisions quickly, opportunities are lost. The fact that trustees are required to act 'prudently' may mean that they don't act at all. After all, no decision means no risk. A delay in decision-making until the next trustees' meeting can slow things down to the pace of a snail.

A couple of times we've found ideal properties to buy, and have lost them because the elected trustees haven't been there to take a decision. On the other hand they do have a degree of sophistication we can't rely on the electorate for.

Membership Charity

Once again it's the smaller charities that find it most difficult to attract people who have time to help and a real commitment to the cause. A charity needs trustees — whatever their title — in order to be established. At the outset, someone starting a charity because they feel inspired to do so will need to be a first-rate salesman to convince their chosen target to support a non-existent organisation, or one in its infancy with a limited income. Then a strong chief executive may be needed to convince the trustees to become more involved! Take these three examples:

CHARITY TRUSTEES

The committee always feel there's nothing for them to do. I think they don't know how to start supporting us. They hear my report and the treasurer's report and congratulate us on the good work we're doing. There are so many meetings . . . I would like them to go out and talk to others. To get cash from those who've no idea of what's going on or what we do.

You used to be able to ask around and people would be delighted — even honoured — to become trustees. Nowadays, it isn't the same at all. People are just too busy. We find it very difficult to get the right calibre of people.

Our trustees are historic and not vastly active. As far as I know they've never been hugely active. We need more.

Each of these charities is relatively small. Two are local, one national. I can almost guarantee you won't have heard of any of them, yet each is doing remarkable work. If you read about them in the national press you'd not hesitate to dip your hand in your pocket. What they have in common is passive and apparently uncommitted trustees.

Committed trustees can work wonders!

Good trustees, who are invariably involved trustees, can make an enormous difference. My vote goes to the trustees of the Acorn Children's Hospice in Birmingham as a good example to follow. The charity's Director, John Overton, explains how they work.

We're run by a committee who move heaven and earth to get things done — even when it means shifting the goal posts. They are an enlightened mix of carers and commercial people. They help us raise cash and do the work.

Trustees need to be recruited in a professional manner. We give an induction course and a job description to every new trustee — which they agree and sign. The chairman reviews the job description with them every year. The main board meet quarterly and at the AGM and are encouraged to keep in contact with senior managers in between. Six of the 14 are on the Executive Committee as well. They take part in monthly operational meetings. It gives them a lot of credibility and is important in showing the team the management is interested. They are also expected to take part in informal meetings, go out and speak on our behalf, collect cheques, and keep up to speed by going to industry events.

Why is it like this? I was a headhunter! At least four of the trustees are still chief executives of their own companies, used to getting their own way at meetings. They expand our resources, they're very constructive and they really know what's going on.

We need to be fleet of foot; to be aware of the changing society and political scene. We can't be introverted. I also believe that a composite team is an enormous asset. Very often charities are set up by a visionary, and when that vision has been achieved the impetus goes. They become protective, defensive and resistant to change. As a team, we have a strong structure. When one person leaves they can be replaced, the structure will survive.

Acorn Children's Hospice

The Acorn Hospice has the advantage of being a visible local charity in Birmingham, an area where business folk abound. So whilst the smaller charities can find it difficult to attract committed and active trustees, larger charities still seem to be able to call the shots. Oxfam, as one of the largest, sets another good example. Despite its size (with income approaching £100 million), only 20 people sit on their main board, one of whom has worked her way up from shop volunteer, and many of whom are elected from the next tier of management, the Assembly:

> *We're incredibly demanding of our trustees – there's an enormous amount of work they are asked to do in between meetings. They meet with management of those departments they're working with and provide input into strategic developments – it's useful to have a fresh eye. Some travel overseas, others become involved in major reviews. Over the past few years we've made deliberate moves to slim down, give clearer roles and responsibilities. The trustee of a regional area is also responsible for pulling together our regional forums – regular meetings where our local supporters can air their views and hear what's going on – they chair the meeting, set the agenda and take information back to head office. I'd say, on average, each trustee puts in at least 20 days' work a year on a voluntary basis.*
>
> *Oxfam*

You don't need any qualifications to be a trustee, although the Charity Commissioners will wish to establish that you are a 'fit and proper' person for the job. The trend is towards fewer people with more involvement. **The Samaritans** is a notable exception to this rule. They manage to keep all 250 trustees very much involved. About 200 are the directors of individual Samaritans' branches, and twice a year all get together over a weekend to exchange views and discuss policy and future developments. It's an essential forum, and everyone turns up.

If you wish to become a trustee, you needn't necessarily wait to be asked. It's becoming more common for charities to advertise for particular skills in a trustee rather than rely on the 'old boy network'. A Trustee Register is available for people wishing to become involved (see Useful Organisations, page 139). As the drive for professionalism continues, everyone is becoming more demanding of their new trustees.

> *Up until 10 years ago it was the old boy network. We went to the Institute of Directors and contacts. Now we've started to move away*

> *from this. Trustees have to bring something and be able to work to our strategy and support it.*
>
> **Action for Blind People**

If you wish to become a trustee and feel you have something to offer, or if a charity has approached you, think carefully about your role and contribution. You don't need to be a high-powered business executive. Most charities are set up by ordinary people determined to create a fairer society, and there's no reason why your experience of life shouldn't make you a caring, motivated and active manager.

As a trustee you are there to make a contribution, to help, guide and support the employees. At least that's the idea.

> *Our trustees are very competent business folk and would never run a business like this. The moment they become trustees they leave all their skills outside the door and apply a completely different set of standards than they would outside the charity – almost as if it's a pastime, a bit of a hobby where they can leave real life behind.*

I recounted this anecdote to a senior fundraiser, who'd been less than warm about his own trustees. It was an ironic response!

> *Yes, it's true. I'm a trustee of two different charities and it's very difficult to apply the disciplines I do to my day job when I go there. It's much nicer to relax and enjoy myself.*

10 Questions To Ask Before Becoming A Trustee

1. **What will my role be? What exactly are you being asked to do? Does your knowledge, commitment or experience make you the**

CHARITY TRUSTEES

right person? Do you want this job? Is there a job description?

2. Can I meet the employees and the person in charge of the day-to-day business? Find out what they're doing, sense the atmosphere and the commitment.

3. Can I look at the governing document? Exactly what is the charity setting out to do? What are the trustees' responsibilities? How long is the term of office?

4. What other charities are operating in this area, and what is the overlap?

5. Can I see the accounts? If in any doubt about your ability to understand them, check them out with a professional. Charities tread the solvency tightrope as much as any other business and as a trustee you may be liable.

6. How much time am I required to commit? The move is towards greater rather than less involvement. If you're only being expected to attend a management meeting every quarter how will you know what's going on?

7. Can I meet the other trustees? What do they do for the charity and would you feel comfortable working with them?

8. What are the long-term plans? Are there any?

How secure is future fundraising? Are funds needed for capital projects?

9. How are costs kept in check? What are the budgets for the next year? Are management accounts available?

10. What information systems are in place? How will you know what's going on? How much feedback does the charity get from the beneficiaries?

6
FUNDRAISING:
A CONFLICT IN EXPECTATIONS

The way it was . . .

Originally, in the early seventies, we fundraised by putting our donors on a simple card system. On the anniversary of their gift we wrote, thanked them and asked for their support again. Eighty per cent responded. We had a system of reminders and very few cards were left at the end from supporters we'd lost.

It worked year after year. I was the Appeals Secretary and fundraising was a very genteel occupation. It seems incredible when you consider it today.

Looking back on it, it was unsophisticated, but it worked. About 22 years ago we decided to move. We found new premises and set about finding £900,000. Nowadays it'd be called a Capital Appeal with Steering Groups and Fundraising Committees. Then, we sat down round the table and put our thoughts on paper. We decided to go to all the trade unions on a theme of workers helping workers. One of the docks unions was the first to contribute. A cheque came back for £20. Others spread the word and within about 18 months we were in sight of our target and — with a bank loan — moved. We paid the loan off in another 18 months and were in the clear. In those days you just stayed with it.

It was with great pride we took people round these premises and with great pride we could say, 'Look what we've done.' We'd had one grant from the Government for £22,000 for a piece of machinery, but all the rest was the result of our direct efforts. We're more professional now, but we've lost that flavour.

The public gave because it was a duty. They didn't question the cause or the money spent. Now people are actively seeking causes, they are motivated to support and question, they are more consumerist.

Eileen Howard, Action for Blind People

How people give

More than a quarter of us don't think about it much. We give a little when we're asked, through street collections and the like. It's not very efficient either – the charities can't claim any tax back and the majority of us give a meagre £2.50 a month: in total about £6 for every £100 raised.

WHAT THE PUBLIC WANT FROM CHARITIES THEY SUPPORT

We're a fickle lot. We like to support a cause which gives us a nice warm feeling: we respond to the innocence of children or the dumb pleading of an animal. We want our emotions to be tapped, to become involved and to know how our donation is used. We trust and give money to causes we know about. (One volunteer carrying out a house-to-house collection for **The Children's Society** raised just over £6, and in the same street just a fortnight later raised ten times that amount for the **Save the Children Fund**.)

We are judgmental in the extreme. Our 'feelgood' factor

often stops short of the homeless or the addicted, whom we believe have brought their troubles upon themselves; or even those whose lives appear so difficult that we can't cope with thinking about them. When accosted by a cause beyond our experience, the most typical reaction is 'It'll never happen to me . . .' even though life's experience shows it can.

It would be easier if we worked purely with those who are blind. We work with those who are blind and have physical disabilities. You can talk to people and watch them switch off. It's more than they can cope with. 'I think you're wonderful,' is what they say and you can see that what they're really saying is 'Don't get me involved.'

But it's often road accident victims that we help. People who go from being a competent professional to totally and utterly dependent overnight. We provide one-to-one staffing and aim to give quality of life. Our core staffing costs and our fundraising needs are remarkably high.

Seeability

Most people we help are extremely difficult to find places for. In the eyes of society they are horrendous. In our eyes very needful. They have been called the unlovely.

It's very difficult for people in society to think that these people are of any worth. They can't see that circumstances might have driven them there.

I don't talk to people about what I do, because I know now they take two steps back. You can see the anger in their eyes. But the people we help are all right. They haven't got two heads. When I first came here and read the case histories, I just cried. The people we help never had a chance from the day they were born.

National Association of Voluntary Hostels

'Don't make me feel helpless'

Charities that advertise know that an emotional advertisement brings in the cash. But this type of appeal has been toned down over the past decade.

> *In the past aid agencies ran fundraising campaigns showing starving, pot-bellied children. They were relatively successful in raising money, at least for a short time. But such poster campaigns were counter-productive. They gave the impression that people sat and waited for food – or death – and did nothing for themselves. It was as if Oxfam was saying the response to famine should be pity; when it should be a demand for justice and action.*
>
> **Oxfam**

> *Sometimes, when I tell prospective donors about our work here they end up in tears. Whilst I need to affect the public, I don't want to make them feel hopeless about us. I don't want to turn them off by making them feel so terrible.*
>
> *There's a legend in the hospice movement that a family who had paid for the refurbishment of a room wanted the room named after them. Their surname was Pyne-Coffin! You can see the problem.*
>
> **Children's Hospice for the Eastern Region**

'Give me something I can relate to'

You've seen it hundreds of times: £10 a week will feed this child, 10p can buy rehydration salts to save a life, £20 will pay for a Jaipur foot – a new limb made out of flexible hardwearing rubber . . . we like the gratification of knowing exactly how the money's being spent, and would rather it were not on a salary or a telephone bill. To take it further, research projects are harder to fundraise for than direct-aid projects, and we like to see an immediate rather than a long-term result. Education and information, so crucial to long-term change, are the poor relations in the fundraising game.

Lack of human interest stories can be a major barrier. 'Knowledge isn't a sexy fundraising purpose' is a cry that's made time and time again. 'Information is vital, but providing information increases our admin. costs and the public doesn't have any sympathy with it.' Or – and what an indictment of human nature – 'We're a Cinderella charity. One in 50 will be affected, but people don't die of it.'

The need to make it easy for people to get information and help is extreme. It's been pointed out that '. . . the middle classes (for want of a better word) are frightfully good at getting money out of charities and the very people we genuinely want to help aren't'.

Let's take three examples:

Community Network is a small charity offering telephone conference calls to needy groups at a very cheap rate. Typically, anyone who has problems getting out and about can chat to others in the same predicament and give each other encouragement, information and support – or just have a good gossip. You may be blind, physically disabled or suffer from agoraphobia. It's a small idea which is also a lifeline.

Contact a Family is an umbrella organisation for 300 different parent support groups. Should anyone in your family suffer with a rare condition, Contact a Family will put you in touch with another family so that you can share your experiences. They will also put doctors and consultants in touch with each other. Their directory of medical conditions is sold to the medical profession and has become a welcome source of revenue. They also help concerned parents who may wish to set up a local charity, so that there's less reinvention of the wheel, but as their fundraising manager points out:

WHICH CHARITY?

People want to know 'What's happened to my money?' They think that if you work for a charity you don't get paid. The Helpline we set up with volunteers, but now have three paid staff. They have become knowledgeable professionals and can give a better service. It's not an easy organisation when it comes to getting money from the public.

Contact a Family

Look is a group of charities that helps parents. They have come into existence to support families of visually impaired children. They now have a central office, to co-ordinate fundraising efforts and raise their national profile.

Many organisations support children. We exist for families. They're often single parents, on benefit, with housing problems, under pressure. The strain of living with a visually impaired child affects everyone. Our fieldworkers are there to go out and do battle; to tackle bureaucracy; to encourage local boroughs to work with us with a whole package of services.

Look, London

The message is that we should look harder and investigate more. Every charity has been set up to meet a need, but causes that can be communicated in a sentence or a single picture make up only a tiny fraction of those trying to raise funds.

Imagine fundraising for a telephone helpline. Helpline services are often a lifesaver, but it's not easy to sell the public the idea of paying for a portion of a phone bill which is likely to get bigger and bigger the more the service is used. Educating teachers so that they know how to work with brain-injured children wherever they live will enable many more children to be helped than at present; but it's easier to fundraise for a dedicated specialist school already in existence even though it's severely restricted in the numbers it can help.

FUNDRAISING

An instant result is more emotive and the purchase of something tangible more satisfying than longer-term goals which aim to make radical changes; but maybe it's just a problem of communication. Research into recent Oxfam TV advertising found their message, which is as old as the hills, was totally relevant to the public. It's certainly one we should listen to.

Give a man a fish, and he'll feed himself for just a day. But give him the means to catch his own fish and he'll be able to feed himself and his family for a whole lifetime.

The public like supporting causes that are emotive, but – it seems – not too emotive! We like them to be safe and above board, and we definitely expect to get something back – a personal thank you and real recognition of the work involved. If a charity can meet these criteria, it will win our approval, support and active fundraising efforts!

Many times we've raised money for charities and had only a receipt and official thank you – not a lot for the work we do and a cheque for about $5,000. The event we did for Womankind was different. We had lots of communication with them and could put a name and a face to the organisation. Obviously the cause, women helping women to help themselves, was one that appealed to the ladies here. I also asked them whether it would be possible to earmark the money. They suggested, and we agreed, that we gave our support to a group of women in Ghana.

The cause meant we raised the awareness of the possibility of working for a charity. It was a cause people believed in. They turned out to volunteer in great numbers. I actually had a surplus of volunteers.

At the meeting today it was decided we want to do another event for Womankind next year. We have a good relationship there.
Amy Barraj, organiser of Jeddah's first Annual Bookfair with The American Ladies of Jeddah, in aid of Womankind

WHICH CHARITY?

'Show us how the money will be used'

Alexandra Rose Day is a very familiar name. As it's been around since 1912, it's easy to assume it's as large as it is well established, although the reverse is true. Alexandra Rose Day exists to help other small charities by doing everything needed to allow them to take part in a national flag day. As a small charity you need only apply for your area, rustle up the volunteers to shake tins and you will get 80 per cent of the proceeds – everything else will be organised for you. Being a catalyst for others – supplying intangible know-how and invisible background work – has made it very difficult for Alexandra Rose Day to generate funds to pay for its own overheads.

The amazing thing is that one small project – which Alexandra Rose Day started to help just 16 children a year – has succeeded by providing a focus for public fundraising support as well as wide publicity. It's a brilliant example of a small initiative which works because it is visible and, in the words of the Director, gives 'enormous spin-off effects'.

The children's camp at Leintwardine started in the pub. I'd been to Shankhill after the bombing. It was different. The atmosphere had changed. You could feel the fear. And I wondered if there was any way Alexandra Rose Day could help.

The camp's now in its sixth year. It brings together underprivileged children from Belfast and London in the middle of the country for a week's camp. The behaviour of the kids from Belfast is better than those from London, but the fantastic spin-off is the effect of bringing together the different cultures. It's a third dimension which breaks down communication barriers.

One of the Belfast kids was going round the group checking: 'Protestant? Catholic? Protestant? Catholic?', when 'Moslem' came out as the answer. You could have heard a pin drop. One of the activities we include is the Dark Walk – a trek through the countryside at night for city children who've never known night without streetlights or traffic noise — to overcome the fear.

The local villages support the camp and it crosses all the social boundaries: the pub, the church and all the families take part. At the end of the week the camp give a party for their hosts. Several of our volunteers have changed the direction of their careers and become teachers as a result of being involved. For a small project we can generate an enormous amount of publicity — in Belfast and London as well as in the Midlands and Wales. At a local level the nearby villages have now become involved in raising money and we, as a charity, can be seen to do something tangible. What's more we do it by co-operating with other charities. (Bryson House in Belfast and the Children's Country Holiday Fund in London).

It's a small project, just one week a year for 16 kids, but with enormous spin-off effects. The seeds of mutual understanding have been planted, waiting to be nurtured through future experience. It's the sort of thing that every village could be encouraged to become involved in.

Alexandra Rose Day

What Charities Would Like The Public To Know

Fundraising is becoming increasingly competitive and professional. It also costs money. As anyone who gives regularly will know, the age of the database and direct mail is with us! Smaller charities — which form the vast majority and are the very ones which appear to be losing out to the Lottery — are finding it increasingly difficult to compete.

The problems of being small

Small charities are fine when you can see the work they do. But how does a small *national* charity attract the public's attention? Without a newsworthy or highly emotive story it's often difficult to attract press and TV coverage. The alternatives – fundraising through national promotion and direct mail – are simply too expensive.

National companies not unnaturally wish to support national charities, although they recognise the benefits of being seen actively to support a local community.

Ironically, the public rather like supporting causes they have 'discovered', which is why many smaller charities are included in the Profiles section of the book. It's good to know that a relatively modest donation can go a very long way, and the personal relationship that can develop between fundraisers and the charity's staff is often very rewarding.

In the end, though, smaller charities tend to rely on the public support they can drum up locally, even when the work they do is national. They can make themselves visible to local Round Tables and Rotary Clubs, and build contacts with supportive local companies to establish the credibility of the work they do. This may sound simple and low key, but it takes time and effort, and good trustees and volunteers can make all the difference. The simpler option is often for smaller charities to ignore the public and approach charitable trusts for funds, but these very funds are under pressure as they're being inundated with an increasing numbers of requests.

The public have learnt to trust household names. The charitable trusts trust us. They know that even small amounts of money will make a real impact. But we can't compete with the bigger charities for publicity. We simply can't afford, for example, to produce schools packs to the standard they do – so we don't do it.
Tools for Self-Reliance (refurbishing basic tools and supplying them to communities in underdeveloped countries)

We live from hand-to-mouth for ever. We never turn anyone down. Parents contribute when they can, but when they can't . . . A legacy would be nice. We're quite good at getting publicity, the families are our greatest fans, but publicity doesn't necessarily get the money. What we do sounds totally unbelievable: to make blind children see, or those who have been written off go to mainstream school. With a legacy we could computerise, set up a proper donor base. The building was cheap when we bought it and is very run down. It would be nice to have a bursary fund to support poorer families.

BIBIC (Working with Brain Injured Children)

It's not necessarily inefficiency that keeps small charities small or out of the public eye. For many the fact that they are regional is as much an asset as a liability.

As a regional organisation our individual donors can come and visit us and feel an ownership of what we do. But we can't benefit from national appeals. The strength of Blue Peter, or even The Week's Good Cause on Radio Four, is lost to us.

Children's Hospice for the Eastern Region

The problems of being large

There are some! Major charities often carry out such a wide range of services that the public never know the extent of their work. The Salvation Army is widely accepted as 'a good cause' but what exactly do they *do*? They are at pains to point out that it's a long time since they ran hostels where the homeless sang hymns, and they can flexibly adapt to the needs of the age!

Large organisations have the luxury of being able to concentrate their wide-reaching fundraising messages to the public on those areas they know appeal. Save the Children, for example, know better than to advertise the work they do with children in the UK. It's far less successful than advertising an overseas crisis appeal. Once you support Save the Children, you'll find out about the UK programmes through their newsletter. Large charities are run as businesses and have the cash available to invest in long-term fundraising programmes as well as a hugely diverse range of fundraising activities.

> *Save the Children has 150 shops and 20,000 volunteers. The country is divided into 750 branches and 40 areas who meet formally with fundraising and operational staff to discover what Save the Children is doing and why, and to feed in any questions as well as hear of any new, planned fundraising initiatives. Involvement can be anything from helping out with a street collection to organising an annual event.*

The problems of sensitive issues

Larger charities can afford the luxury of being totally honest with their fundraisers. They're likely to have a varied portfolio of projects at any one time, and people trust them enough to do what is right with the money.

> *The message we give and the work we do need to be one and the same. We explain this is what we're really doing and, yes, it does lose us some cash. Research amongst those who support us indicates they trust us to do the right thing.*
>
> *Trust comes with size and the length of time we've been around. Even if you put all the major children's charities together the services we provide are minute compared to the services through the statutory system. We do the things we can do better — for example, our campaign to help child prostitutes — where the statutory services aren't trusted.*
>
> **The Children's Society**

Smaller charities that focus on sensitive issues may choose to take a low public profile. **Fairbridge** picks up inner-city, at-risk teenagers from 'the bottom of the pile', and works with them to develop life skills. They're very aware that the high public profile that comes with public fundraising could backfire on them. Unemployed youngsters accept Fairbridge as a good place for courses, not as a charity.

Who is getting the money?

This may sound like a basic question but it's one to ask more often.

Charities we consider national are often far from that. It's common for a charity to use a single name even though it's really hundreds of independent fundraising units; because historically groups around the country set up local charities before eventually working with the developed parent organisation. People tend to know the national name and give to the national charity – whose objectives may be political lobbying and overall policy making. The local branch – which does the grass-roots provision of service, day in, day out, year after year – may get nothing from money sent into the national office *unless you specify exactly where you wish the money to go.*

> *There's huge misunderstanding. A great many people think that money given to the national society will come to us, but it doesn't. Ask who's going to get the money you fundraise. As a local society we are affiliated, use the logo and pay a sub, but don't get the central funds. At the same time people are moving into this area because of the quality of schools we provide.*
>
> **Hampshire Autistic Society**

Very few charities have enough money in the pot to do all they would like. As with the Government or the NHS, priorities have to be sorted out. Discerning supporters should check just how the money will be used. It's easy to give to the person you know, but not necessarily the right decision.

WHICH CHARITY?

> *Patients who want to say thank you often give to their local consultant or hospital, but where does that money go? Quite often on a short-term programme or not to the renal unit at all. We fund social workers, get them going and once the need has been established we make sure that service continues to be funded by the local district. It's much more about making a significant difference long-term.*
> **British Kidney Patients' Association**

Charities are constantly putting together schemes for large companies, adapted to make sure the company benefits with the charity. But they are resigned to the fact that the majority of the public aren't too informed about the charities they give money to and, in the age of the sound-bite, it's difficult to get a long-term or complicated message across.

Fundraising is expensive

Thousands of charities are out there in need of your money and competition makes raising it expensive. As any volunteer knows, even the smallest event needs publicity, some information about the cause, telephone calls to be made and paid for and more. Put simply, raising money costs money.

> *When I was appointed as the first fundraising director in 100 years I asked what the fundraising budget would be. 'Budget?' the trustees chorused in amazement. 'We thought you were here to raise money, not use it.'*

Charities may employ their own fundraisers or use outside companies and individuals to organise events on their behalf. Inevitably, what seems like a good idea at the time can go wrong. Charities know that the costs of running events can totally overtake the money raised. Everyone's been to at least one soggy Fun Run or village fête which has been rained off.

Using a professional fundraiser isn't foolproof either. The 1994 Aerobathon was a professionally organised event which encouraged thousands of people to take part in mass aerobics sessions across the country and be sponsored for doing so. The plan was that all the money raised – less the costs of organising the event – would be divided between participating charities. However, the costs overtook the organising company which collapsed. Although the charities hadn't paid for anything, they did lose out on potential income and were left with an embarrassing situation, as far as their supporters were concerned. Putting on events is risky, and charities who are asked to contribute to the costs of setting up an event by an outside company should be very wary about doing so. Written contracts don't guarantee success.

10 Questions To Ask Before Making A Major Donation

1. **What sort of an organisation is it? You could be dealing with an affiliation, membership charity, society, etc.**

2. **Where does the money go? Your local branch of a charity may be totally independent of the national parent and unless you specify, the money may never reach the local branch. Likewise, if you give money to a hospital specialist, it may not be used for the charitable work intended.**

3. **What does the charity do? Some charities are purely grant-giving or fundraising. They are often in the best position to assess which**

charity in a particular field is in need of the funds you wish to raise.

4. Who else is doing it? It's normal for several charities to operate in a single field. This makes for healthy competition and greater public awareness, but establish first who you wish to give to – a cancer research or care charity, for example.

5. Have you established why the money is needed? It's more than life is worth to mention the major charities with an excess of funds, but there are some. As needs change a charity can change its objectives, but some continue to raise funds, even though the money they have invested more than meets the need.

6. What is the ratio between fundraising and other overheads? Administration costs can vary, as explained, but if the fundraising costs are high compared to those of other charities in the same area, you should ask for further information. It could be inefficiency, and if so the charity doesn't deserve your support.

7. Can I see the latest accounts? Public companies try to make as much profit as possible, whilst charities don't want to be thought of as fat cats. They are there, after all, to distribute the funds raised for their beneficiaries. It's worthwhile getting an accountant

to look through the accounts, and if you've any questions, ring up and ask. Remember, though, that it's difficult for smaller charities to maintain their income/overheads ratio at the level of their larger counterparts.

8. Can I visit you and see what you do? It's not something many fundraisers bother to do, but why not? Charities have nothing to hide and you will immediately sense an air of efficiency or otherwise. You can see for yourself the energy and sense the commitment.

9. What is the policy on reserves? The Charity Commissioners feel any charity with over two years' worth of reserves may not be fulfilling its primary purpose, which is to give money away.

10. What are your future plans? Soundly run organisations should know where they're going.

7
Inspirational Stories and Quotes:
From Founders, Volunteers, Workers and Beneficiaries

'I shall select you and supervise you and discipline you and sack you if necessary, and see the clients who need something more than your befriendings, and I shall make the decisions you're not competent to make. But you are the life-savers'

Chad Varah's debut as a minister was burying a 14-year-old girl who'd killed herself when her periods started, thinking she had VD. As a direct result he'd seized every opportunity to teach people about sex, and found it led to youngsters joining his youth clubs and young couples coming for marriage preparation. It was not until 18 years had passed that the catalyst for The Samaritans came to him.

'. . . I read in some digest that there were three suicides a day in Greater London. What were they supposed to do if they didn't want a doctor or social worker? What sort of a someone might they want? And how would they get in touch at the moment of crisis? There ought to be an emergency number for suicidal people, I thought. Then I said to God, "Be reasonable . . . don't look at me . . ." and having settled that, went on a busman's holiday to Knokke.

'While there, out of the blue I got a wire inviting me to apply for St Stephen Walbrook, in the heart of the City . . . Interviewed by the Patrons, I told them of my crazy scheme. The decision was made to appoint me, because they thought it was worth a try. A decision which gave me immense confidence.

'All I had to do was stand drinks to my pals in Fleet Street to get all the publicity necessary if the idea was to work. The telephone number of the church turned out to be the one I'd planned to ask for, MAN 9000. With my secretary I coped with callers-up and callers-in for some weeks from November 1953, but then useless amateurs began offering to help. I graciously allowed the ones I found agreeable to run errands for me and keep the clients amused while waiting to be ushered into the Presence.

'It soon became evident that they were doing the clients more good than I was. Everybody needed *befriending*; only a minority needed my Counselling or Referral for Psychiatry. By February 1954, I called these amateurs together and said, "Over to you, Samaritans. Never again shall I pick up the phone, nor be the one to say come in and have a coffee when a client taps at the door. I shall select you and supervise you and discipline you and sack you if necessary, and see the clients who need something more than your befriendings, and I shall make the decisions you're not competent to make. But *you* are the lifesavers, and one day everyone will recognise what suicidal people need."'

Chad Varah, Founder of The Samaritans

> *Go to the people*
> *Live with them,*
> *Love them.*
> *Learn from them*
> *Start from where they are,*

Start with what they have,
Build on what they know.

And in the end,
when the work is done,
the people will rejoice and say,
We have done it ourselves.

Words from a Chinese philosopher – from the Ockenden Venture

'Theirs is a spirit that makes the world worth living in'
Lord Tonypandy

In 1943, nine friends gathered around Eddie Price as he lay critically ill in hospital after an accident. His family was told there was no hope of recovery. Yet, with skilful nursing, he got better. Those who had watched over him sat around his bed and together they and Eddie decided there must be some way they could show their appreciation of the care he had received.

The first idea was a simple one: a fundraising drive to buy radio sets for the use of patients in hospital. It was wartime and there were many shortages, but money started rolling in and the 10 realised something more formal was required: a proper organisation. 'Since we are ten, why not call ourselves Tenovus?' So Tenovus, a charity dedicated to medical science and welfare, was born.

From the outset Tenovus made a huge impact in the Cardiff area, building a nurses' home, a convalescent home for repatriated British prisoners of war returning from Japanese camps in Burma, an extension to the Craig y Parc spastic school in Cardiff, and the Sunshine Home for Blind Babies at Southerndown. Tenovus also funded a purpose-built unit for spine bifida babies in Cardiff, having discovered that spina bifida was, at the time, more prevalent in South Wales than anywhere else in the UK.

Tenovus has tackled problems as they arose. About 20 years after foundation, aggrieved by the ravages and distress of cancer, Tenovus set out to raise the money to build and equip the first centre in Wales for cancer research. In 1967 that dream was fulfilled and the Tenovus Centre for Cancer Research was opened in Cardiff. Now, Tenovus is a major cancer charity, supporting research at four different centres in the UK: Cardiff, Southampton, Bournemouth and Aberystwyth.

More than 50 years after that first decision was taken, thanks to the early work, and great strides in the treatment of the disease through research worldwide and at Tenovus's own laboratories, many thousands of cancer sufferers are alive and well today.

One of the original 10, asked if any of them were tempted to complain about the demands on their support, reminded himself of the quotation: 'I cried because I had no shoes, until I met a man who had no feet.'

Eddie Price is now 86. Ten ordinary citizens – a butcher, baker, retailer and insurer among them – have not only changed their own lives, but established a philosophy which has become their *raison d'être*.

The Foundation of Tenovus

But God chose the foolish things of the world to shame the wise; God chose the weak things of the world to shame the strong. He chose the lowly things of this world – and the things that are not – to nullify the things that are, so that no one may boast before him.

1 Corinthians, Chapter 1, verses 27–28

'Even today, the ultimate step, the final thing that counts, is not what the great national or global organisations do – but the individual action and personal courage of a single volunteer'

WHICH CHARITY?

Alec was always passionate – an inspiring and uncomfortable quality, perhaps more in British culture than elsewhere. He had the publicist's ears for the words and pictures that would claim attention to his passion, as here, describing his work with a group of young volunteers on the Hungarian frontier in the winter of 1956:

'The cold was so intense that the hairs in one's nose went stiff like needles. We had to cover our ears to prevent them freezing and there was often the risk of the water in the radiator of our Jeep becoming a block of ice if we did not keep the engine running.

'We worked at night – for it was under cover of darkness that refugees could make their escape into Austria. When we heard these groups approaching in the snow we would stumble towards them, shouting, "This is Austria, this is Austria, you are safe here!" At the sound of our voices they would stop still in fright, fearing that this might be some trap. Then, as we came out of the blackness and they saw that we were friends, they would throw their arms around us and warm tears of relief streamed down their icy faces. Not once but a dozen times every night we would be kissed by children, old men and women as at long last they knew themselves to be safe.

'Often the babies that men carried on their backs would be drugged, so that no sudden cry could betray the position of the group to the Hungarian frontier guards, and the women's legs would be half frozen from their march through the snow.

'We had taken up a position beside a canal that marked the border in this area – and night after night, when we thought no frontier guards were near, we would push across a small rubber boat to bring over refugees.

'How did that boat come to be there? Dozens of international relief organisations had hurried to Austria to help in this tragic situation. There were Red Cross teams from about 20 different countries and of course there was the United Nations Commissioner for Refugees, with train loads of emergency supplies. But it was none of these bodies which had supplied the boat . . . One of our young volunteers, a student, had gone into a sports shop in Vienna, purchased the boat with his own money, brought it by bus to the frontier area, and hidden it in the reeds beside the canal . . . It was thanks to *his* initiative that hundreds of refugees owed their escape to freedom.

'My conclusion? Even today, the ultimate step, the final thing that counts, is not what the great national or global organisations do – but the individual action and personal courage of a single volunteer.'

The individual volunteer – that was always at the centre of Alec's vision. And everyone could be one. Not for Alec the elitist priorities of society, either at VSO and especially at CSV. To a VSO volunteer in 1959 he wrote:

'Those who themselves have known what it is to have doubts and misgivings may perhaps ultimately have some of the best contributions to give. The race is not always to the swift, nor the battle to the strong, and it is not just beefy extroverts that we are looking for, but people with a warm heart who are sensitive to human situations and who can give their affection in rich measure.'

Alec Dickson, founder of Voluntary Service Overseas.
Extract from the address at Alec Dickson's memorial service,
December 1994

There are over 40 million refugees and displaced people in the world. Over 50 per cent of them are children.

Concern Universal

'There are some things in life which seem to happen to you. You follow your nose when the door opens, but events take over'

WHICH CHARITY?

Back in 1988 I was at a Christmas party when the host, who worked for one of the companies sponsoring the London Marathon, challenged us all to run a marathon. 'Who's game? I have 12 running tickets and they're like gold dust.' (He'd sensibly waited until halfway through the party!)

'Fine. We'll do it!' chorused the assembled unfit, including myself, and without much more thought changed my life!

Christmas came and went. In January a fax arrived at the office. 'Here is your training schedule.' To put it in context, I am no athlete. I was in my forties and a couple of stone overweight. 'A good reason to get fit,' I thought. 'If I start I will at least be in better shape in a couple of months.' That night, over supper with friends, I regaled them with the unlikely scenario.

'If you do it, we'll give you £1,000.' You could have knocked me down with a feather. 'Our company gives money to charity every year. You can be our charity this year. Any charity of your choice.'

Training progressed. Slowly. I was very busy at work and managed about six miles for my longest run, but my GP said it was attitude that counted! I roped in a friend to train with – by total coincidence a paediatrician at Great Ormond Street Hospital – and two weeks before the event went in search of a cause. I'd seen a very sophisticated wheelchair in a shop a few years back and was fascinated by it. I rang up the manufacturers. 'Have you a waiting list of people who can't possibly afford it?' I asked.

'Over 100,' was the reply.

And so I went to visit Sammy, who suffers from cerebral palsy, came home and wrote begging letters to everyone I could possibly think of, having first checked out exactly what cerebral palsy was.

As I set off on Marathon Day, reeking of Vaseline and confidently predicting a four-and-a-half to five-hour finish, my wife pointed out that if I didn't make it we'd have to find the money somehow. We couldn't let Sammy down.

I crossed the line in six hours 40 minutes. Friends, neighbours and colleagues were amazed. I went home to bed! Nine thousand pounds was raised and Sammy got her chair. My supporters kept on at me. 'What's going to happen to Sammy now? What happens when she grows out of her chair?'

'There must be a charity that specialises in this,' was my reply. 'I'll check it out.'

The next coincidence. We met a friend of a friend, who'd just lost her job. As we got talking, she told us she'd spent 12 years with major charities. 'I've got time on my hands and know the right people. I'll check it out for you. You're quite right, there are far too many charities.' Three months later we were sitting round a table in the Institute of Child Health with representatives from six major disability charities. 'No one's doing this properly. We'll help you. Please start it,' was the unanimous vote.

To form a charity costs money. We should go ahead, but how? A successful business friend offered £5,000 unconditionally – I hadn't even asked him for the money, just filled him in on the details.

In the meanwhile nine friends had been cajoled into running the New York Marathon that November and between them raised £45,000. We didn't have a charity established, but we had the name – they ran for Whizz-Kidz. As the phone started ringing and wheelchairs needed to be ordered in the New Year, my wife's office found a spare desk and a friend who'd worked for a GP for eight years found she could spare us some time. In 1990, just a year after that first effort, Whizz-Kidz was a registered charity with a desk and a phone. In 1995, the turnover hit £1 million. We're still just touching the tip of the iceberg, but I have great faith in the charity's future, because so many trip-switches seemed to cause it to start.

Michael Dickson, joint founder of Whizz-Kidz

Sometimes I look about me with a feeling of complete dismay. In the confusion that conflicts the world today, I see disrespect for the very values of life. Beauty is all around us, but how many are blind to it! They look at the wonder of this earth and seem to see nothing.

Each second we live is a new and unique moment of the universe, a moment that will never be again . . . And what do we teach our children? We teach them that two and two make four and that Paris is the capital of France.

When will we also teach them: do you know what you are? You are a marvel. You are unique. In all the years that have passed, there has never been another child like you. And look at your body – what a wonder it is! Your legs, your arms, your clever fingers, the way you move. You may become a Shakespeare, a Michelangelo, a Beethoven. You have the capacity for anything. Yes, you are a marvel. And when you grow up, can you then harm another who is, like you, a marvel? You must cherish one another. You must work – we all must work – to make this world worthy of its children.

Pablo Casals, for Life Education Centres

'We did it because we were interested in cycling, safety and the environment. We'd never realised we'd unleash this huge suppressed demand'

In 1979 John Grimshaw was in his mid-thirties, a successful civil engineer bursting with energy and vision. He was also totally exasperated! For years he'd been trying to get local councils to make the Bristol roads safer for cyclists, but without success. He'd identified the rubbish tip of the old Midland Railway line as a perfect potential cycle path and still nothing was done. Finally, enough was enough.

'If we have to do it ourselves, we do it ourselves.' John was so clear in his vision that he left his job, leased the old railway for a peppercorn rent, rounded up dozens of fit and able volunteers and for the next three years cleared, levelled and put to rights eight miles of path.

'We did it because we were interested in cycling, safety and the environment. We were a group of mainly young, strong and able-bodied people. What we never realised until the path opened was that there were enormous numbers who'd been almost housebound because of the traffic. Of course cyclists use it, but also young children, old ladies, people in wheelchairs and with prams. The pleasure of taking a traffic-free route straight through the city appeals to everyone. We'd never realised we'd unleash this huge suppressed demand. The original route now runs the 16 miles from Bristol to Bath and over a million journeys a year are made on it.'

'That was when Sustrans was formed. We had to become a charity if we were to carry on the work and apply for grants from local authorities.'

Sustrans (which stands for Sustainable Transport) carried on working steadily and by 1995 had built 300 miles of motor-free routes with John Grimshaw at the helm as director. In 1995 Sustrans's vision of a National Cycle Network was chosen by the Millennium Fund as its first major project to mark the year 2000. An award of £42.5 million was made to complete 2,500 miles by the year 2000. It seems like an enormous sum, but is still only 23 per cent of the cost and less than half the length of the National Network which Sustrans hopes to complete by 2005. This will deliver 6,500 miles of cycle routes across the country.

As Carol Freeman, Sustrans Deputy Director, points out: 'There is no other way we could possibly have raised that amount of money. For us, the Lottery has been a godsend. But it does mean we'll need an army of volunteers, donations and fundraisers to get everything finished, just as we did when we rebuilt the first path.

'This is a real rags-to-riches story. Without John's single-minded decision to do those first eight miles, Sustrans would not exist. It's not just environmentally sound. We estimate £350 million-worth of revenue will go to local businesses from holidaymakers and tourists using the routes when the National Network's finished.'

John Grimshaw and the foundation of Sustrans

Unless you are willing to change yourself, you cannot bring about change. If something is important then one has to pay a price for it — nothing comes just like that. And it's not easy!

Valli Shesham, Oxfam, Southern India

We were given a violin once — I was convinced it was a Strad or something equally wonderful and took it off to Boosey & Hawkes. The man rather looked down his nose at it, until he spotted the bow which was inlaid with mother-of-pearl. The bow was worth more than the fiddle!

Eileen Howard, Action for Blind People

'This is the story of many people, but most important are those children and families who unknowingly initiated the idea through their sadness'

Most people think that nurses get accustomed to illness and death, but in my experience, this is not so. I can vividly remember those who have died and those who have survived against all odds.

Anita was brought into the British Military Hospital in Kowloon, Hong Kong, on my first day as Sister in charge of the Children's Ward, back in 1979. She had tumbled out of her father's bicycle basket as he negotiated the traffic and hit her head on the kerb. She was unconscious on arrival and died that evening. Her father, a Gurkha soldier, was distraught; her mother — who spoke no English — disbelieving; she rocked her baby, imploring her to cry.

This tragedy made me consider more seriously an idea that had been at the back of my mind for some time. How do families cope with the death of a child? How do parents manage if their child is so seriously ill that he or she needs constant attention? An acute children's ward is not the right place for children with progressive, degenerative conditions. The care received is perfectly adequate, but there is insufficient time to give every child the individual attention ideally required.

When Anita died, the language problem and cultural differences made comforting her parents even harder. I realised it was no good to just keep thinking about what was wrong, I needed to get on and do something.

The idea of a children's hospice started to develop – a place where families could take refuge from the stress and anxieties that looking after a child with a life-limiting condition can engender.

It was not until 1984, when I had returned home to Essex, nursing in a private clinic near Cambridge, that I started evaluating the need. I did a great deal of research, and there was unanimous acceptance of the idea – if only it could be financed.

I approached my solicitor for advice and set about writing letters. The replies were not forthcoming. Some people obviously felt I was some sort of crank. I started to feel despondent and for some time did nothing more.

And then, a phone call, from a total stranger called Barry Coup. He'd learned of my plans from my solicitor and as Chair of the local Round Table, was interested in making the hospice the cause they would fundraise for in the coming year. Another member of the Round Table suggested an empty rectory as an ideal site and the seed was firmly sown.

The hospice has now been going and growing for 10 years. The seed that was sown has been brought to life by others. It is the story of many people, all playing a part in the overall plan, but most important are those children and families who unknowingly initiated the idea through their sadness.

Sue Potter, Founder, Children's Hospice for the Eastern Region

Every generation of children offers mankind anew the possibility of rebuilding the ruin of the world.

Eglantyne Jebb, Founder of Save the Children

Childhood is a time when we form our view of the world and how to act within it. We learn whether to trust others or to fear them: whether to seek love or avoid pain; whether to use force or kindness to achieve our goals. What happens in childhood shapes the people we become.

Concern Universal

By halting a demolition order the citizens of Farnham are now rewarded for 'imaginative use of a redundant industrial building for the benefit of the community'

The demolition order had been approved and it was only a matter of days before the old maltings was to be destroyed to make way for housing development. The news so alarmed residents of Farnham that a core group of 30 people decided to act to save the 18th-century listed building. To them, it didn't matter that the building was semi-derelict and had been standing empty for 12 years; it was part of the town's heritage.

'A public meeting was called and the school hall was packed. More than 500 people turned up,' says Bob Blackman, general manager of what is today a thriving Farnham Maltings community centre. A rescue plan was put to the owners, Courage Brewery, and a frantic fundraising effort was launched to raise the agreed £30,000 sale price within six weeks.

'The place was crawling with volunteers,' continues Bob, 'but with days to go before the expiry of the deadline in 1969, there was still a shortfall of £12,000, and it was decided to sell nine cottages adjoining the maltings to raise the full sum. Then began the huge task of renovating and refurbishing the building.

Needless to say, public funds were lacking and there was growing hostility towards what some saw as a reckless venture.' Nevertheless, the volunteer force stuck to their guns, and The Maltings, 85 per cent of which has now been converted, has grown to be an extraordinary success story.

A market that started with six or seven vendors now hosts 150 stalls every Saturday, attracting about 7,000 people every weekend to the town. More than 320,000 people visit the Maltings every year to attend a variety of events – from antique fairs, a bridge congress, model railway exhibitions, blues and jazz festivals to toy fairs. About 40 groups use the venue for their activities, ranging from keep-fit classes, toddlers' playgroups, film society, to workshops for the retired and start-up offices for small businesses. Success does breed success, and the spirit of enterprise has led to the Farnham Maltings Association being awarded various honours 'for the imaginative use of a redundant industrial building for the benefit of the community'.

As Bob Blackman says, 'This is a prime example of local people coming together to preserve a superb industrial building from certain demolition. It is also a leading example of just what can be achieved given the vision and determination to succeed. It's only a pity that we're now so much part of the local community that people have stopped thinking of us as a charity in need of cash!'

The Foundation of Farnham Maltings

In charity there is no excess.

Francis Bacon (1561–1626)

Everywhere, in every human being, there is talent and creativity. All they need is the space to develop. Do not think you can change the world, or the whole of society, but work to change things little by little at your own level. Do something, do whatever you can do. This gives others the inspiration to stand and to stay.

K.N. Tiwari, Oxfam, India

WHICH CHARITY?

'Sometimes I just feel I'm lucky to be able to do all the things I don't want to do'

Elizabeth Ward is clearly not giving up her role as the driving force behind the British Kidney Patients' Association until she's got someone in her sights she considers a worthy successor. She founded the charity in 1975, following the death of her son Timbo from kidney failure. At 69, she's still a remarkably good-looking woman, with the sort of no-nonsense approach, clear gaze and firm handshake which gives you the impression you'd better agree with her, or else . . .

Before it was fashionable to be so, Mrs Ward combined being a successful businesswoman with motherhood. She brought up her family and was there for Timbo through kidney transplants which failed and during many years dominated by emergency dashes to hospitals. Today, she runs the BKPA from her former family home in the Hampshire countryside, a short walk from the smaller house she and her husband have built in the grounds.

'When I started BKPA, patients under 17 and over 50 weren't treated. Now it's everyone's right, although there's still a shortage of donors.

'I came at the problem from personal experience. In the beginning I wrote a letter to the bank asking them to let me know when the account got over £100. Our income now is about £2 million a year. We started in a small way, then 17 years ago a TV appeal brought in 3,476 sacks of trading stamps. My assistant went to the market for plastic containers to sort them. I didn't say anything but wrote to the manufacturer for exactly the same number of bins, which were supplied free. It's something that's never discussed and always remembered. It's the principle on which this charity has been built. Much of our support is from patients and their families and I hate spending their money when I don't have to.

'We have no salaried fundraisers and no regional branches. I am unpaid. We built ourselves up to 33 branches and then got complaints from the patients that the volunteers were fundraising on their patch. I didn't want to upset the patients. They put up with such a lot they must always come first.

'I've always had a cause. I feel privileged to help and speak for the people who can't. I used to pray in bed that a politician would go into renal failure, because then someone in power would understand what it's about. It happened, but I didn't expect that politician to be a close friend of mine.

'Sometimes I just feel I'm lucky to be able to do all the things I don't want to do. When I talk to children I often suggest that if they hate getting out of bed they should just once in a while be grateful that they can. When they moan about lack of chips they should stop and think how lucky they are not to be restricted to a special diet.

'But then, until it happens people think, "It'll never happen to me."'

Elizabeth Ward, founder of British Kidney Patients' Association

The more you give,
The more you get,
The more you laugh,
The less you fret,
The more you do unselfishly,
The more you live abundantly.
The more of everything you share,
The more you'll always have to spare.
The more you love,
The more you'll find
That life is good and friends are kind.
For only what we give away,
Enriches us from day to day.

Helen Steiner Rice

WHICH CHARITY?

> *'From my own disaster has come a richness of*
> *experience I could never have dreamed of...'*

At 18, instead of spending my pre-university year working and travelling, I spent it in and around a burns unit. A serious car fire that I was lucky to survive had seen to that. So when I went up to university in 1971 I was looking very different. Instead of my previous good looks, my face was severely scarred and disfigured: I had changed faces.

Five years of plastic surgery couldn't put my face back together again, but people said it made me look 'a lot better'. It was an extraordinary experience meeting people I knew before and seeing them shy away, and meeting others I didn't know who didn't want to know me – or so it seemed. I felt isolated, ugly and bitter. But then a strange and simple truth started to dawn very gradually. My appearance was actually far less important than I imagined *if* I cultivated the skills and strategies to help other people cope with it and me. It was an enormous IF. By trial and error, I worked out what I had to do to get a positive reaction – and it gave me a real 'high', of course, when that happened! I was changing the way I faced others and helping them to change the way they faced me!

I got work after university, got married even, and by the late 1980s was quite settled running a small dairy farm in Guernsey and teaching economics in the local girls' school. It was the time of the tragic fires at the Bradford City football stand, Piper Alpha oil rig and King's Cross Underground station. One day, quite out of the blue, I opened a letter inviting me to write a book about my experiences – a sort of 'DIY guide to disfigurement', it turned out to be, not solely about the experience after burns, but coping with any facial disfigurement.

I called it *Changing Faces: the Challenge of Facial Disfigurement* (Penguin, 1990) and it sums up my approach. As well as tolerating essential surgical reconstruction, anyone who lives with a disfigured face needs to discover and develop what I now call 'the life skills of disfigurement'. These are basically positive self-talk and robust communication skills to deal with the reactions of other people to your appearance.

Little did I think there was another change in the offing. In the aftermath of the book I met many who asked 'What are you going to do next?' 'Milk the cows' was my usual response . . . but a germ of an idea had been sown and I found myself thinking about it at every milking! Was there something that I could do to make a difference – that would make the recovery process less painful for others? A charity could be launched . . .

The changes started to impinge on my family. Exciting ones in some ways, but difficult too. In the summer of 1991, after the herd had been auctioned, I received the catalyst. An amazing donation of £5,000 from a supporter, who simply said: 'Do it.' And I did!

Changing Faces, the charity, was launched in May 1992. It was in some ways another challenge successfully negotiated – with lots of luck and not a little entrepreneurial risk! It meant we had to move from Guernsey, too.

By 1995, Changing Faces has become a recognised voice for anyone with any facial disfigurement, offering supportive help and training as well as campaigning for better NHS facilities and more informed public attitudes. A small team of counsellors/trainers is employed and I have been active in the media, getting the message across. Is it acceptable for anti-heroes in film and TV to be portrayed as having disfigured faces? What does this do for the self-esteem of those affected? In my case, it just makes me even more determined

From my own disaster has come a richness of experience I could never have dreamed of . . . I hope I can convince a few more people to help me help others.

James Partridge, Founder of Changing Faces

WHICH CHARITY?

Everybody has something good inside them. Some hide it, some neglect it, but it is there.

Mother Teresa of Calcutta

'You have to reach out to people in their distress, learn what their pain is and how to get through it'

When I was first told about Rhaune O'Brian, she was simply described as an amazing lady. She has set up and sits in the driving seat of Camden Housebound Link. Sits is the operative word, because she herself has angina and multiple sclerosis and can only work from her bed.

The charity operates in North London, providing support and help for the housebound elderly. There are 10 paid staff including a professional counsellor and trained carers who visit 120 people regularly and when they can't visit, phone daily. This seems a simple enough service, but as you talk to Rhaune (a name attributed to her American Indian ancestry), you are aware of the passion she gives to the cause. 'I try never to refuse help. I'm always aware of how they're feeling. Nowadays people aren't kept long in hospital and the loss of dignity and the loneliness which come with being back at home, severely disabled post-fracture or post-coronary, and seeing that home become dirty and tawdry because you can no longer clean it, having to deal with agencies where the staff are on working holidays and not long-term . . . we're helping people who haven't got neighbours, very few have family or friends – we try to become the family they don't have.

The 24-hour Crisis line is a phone by my bed. I can't sleep with that little quivering voice. You have to reach out to people in their distress, learn what their pain is and how to get through it. I have a deeper understanding of the psychology of pain. I know how it was for me.

The reward? Little things like that voice that says, 'I don't believe it. It's never happened to me before,' when we've delivered a Christmas hamper. We remember birthdays and send cards for Jewish New Year. Simple things which show we're here for them. We embrace all religions and beliefs. We run a newsletter with a nature watch column, articles about medication and spiritual matters. We'll help arrange people's financial affairs.

I'm a doer. I don't believe in committees. I used to run a settlement for 36 adolescents which had to close when the council wanted the building back. As I lived there I was homeless for a bit and, shortly after, became confined to a wheelchair . . . a very determined person stuck in a wheelchair, but confident a door would open. I became dependent on my husband and children. I didn't understand how to apply for benefits, or about the medicines available.

Without this work that I do I would end up in the psychiatric hospital. I started life as a nurse and I do get a lot out of this. We never have enough money, but it's good for us. Life wasn't meant to be easy. I'm sure we wouldn't get the committed people we do working here if everyone was paid well. I feel my life is fulfilled.

Rhaune O'Brian, Founder of Camden Housebound Link

I expect to pass through this world but once; any good thing therefore that I can do, or any kindness that I can show to any fellow creature, let me do it now; let me not defer or neglect it, for I shall not pass this way again.

Stephen Grellet (1773–1855)

'We all get so much satisfaction and joy from helping our guests I wouldn't have it any other way'

It was the early fifties. I started by helping a lady I knew who was struggling to care for five disabled relatives at home: a sick husband, a sister and sister-in-law with multiple sclerosis, an arthritis-ridden mother and paralysed brother.

I simply asked what social services were doing. They were sending a district nurse over once a week. The lady was on the verge of a breakdown; she badly needed a rest. So I searched throughout London for a hostel that the family could stay at, enabling her to have a break.

I went home to my husband so angry: 'Why aren't people doing things? There must be more families like this.' His reply was, 'If you feel so passionately, shouldn't *you* be doing something?'

Was there anything I could personally do? I rang the Charity Commissioners and asked them how I should start. Then I went to see Lady Hamilton; a very great person who set up the Disabled Living Foundation. She agreed to become a trustee and her husband – then chairman of Lloyds Bank – wouldn't become a trustee but agreed to guarantee any bank loan (I had begun with eight shillings from the housekeeping). I needed useful trustees who wouldn't charge for their services.

It was later I had the idea of converting a house for severely physically handicapped people to provide holidays and respite breaks. And, despite having no funds, found and bought the house and paid for it as we went along.

That was the best moment, when that first house was finished; showing people round. My biggest disappointment in all this? Well, you know, it's people. Everyone pulls together and works wonders when there's something major going on, but in the little things, they can be very petty and can let you down.

Now – I'm very much a totem pole. I insist on getting to one centre to join volunteers as a worker on Saturdays. Saturdays are written off, but we all get so much satisfaction and joy from helping our guests I wouldn't have it any other way. I'm known as Mrs B. The energy comes from doing it.

Joan Brander, Founder of Winged Fellowship Trust

'I did something I really wanted to do and got a reward I'd never dreamt of – my health'

In 1985 I was ill with heart problems – I couldn't walk to the end of the street and was told I needed a heart by-pass operation. I had long wanted to organise a festival for Chaucer and the illness got me going, because I felt it might be my last chance.

Chaucer had been a lifelong interest. I had produced and directed my own play, *The Canterbury Tales*, at the Oxford Playhouse in 1964. Later, in 1968, I produced a hugely successful musical version in the West End of London. I'd done it because Chaucer's work was something I cared about, not something just to make money. I'd backed it with just one other person, co-directed it and produced it on the basis that we'd be prepared to write off the money we'd put in. If, by some miracle, it was a success, we'd give the profits to charity which we did.

Canterbury Tales ran for over five years. It was a tremendous success. The manager of the Phoenix Theatre said she'd never known a show that appealed to so many different types of people. I hope we got some of the spirit of Chaucer across. To most people Chaucer is something they do at school then forget. I feel the spirit and joy of Chaucer is something everyone needs. He had a love of life and an extraordinary acceptance of every sort of human being. His father was a wine merchant and he was originally a page to the royal household. He became Head of Customs of the Port of London, then Chief Clerk of Works for 10 royal palaces, then a JP and MP for Kent. He was someone who wrote in his spare time, and his writing has a spiritual quality, even though he's best known as a comic writer and storyteller.

Back to 1985. I'd had an unexpected financial windfall but didn't think that I had much longer to live, so it was now or never for the Chaucer Festival in Canterbury, and so it was born. It was a tremendous success. Everything we did was packed out.

WHICH CHARITY?

We had a huge exhibition and a full-scale production of *Canterbury Tales*. But most of all, doing the festival transformed me. Helpers appeared as if from nowhere. We all felt a wonderful sense of achievement. It was clear Chaucer had a meaning for people's lives today. So next year we did it again, this time in London as well as Canterbury. I was so busy I didn't even think about being ill and then I found I was so much better. The amazing transformation was to have done something I really wanted to do and got a reward I'd never dreamt of. I'd got my health and energy back. The doctor couldn't explain it, but said, 'These things happen.'

The past 10 years of my life have been the happiest. It's not just the doing. I've been involved with all sorts of people. Happiness resides in being really fulfilled within oneself. Nothing can take away these past 10 years which have been so rich for me. Not in financial terms, because the money has been spent. But then, I believe money's to use, not to hoard.

Martin Starkie, Founder, Chaucer Heritage Trust, established in 1992 to fund the work of the Chaucer Festival

> *Seeke out ye good*
> *In everie man*
> *And speke of alle*
> *The best ye can.*
>
> **Geoffrey Chaucer (1343–1400)**

One morning a parcel arrived from a lady whose mother had died. She had sent her set of gold-filled false teeth. Well, what was I going to do with them? Fortunately, gold bullion prices were up, so I set off for the bullion merchant and queued up in a long line of people with things to sell. I was rather embarrassed to hand them over, and explained about us being a charity but the girl didn't bat an eyelid, took out a hammer, smashed the teeth, weighed the gold and gave me the money!

Eileen Howard, Action for Blind People

'Cut down the forest and you kill culture. It took five journeys of 13,000 miles each before we reached this stage of enlightenment'

In 1988 friends Richard Edmunds, a playwright, and Nigel Hughes, an actor, realised their lives were stuck in a rut and felt the need for a challenge. Beckoning them was the primeval instinct to walk in a virgin rainforest, which led them in due course to the misty forests of the remote Hunstein Range in Papua New Guinea in south-east Asia. The experience was a dramatic one, as Richard illustrates: 'We saw the birds of paradise in their full breathtaking beauty. The Melanesian people believe the birds of paradise are higher beings than us. Now I understood what they meant. Pure heaven was somersaulting over my head.'

The joy of witnessing such beauty of nature posed a dilemma as Richard and Nigel discovered that the entire 2,000-square-mile range was earmarked for industrial logging. During their journey up the mighty Sepik River to the Hunstein they had experienced the rich hospitality of the indigenous peoples and made many friends among them. These people now looked to Richard and Nigel to help them save their heritage. William Takaku, a tribal elder, reminded them: 'Cut down the forest and you kill culture.' As Richard says: 'We couldn't just go home and ignore what was going to happen to the trees of paradise.' He made up his mind that somehow they would help these people help themselves to save one of the last great forests.

On their way back to England, they wondered how to avoid falling back into the old ruts. Richard says: 'Though I had not fully realised it at the time, part of my original purpose in travelling had been to find motivation to become an active player in fighting environmental destruction. But what could we do?' Their response was to form Green Light Trust. 'Enough hanging around at red lights. Green for go and green for our love of the natural world,' recalls Richard. It was the start of a unique programme to enhance environmental and cultural understanding while at the same time reawakening people's link with nature. Using their favourite medium of the stage, Green Light Productions took plays on environmental conservation to Papua New Guinea, travelling upriver in dugouts to remote jungle settlements. They involved the local people in acting out the plays themselves.

In 1991, at the request of the people of the Sepik, Green Light formed Friends of the Sepik to preserve the Hunstein Forest Range and the little-known cultures of its indigenous peoples. The drama tours in the jungle have brought traditional landowners out of the deep forest to view a logged area and thus understand more clearly what logging means. The Friends have set up a sustainable forestry training programme, established a market for local carved handicrafts and published a picture book in pidgin for the forest children.

In trying to save one forest, Richard and Nigel realised that most of England's own forest cover had been destroyed centuries ago. 'It took five journeys of 13,000 miles each before we reached this stage of enlightenment,' says Richard. 'To our tribal friends in Papua New Guinea, who believe that everything must be roses in the West, not to have forests was the ultimate poverty. To help redress this poverty in England, Green Light initiated a woodland restoration project in the Suffolk countryside village of Lawshall. We then completed the circle with Papua New Guinea by inviting tribal elder Takaku to plant the first tree.' The Suffolk community woodland project, called Forest for our Children, is planted and maintained by pupils from local schools and adult volunteers. So far, two woodlands, Golden Wood and Crooked Wood, have been planted on set-aside land partly donated by a local landowner, and partly purchased by fundraising efforts and an Adopt a Plot scheme.

For Richard and Nigel, what started off as an adventure has inspired them to make a real impact on environmental awareness with a simple formula and without sober lecturing or militant campaigning.

**Richard Edmunds and Nigel Hughes,
Founders of the Green Light Trust**

Where is the man who owes nothing to the land in which he lives? Whatever that land may be, he owes to it the most precious thing possessed by man, the morality of his actions and the love of virtue.
Jean Jacques Rousseau (1712–1778)

'I never realised how much human effort was involved. I didn't realise it would be as tough. I still hankered after the thought that if you've got something good, people will beat a path to your door. I forgot how many people lay mines in your path and put "closed" in front of the door you're trying to open'

The Foundation for Conductive Education is a system of specialist education for children and adults with motor disorders which originated in the Pets Institute in Hungary. At the time it was 'discovered' by half a dozen colleagues in Birmingham, they felt it had already been reinterpreted, misunderstood and consigned to the dustbin by others in the UK. Andrew Sutton, Founder of the Foundation, takes up the story:

'We decided to be revolutionary. We needed a modest investment so that we could deal with Hungary behind the Iron Curtain, and bring this amazing system into the UK.

'Dealing with Hungary was easy, getting the cash to set up in the UK wasn't. The system was new. We felt the existing structures would try to reject it because it didn't fit. Support was promised *when* it was proved worthwhile but not before. We decided we could only get it off the ground if there was public pressure to do so. We deliberately seeded articles in the press, which led directly to a human interest TV documentary broadcast at prime time. The documentary made the news and the Establishment tried to defend their stance – so even more stories were printed and broadcast and parents started to articulate. Finally, a meeting was arranged at the Houses of Parliament of the organisations that had promised us some cash conditionally. We wanted them to pledge half a million pounds. A *Newsnight* TV crew was outside the door and we had two press releases prepared. We got the money.'

**Andrew Sutton, Founder/Director,
Foundation for Conductive Education**

Where there is charity and wisdom, there is neither fear nor ignorance.

St Francis of Assisi (1181–1226)

'Being able to change, and being able to bring about change, is wonderful'

I have met extraordinary individuals over these years. They came from all sectors of society – a lot from underprivileged societies – and meeting them, you know, has been encouragement for me. Working with people involved in problems was one big factor in my life. The other thing is that one is constantly growing – so that you still feel very young. I am 61, and that amazes me! Being able to change, and being able to bring about change is wonderful. We are talking about working with people in villages and not in the cities – such powerful, unknown, unseen people; I feel very fortunate for having been involved. I have always said that it is good to work in development, and I wonder, do the people involved understand how very fortunate they are?

When we help someone or something we grow and gain tremendously – and maybe, incidentally, give something in return.

If I were going to start a programme, first I'd listen. Just listen and talk. Starting some work with street children would be good. I would say to them, 'What do you want to do? Would you like a club? Or would you like to be a group? What do you want to do about your life?' I would explore the potential and the capacity they have and their own aspirations, and then we'd go from there. And children, because theirs is an open mind, are not prejudiced and not frustrated.

Valli Sheshan, Oxfam volunteer in southern India

Have you had kindness shown?
Pass it on.

Henry Burton (1840–1931)

As a homeless teenager Colette knew the strong bond and stability an animal provided. Today she's an international speaker on animal welfare

As a homeless teenager in London, Colette Kase was told to 'get rid of your dog if you want to be housed'. She refused, because 'A dog is for life. People don't realise how strong the bond is between pets and owners. Having an animal provides stability in one's life, especially when you are homeless and vulnerable on the streets of London.'

Colette's predicament spurred her to initiate a service for homeless pet owners for whom the costs of preventative care such as vaccines and worming are often prohibitive. With the help of animal welfare charities, she started a care project, Hope, in 1991: soon even landlords and resettlement workers were contacting her for advice on how to manage pet problems. By 1993, the demands on the service were so overwhelming it nearly folded. For its continued success, Colette's Hope project needed more sponsorship, volunteers and financial backing. She approached the National Canine Defence League, the UK's largest dog welfare organisation. The League adopted the project at the end of 1994 and officially launched it in 1995.

Colette is now busy giving legal seminars on pets and housing, developing guidelines for those providing housing, advising tenants with dogs who face eviction, holding regular clinics offering free health check-ups for pet dogs and, given the transient nature of the homeless population, visiting travellers' sites. The project is in the process of drafting literature for homeless people seeking shelter with a pet, and planning an award for pet-friendly housing providers.

Colette, who is now housed and has completed a psychology degree, says of her achievement: 'I feel incredibly lucky. Like all typical adolescents, I wanted to work with dogs and horses. Now, I have the job that I always wanted.'

Colette Kase, National Canine Defence League

> *Whatever you can do,*
> *Or dream you can, begin it.*
> *Boldness has genius*
> *Power and magic in it.*
>
> *Goethe (1749–1832)*

'The work has become an integral part of my life, so much so that I cannot live without going to the garden two days a week. I'm now as dependent on them as they are on me'

'When we came back to England, my husband had a job to go to. But I was not enthusiastic about getting dull, low-paid work; my priority was to establish a home before looking for something to do, since we had been out of our society for seven years. I also wanted to put something back into the community after a highly paid, good job with a pharmaceutical company in Switzerland.'

It was 1993, and 52-year-old Hilary Miflin, a trained botanist, decided to visit Charity Fair to look for a community project that appealed to her. 'I was looking for what I call my Bash Street Kid to adopt, but couldn't find any.' Her search led her to Reach, which puts people who want to offer their expertise to hard-pressed voluntary organisations in touch with such organisations. She was given a form which 'took ages to fill in'. Within a week, Hilary was given a choice of six charities, four of which she thought were really interesting. Hilary plumped for a post with the Chelsea Physic Garden, since 'I loved plants; although it was quite different from what I had in mind, since it was not a Bash Street Kid project.'

The Chelsea Physic Garden, founded in 1673 by the Society of Apothecaries when plants were a main source of medicines, needed a receptionist. Hilary talked to the curator, suggesting that the garden could use her knowledge of plants. Two years on, Hilary is still there working two days a week and is 'now virtually responsible for all the plant database'. There are 7,000 species to be indexed, and the work is crucial to the garden. To date Hilary has completed 4,000 with support from a consultant from Kew Gardens. 'The work has become an integral part of my life, so much so that I cannot live without going to the garden two days a week. I'm now as dependent on them as they are on me.' Hilary enjoys the combination of the administrative work and the gardening. 'When I get bored, I go out and look at the plants. The garden of the apothecaries is a really, really charming place, and has a long history in medicinal herbs.'

Working at the garden has inspired Hilary to start a four-year correspondence course in herbal medicine. 'The Chelsea Physic Garden was instrumental in showing me a new direction. It has definitely been a stepping stone. I came in as a volunteer, and will stay on as a gardener if need be. The garden has been in desperate financial straits and could have been lost.' It is now having to balance being a venue for society weddings and industrial functions with being a garden of medicinal herbs. Hilary believes that her small contribution will give the garden a boost to function better in the future. And when she has finished cataloguing the 7,000 plants, she will have to start all over again. 'It will be like painting the Forth Bridge. Information changes year by year.' She will also continue to work in the garden, growing specialised plants. 'This is a garden of world medicine; the plants look ordinary, but they are integral to different systems and cultures of medicine, from Europe, India and China.'

For Hilary, the search for something meaningful to do has greatly changed her life. 'I have to be motivated by something other than money, and it is worthwhile doing something for my own satisfaction.' She also ponders how a long time ago she wanted to be a doctor, but ended up doing botany instead. 'Now, with the course I'm doing, I'll be eligible to practise medicine.' Her eldest daughter, a hospital registrar, gently mocks her by stating, 'Just trust her to do this at this stage in life.' Hilary knows that Reach has helped to expand her horizons. 'I'm a nicer, kinder, more patient and interesting person.'

As for Reach, she says, 'It is very efficient, and does find the right jobs for people. But you have to start as a volunteer.' If the Chelsea Physic Garden were not so short of money, Hilary would have pushed to be paid. But she says: 'Reach is a stepping stone, and it has enabled me to acquire new skills. Last week, I saw an advertisement for a paid job for what I am doing . . .'

Hilary Miflin, volunteer with Chelsea Physic Garden

The best portion of a good man's life, his little, nameless, unremembered acts of kindness and of love.

William Wordsworth (1770–1850)

T.E. Lawrence was an airman in the ranks of the RAF after the 1914–18 war and gave the royalties from his books to the RAF Benevolent Fund – privately making sure the Fund knew about the needs of his barrackroom comrades.

'You start in the morning and you could be soaked through at the end of the day. It's a wonderful feeling when you know you have helped others'

'What are you doing this weekend?' As a result of that query, Esmee Salkeld found herself whisked off to visit a coal mine in Wales. As she crawled on her belly down a pithead, Esmee couldn't help wondering what she was doing down there, but when someone yelled, 'Are you enjoying yourself?' Esmee shouted back, 'Yes', and the response came back: 'So, why don't you join us?' That was in 1960, and Esmee has since dedicated more than 30 years of her life to voluntary service with St John Ambulance. 'I've thoroughly enjoyed every minute, whether on duty at the Royal Opera House or in a muddy field.' The friend who asked her to come along is still active at 83.

'Once you join, it is like a big family. As a radio operator we all chat like parrots, about everything. On duty, a member has to be prepared to cope with anything. You start in the morning and you could be soaked through at the end of the day. It's a wonderful feeling when you know you have helped others. My most challenging moment was while on duty at Biggin Hill when two small aircraft collided. The crowd was shocked, some injured. We worked calmly as a team, attending to the injured, and no one needed any counselling after that.

'It's a pity that fewer young people are joining up. But there are still some young coming in, especially those who want to pursue caring as a career. It is a stepping stone to the future. There is a lot that they can get out of the Order. I know. I have got more out of it than I have put into it. I have expanded my interests, and have helped people. I do like helping people, and this is an opportunity to do it. It has also given me a lot of companionship.'

Whether on duty at a rally, a football stadium, a West End

theatre or a fete, wet or cold, for Esmee 'it has been very worthwhile'.

Esmee Salkeld, volunteer for the Order of St John (St John's Ambulance)

Ninety per cent of war victims were military. Today 90 per cent are civilians.

Health Unlimited

'Helping other people, who are frightened by the sea, is a satisfying experience'

The weather had been steadily getting worse; so much so that a Christmas fun and fundraising event for children, when the Porthcawl lifeboat crew planned to save Santa from drowning, had to be scrapped. By December 30, the winds were howling at gale force nine; the Severn bridge was closed to all traffic and the Swansea–Cork ferry service was cancelled. Stuart Roberts, helmsman of the lifeboat station and a police officer by occupation, decided to take a drive along the promenade. He spotted a fisherman at the end of the breakwater, became anxious, and decided to stop at the lifeboat station. 'I wanted to have a word in his ear that he was being an idiot. The swell was crashing over the breakwater and the weight of the water could have dragged him into the sea. But just then a man came running up to tell me there was someone in the water waving for help. I thought that it was the fisherman, but when I looked around I realised it was not.' The victim was a 17-year-old, who'd been given a surfboard for Christmas, and was now out of control, caught in a rip tide which was dragging him out to sea.

Despite the appalling weather, Stuart was determined to launch the station's inflatable lifeboat, and the crew's pagers were activated. 'The first lad to arrive was suffering from 'flu and had literally got out of his sickbed. The second had only a few months' service. I told them that they couldn't go. A couple of other lads arrived, but even then everyone shook their heads in disbelief about launching in such atrocious conditions. The waves were by now 12 feet high. But I knew that if I delayed the launch any longer, the boat would be ripped to bits on the rocks. With great reluctance, the secretary in charge of the station decided to let us go.

'The wind was very strong, but we had a perfect launch. Since we can't start the engine till we hit water, the wind pinned us to the pier. It was wicked. The breakers were coming in. On the third pull, the boat started, but when we were in the water, I couldn't see the surfer. The waves were awesome. We had to zigzag amid the swells to reach the victim. It's standard practice to put the engine into neutral when trying to get the victim on board, but I looked ahead and saw this wall of water hurtling towards us; if I had put the engine into neutral, the swell would have picked us up and tossed us like a cork. I yelled to crew member Wayne Evans to let go of the surfer and powered the lifeboat through the wall of water. It seemed for ever and a day. Wayne and Carl [the other crew member on board] were tossed into the stern by the weight of the water. There was so much white water that the engine just revved without engaging gear. My heart was in my mouth. It was the worst moment for me.'

Stuart, who sails as a hobby, drew on all his seamanship skills to reach the surfer on the third attempt. As the victim was being dragged on board the waves picked up his surfboard and tossed it like a plank into the boat, cutting through the visor of Stuart's new helmet. 'If I'd had my old helmet on, it would have split my face open.'

With the victim on board, Stuart ran the boat straight onto the sandy beach. The entire rescue had taken less than five minutes, but for those watching from shore, seeing the punishment the crew and the boat were taking, it seemed like a lifetime.

WHICH CHARITY?

For Stuart, this outstanding lifesaving act won him the Lifeboatman of the Year award, but he regards what he did that day as no different from any other day. From the age of five, when he held one end of the tape at the official inauguration of the Porthcawl station in 1965, Stuart's been interested in the Royal National Lifeboat Institution. His father was one of the original crew but Stuart didn't join up until 1978 because 'My mum wouldn't allow both of us to serve as crew at the same time.' Over the years, Stuart has honed his seamanship skills under various conditions. 'For me, the rescue gave a sense of wellbeing. Helping other people, who are frightened by the sea, is a satisfying experience. Seeing the look of relief on the faces of those rescued is reward enough.'

Stuart Roberts, volunteer lifeboat helmsman, RNLI

With malice toward none, with charity for all, with firmness in the right as God gives us to see the right, let us strive on to finish the work we are in, to bind up the nation's wounds, to care for him who shall have borne the battle and for the widow and his orphan, to do all which may achieve and cherish a just and lasting peace among ourselves and with all nations.

Abraham Lincoln (1809–1865)

'Yes, I've been able to "put something back into life", but it's also brought generous rewards. I enjoy the treat of the love and warmth I get from John's visits'

Tom, a retired police inspector, answered a local MENCAP advertisement to become a MENCAP visitor.

He was asked to visit John, who was then 35 and had been in hospital since he was 11. John was disturbed and antisocial, kept in a locked ward and left alone for long stretches of time. He had no visitors, was lonely and desperate for affection.

'On my first visit I tried not to think how grim it must be to live on a hospital ward. The staff member with me unlocked the heavy door to John's ward and let me in. A grown man was sitting hunched on the bed, refusing to look at either of us. He was frighteningly withdrawn and wary. I didn't feel that anything I did or said really got through – except at the end, when I said goodbye. The feeling of recognition I got then is probably the only reason I made it back.

'That first visit was over five years ago. The second and third weren't much better. Very slowly, though, I started to notice the difference. The first major breakthrough was the day I got John to come for a walk with me in the hospital grounds. Then we made it to the shops. It was certainly progress of a sort; I knew it must be providing some sort of much needed contact. But I still felt that in some ways John was still in a locked ward of his own, but by now I was determined to get him out. At my wits' end, I finally talked to the MENCAP District Officer. What was John really like? I asked. Was there something he did really care about, something that someone had noticed? Rather to my surprise, I was told that yes, he did have a passion – for trains. Something about the bustle, the noise, the people and the engines gave him real pleasure. After that it was simple. On my next visit we went to the local station.

'We're a regular sight there now. Would anyone, I often wonder, recognise the outgoing and affectionate man standing on the platform with me as the withdrawn, anti-social figure I first met? And would anyone knowing John believe that these days I don't return him to the hospital – where he's now living in an open ward – but we go back to my house for tea? Or that he's become a part of the family – someone who joins in and makes us roar with laughter?

'Yes, I've been able to "put something back into life", but it's also brought generous rewards. I enjoy the treat of the love and warmth I get from John's visits and I know that this is positive affirmation that I can do this, and do it well. There is also the joy of becoming part of John's "family" on the ward and being involved with his friends. The openness and honesty of feelings there are a lesson for us all. He's helped me to see life from his viewpoint, and that too has been very important to me.'

A MENCAP volunteer's story

> *What we think,*
> *or what we know,*
> *or what we believe is, in the end,*
> *of little consequence.*
> *The only consequence is what we do.*
>
> *John Ruskin (1819–1900)*

Our society values achievement, success, technology, physical beauty and prowess. Where does that leave those who do not succeed? In L'Arche we learn the unique value of every person, however handicapped; we learn to appreciate their gift. When we slow down to their pace we gain a new perspective on life and learn what really matters. We learn to value relationships and the things of the heart. People are important, not status or success.

When the element of competition is removed and a place is made for each person, there is a place for me, too. I was able to open up, and to share my vulnerability. Living with handicapped people I discovered my own handicap, my own broken-ness. I was also accepted and loved. I came to L'Arche with little self-confidence and although I still have a way to go, I gained an enormous amount.

To discover how much I share with those we call handicapped was extremely important. It brings me to the basics: to affirm the dignity and value of each person.

From* Living in L'Arche *by Clare Hall-Matthews

L'Arche is French for The Ark, as in Noah's Ark. L'Arche communities are places where adults with learning disabilities and those whom society calls normal live together, sharing their lives, their work and their leisure.

'It's a commitment, but that's what volunteering's about'

I spent three weeks in the office as a volunteer and now I've been a penfriend for about four months. It's not something I mention much to friends – they might think it silly, or wonder at my motivation for doing it. People often think you write because you have a father or brother inside.

It's the other side of the Trust. The main part of their work is dealing with the people who've got control – issuing reports and targets. The penfriends involve people on a one-to-one basis. I was a bit dubious at first – writing to someone you don't know – but it's only when you start writing you realise how important your letters are. The Prison Reform Trust take great care in matching people. If there isn't a match they will ask you to wait – whether you're prisoner or penfriend. Absolutely anyone can do it, but I was warned it could be quite demanding. Of course it's changed my attitude. My penfriend has taken me into his confidence enough to tell me why he did what he did. It's easy to be judgmental when you don't know the background. I realise that even someone with a lot of family support can be very lonely. That even though it may only take me ten minutes every couple of weeks to dash off a letter, I know it will mean an enormous amount. A friend of the prisoner I write to wrote as well, to ask to be included on the scheme and I was happy to point him in the right direction. Everything's handled via the Trust, so there's no pressure.

It didn't mean a lot to me initially, but now I'd feel very guilty if I didn't reply. I usually try to write back within a day or two, and I'm happy to find I'm building a friendship. It's a commitment, but that's what volunteering's about.

Kate Hobbs, Volunteer with Prison Reform Trust

WHICH CHARITY?

To be able to practise five things everywhere
Under heaven constitutes perfect virtue . . . (they are) gravity,
generosity of soul, sincerity, earnestness, and kindness.

Confucius (551–471 BC)

'Volunteering has created a sense of community in the way we help each other'

I was fairly new to the town when I was asked to help, 13 years ago. I'd say it's mainly through my work with Save the Children that I now know a tremendous number of people; I can hardly walk down a street without bumping into someone I know, and this enormous friendship between all of us is one of the main benefits.

We help other volunteers – an 84-year-old lady went over to visit my wife while we moved house for her; another was enormously depressed, alcoholic and getting no help from her doctor. I think I can say that being involved with us and getting support at a personal level, counselling and the like, has made the difference. She's made a real recovery. As for me, what I've got out of it is a wife!

A lot of people work very hard for the Fund in all sorts of different ways. Thirteen years ago fundraising had reached a plateau of about £4,000 a year. I knew the Secretary of the local branch – I wasn't involved at that stage, I was her lodger – and suggested a house-to-house collection during Save the Children Week. Everyone was a bit worried as they'd never done it before. Neither had I, but I made a few suggestions and ended up agreeing to organise it! We didn't have a lot of time to get going, but all the same raised about £830. The next year we had more time and raised a bit more, and it's gradually built up so it's now about £4,000. Then, because we're better known, people help in all sorts of ways. One trader gave us all the profits from his

Christmas tree sales if we agreed to man the site. Someone phoned to ask us to organise a concert: he had the venue and the musicians. We now have enough helpers we can call on, and I was immediately able to say, 'Yes, we can do it', despite the amount of work I knew it'd be. We sold 65 tickets for £25 each, which takes some doing in this economic climate!

It's very much easier collecting for Save the Children than many other charities. Children are readily accepted. Above all it's the sense that we can make a difference to some children's lives. If someone's a bit down because they don't feel they've raised much I can say 'Ten pence can buy a sachet of dehydration salts and save a child.' You have to bring people back to the primary purpose. Every little helps.

Les Hodges, volunteer for Save the Children Fund; Chairman, Hitchin branch Save the Children Fund; Deputy Area Rep., Hertfordshire and Bedfordshire; Member, Save the Children Week working party

> *In necessary things, Unity;*
> *In doubtful things, Liberty;*
> *In all things, Charity.*
> **Richard Baxter's Motto (1615–1691)**

Eighteen years of volunteering and still going strong

It's unheard of for anyone to stay in the same job for 18 years without being paid a penny for their work. But that's what Jean Harrington has been doing as a childcare volunteer with Barnardo's at Ravensdale in Tunbridge Wells since 1977. Now past retirement age, she continues to work at the project at least two days a week.

'I wrote to the project all those years ago because I care about children. I've been here ever since.' Jean organises activities and play sessions for a group of children and quite often, she says in good humour, 'My clothes are splattered with flour when the children have been making dough.'

The Ravensdale project works with children under five who are slow at learning or who have a difficult home life. Jean says being a volunteer there has widened her outlook. 'I've never had contact with disabled children before,' says the mother of four grown-up children. 'I didn't want to work when my children were small, I liked being a mother and a housewife, so until they were older, I did not think about working.' Few mothers of Jean's generation went back to work anyway.

Jean now realises that if she had wanted she could have had a successful career in childcare. 'If I was younger, I probably would train as a social worker, but you can't do training when you're my age. Still, I wish I had.'

After 18 years working for Barnardo's, Jean is now planning to expand her volunteering even further and help in the kitchen at a centre for disabled adults that is opening near her home. 'I hope it gets going soon, otherwise I might make use of the services and need looking after myself,' she laughs.

Jean Harrington, volunteer with Barnardo's

No act of kindness, no matter how small, is ever wasted.
Aesop (c. 550 BC)
The Lion and the Mouse

'As a wife and mother, I'm a diabolical cook, I can't sew on a button and I hate housework. But, ask me about diabetes, and you can't stop me. And, by God, I'm a bloody good Big Chief Yellow Frog'

If it were not for Barbara Elster, there would not be a Big Chief Yellow Frog or Tadpole Club. The club for diabetic children, their brothers, sisters and friends was formed in 1992, but Barbara's involvement with the British Diabetic Association began more than 26 years ago, when the youngest of her four children was diagnosed with diabetes. 'It was traumatic, unbelievable,' says Barbara, recalling how she was stricken with guilt. 'Why me? Why my child?' There were no support groups then and Barbara found books gave little practical advice. Children were put on a strict diet and had to have two insulin injections a day, and that was the sum measure of their lives.

For Barbara, that was not enough. As a teacher, she had always been interested in children and was involved with youth clubs. Her interest and involvement inspired her to do something for diabetic children. 'There was nothing for them then; when parents got together, children got together.' Through her involvement Barbara set up a Parents' Support Group, and although she started off as a volunteer she is now a trustee of the association.

The Tadpole Club was an idea she had which came to fruition in 1992. The message for children is that good little tadpoles grow into healthy frogs. Club members receive the *Tadpole Times*, which gives practical advice about living with diabetes, has its own 'tadtoon', a cartoon about their mascot Frankie Frog, and other goodies, such as a frog puppet, colouring book, badges, and a birthday card each year from Barbara, who is Big Chief Yellow Frog and lives in Marsh Cottage, by the Lily Pond. There are now 3,000 members all over the world, and both Barbara and the association are over the moon. 'No one else anywhere in the world has anything like this for children.'

Through Barbara's efforts, children with diabetes and their families get to attend holiday camps at resorts such as Clacton-on-Sea three times a year. These longish weekends cater for about 100 families and there are 20 medical staff on hand to help and give advice. The club also organises pond parties and 'splashathons', which encourage 'tadpoles' to learn to swim.

Awards are given to children who can swim the width of a pool unaided, as well as to those who care for pets or wild animals. Big Chief Barbara acts as agony aunt, listening to children's problems and answering their letters. 'It gives me a terrific buzz, I love children, and I will give them 25 hours every day, and I still can't get enough.'

Besides her varied roles Barbara, who still does supply teaching, lectures to the Royal College of Physicians and appears on television to talk about diabetes. 'As a wife and mother, I'm a diabolical cook, I can't sew on a button and I hate housework. But, ask me about diabetes, and you can't stop me. And, by God, I'm a bloody good Big Chief Yellow Frog.'

Barbara's diabetic son, now in his late twenties, works as a cameraman. She, however, can still remember the fear that gripped her in the early days: 'I have always been a coper, but what about my son, could he?' But now, she adds: 'There is a future with diabetes. We can live with it, a good life.' Barbara should know, for her dogged determination has played such a significant role in inspiring that belief.

Barbara Elster, from parent to volunteer to trustee with the British Diabetic Association

If 1,000 children are starving and you can only feed one, then feed one. Do whatever you can, however small it seems. A kind word. A friendly gesture.

Concern Universal

'It was a courageous decision, to take on the retired director of a 1,000-bed hospital as a staff nurse in a 24-bed hospice'

Let me give you a potted history. I was Director of Patient Services at the Belfast Hospital, having been a senior manager in the health service, when suddenly my mother died. Within two months my father was diagnosed with cancer and dead within the month. At the same time my brother was diagnosed with cancer of the prostate. So, as we buried my father, I had knowledge of my brother's cancer and a real desire to give up the hassle of trust status.

I'd had 13 years in nurse management, commissioned a new hospital, spent two years getting it running, helped it become a trust, been a surveyor for the King's Fund Organisational Audit . . . but despite all that I felt I wanted to get back to my roots: to provide hands-on cancer care and share with families and patients the personal experiences I had been through and my years of professional experience.

I negotiated early retirement, designed my own clinical refresher course, went back into my own wards and asked the sisters I'd been in charge of to pass on their skills and refresh me.

That done, I saw an ad and applied for the Beaconsfield Marie Curie Hospice Centre. The Matron very courageously took on the retired director of a 1,000-bed hospital as a staff nurse in a 24-bed hospice, but I was very fortunate to have Sister Armstrong as my team leader and mentor. I fitted in and very quickly it seemed I'd never left nursing.

I think more than anything else the Christian ethos makes it easy for me to listen, to be there, to share my knowledge. When people know what to expect they can cope 70 per cent better, because they know what's about to happen. I can prepare them for the little things. I can reassure them that although I might be busy, 'You're important. I am here to be with you.' The secret is not the length of life but the quality of life. We can make those last days and hours that bit more pleasant. And if someone is comfortable and sleeps away, it's much easier for relatives to cope with the death. Knowing that cancer doesn't have to mean pain.

For me, I've completed the circle. Senior nurses very rarely have the opportunity to share their experiences with people at the grass roots. I can act as a mentor to younger staff and somehow share my mistakes, not only my successes. They can share with me some of the research they're doing. It's a symbiotic relationship, as well as learning every day from patients and relatives.

It's amazing how courageous patients can be when facing terminal illness. To be part of their struggle and see how they cope, taking a day at a time, an hour at a time, is a great privilege.

Our principle is that money's never mentioned. There is no cost to the patient or the carer even though the NHS covers only about 48 per cent of the costs. So we go out in our spare time and fundraise. But I am cutting back my hours now, so I can spend that bit more time with my brother.

Marie Curie Nurse of the Year, Robert Wilkinson, Co. Antrim

> *Do all the good you can,*
> *By all the means you can,*
> *In all the ways you can,*
> *In all the places you can,*
> *At all the times you can,*
> *To all the people you can,*
> *As long as ever you can.*
>
> *John Wesley's Rule (1703–1791)*

An unexpected heavy brown paper parcel was opened in the 1939–45 war to reveal 100 ounces of gold from the Emperor Haile Selassie of Ethiopia, in gratitude to the RAF for its role in restoring him to the throne.

'The trustees, all parents of deaf children, deserve credit for appointing a deaf chief executive'

Susan Daniels is an excellent role model for those born with a disability. Susan's deafness never stopped her from striving to fulfil her potential. As she says: 'My personal view is, always have a go at something.' And, indeed, she has. Now in her mid-thirties, she has become the first deaf chief executive of the National Deaf Children's Society.

'From a very early age, I was a very determined person, and I have had tremendous support from my parents.' Susan is now setting out to sell her message to other deaf children, that 'you can do it, too'. But she knows from her own experience that deaf children and their families ought first to be provided with the proper support. 'I was the only deaf child in the mainstream school that I went to, so my parents didn't know what support was available, or even if there was any available. Some teachers told me that I wouldn't be able to sit for my A-levels. When you are deaf, you are constantly being told what you can't do.'

Susan overcame these barriers, went on to university and did a degree in history and politics. 'I thoroughly enjoyed my undergraduate years. University students, being more mature, are more understanding of your needs, unlike schoolchildren.' After her degree, Susan had the option of doing personnel management at the London School of Economics, but instead took a job in a large food company. 'I needed the money more but I decided never again to do a job where I need to use a telephone.' A stint with Islington and Camden area health authority followed which involved paper work, before she moved on to a computer company.

'A fortunate experience happened when I met a man teaching at the City Lit. Centre for Deaf People. I had been thinking of working with the deaf, but had no confidence.' That meeting encouraged her to become qualified in teaching deaf children, and Susan moved on to be higher education officer at the Royal National Institute for the Deaf, before becoming its head of policy. 'I love teaching and working with deaf students, but I also realised that my ability to campaign on behalf of deaf people was incompatible with a lecturer's role.'

When she was offered her present job, it was 'A surprise and delight! The trustees, all parents of deaf children, deserve credit for appointing a deaf chief executive,' says Susan, who is only the second woman to head the 51-year-old society. 'That is a milestone.' Now, Susan works with a staff of 35 people, only six or seven of whom are deaf. 'I very much want to increase the number of deaf members of staff, but the interaction between deaf and hearing staff is beneficial for the Society. Since staff have to work with a deaf chief executive, they develop a clearer understanding of the communication needs of deaf children and adults.'

Susan's goal is to help the country's 65,000 deaf children achieve their potential. 'I feel strongly that if deaf children are to be integrated into schools there must be proper support from teachers and the other children. There is no point putting deaf children in a class and expecting them to get on with it. Teachers don't think that when they are talking to the blackboard, with their backs to the class, deaf children cannot lip-read. There has definitely been an improvement but there is a long way to go to change attitudes. The 1993 Education Act sets out a code of practice, but there are insufficient resources to implement it. A deaf child in a mainstream school may need 10 hours' support a week, but a local authority may only give two hours because of a lack of funds.' Susan also wants to build a higher profile for the Society so that parents of deaf children immediately know where to go to seek help and advice.

'I will achieve what I set out to do. The challenge of deafness is faced by both deaf children and parents who have no experience of a deaf child and I can't imagine doing anything else but enabling families to help deaf children develop their potential.'

Susan Daniel, Director, National Deaf Children's Society

Ideals are in the stars, but the reality is on the ground.
Elizabeth Fitzroy (1940)

> *'One firm even told me that taking me on would destroy the image and credibility of the company'*

Kirsten Battle walked down the aisle on her wedding day. 'I sort of glided. I can't remember actually walking because the day passed in a kind of haze. Afterwards, my legs were killing me.'

Kirsten was 21 when she married Mark Battle at Oulton Church in Leeds. She was born with spina bifida, a neurological condition which can paralyse the legs and cause other complications, so she's normally confined to a wheelchair. This she was determined to leave behind on the big day. Nothing was going to hold her back.

'I had been absolutely determined to be like any other bride. And with this in mind, I went looking for a physiotherapist who would help me. When I found one, the first thing I asked was, "Do you want a challenge?" She did me proud,' said Kirsten.

Sheer guts have carried Kirsten through ever since. She moved south to Burnham, near Slough, for married life with Mark and went job hunting in a big way, determined to pull her weight, and not become dependent on Mark for income.

'From the April after I came down here, I sent off at least 2,000 applications for jobs. Looking for work turned into a 24-hours-in-the-day job. I must have spent £1,000 on buying newspapers and stamps and visits to the Job Centre. It cost me a small fortune.'

With a clutch of GCSEs, RSA typing, a certificate in computer technology, an NVQ in business and administration and over two years' office experience in Leeds behind her, you would have imagined bosses would be crying out for her skills.

Not so. Most employers failed to reply and rejection was the norm.

'Basically, people discriminated against me because I'm a

wheelchair user. One firm even told me that taking me on would destroy the image and credibility of the company. I had to wait until my story was told in the local paper before firms took any notice. Then I had a queue of people wanting to talk to me. There were eight job offers very quickly.'

Kirsten eventually accepted a full-time job with a translation company as an audiotypist, working at home. She feels that someone down south is at last valuing her skills.

She has got at least one other marvellous thing to look forward to in the near future. Mark and Kirsten expect to make their family complete with a baby. She's made sure she took enough of the B-group vitamin folic acid to greatly reduce the risk of her baby also being born with spina bifida.

Kirsten Battle is supported by ASBAH

Nothing is more terrible than ignorance in action.
Goethe (1749–1832)

Is it right to dream?

Dhanalakshmi is 19, bright, attractive and in her final year at school. All her life she has struggled against three facts of her birth which have been seen as handicaps: she was born into a family of landless labourers, the poorest of the poor in rural India; she is a woman; and – from polio in infancy – she cannot walk.

Her family were unable to pay for her to go to school. Why waste resources on someone who was both a cripple and a girl? So, it was not until she was 12 that she was spotted by a pastor at the Church of South India, who saw her as Dhanalakshmi and not as three problems rolled into one.

As a result a place was found for her at the Lucy Perry Noble School in Madurai, run by the Church of South India to give first place to the marginalised people of society. Classes integrate physically disabled children with those more able. Half the curriculum involves learning income-producing skills, such as basket- and toy-making, machine and hand-loom weaving, to guarantee a living after school. The other half is the more traditional school curriculum which takes the students up to the general certificate they need to get them into government colleges and technical institutes.

When she arrived, Dhanalakshmi's legs were a mass of persistently infected sores, caused by crawling. The problem was solved when the school organised a specially converted tricycle she could operate with her hands. She was an eager pupil right from the start and did well, announcing her ambition to become a doctor.

Seven years on, the good luck tale is just that. There is no happy ending. Dhanalakshmi still has her ambitions, but her enthusiasm has failed her. She is only too aware of the enormity of social prejudice which will prevent her realising her dreams. That, tragically, is another fact of life she has to struggle with as she prepares to leave school.

So was the Church of South India right to give her — and thousands like her — a chance? What value can you place on dreaming?

Case history supplied by Council for World Mission

Creativity is a struggle — and the creative side of charity work can feel like going in the wrong direction up a busy one-way street. Every time you write an article, create an advert, invent a new campaign idea, help in some way to rebuild a person's life, you're creatively opposing the forces of disorder and decay in the world. But this struggle is worth it to see one person lifted up the ladder of hope.

**Debra Chand, Director of Communications,
The Leprosy Mission**

WHICH CHARITY?

> *'I wanted to trust you, to like you, but I was frightened about getting close to you because everyone I'd trusted or loved in the past had either gone away or hurt me'*

It has been a long time since you walked into our lives – five and a half years to be exact. The first year you started visiting from Home-Start, my life was such a blur. I was numb, dead, nothing mattered. Things were really rough for me then, with one baby dead, a miscarriage at 17 weeks, a couple of overdoses behind me and a violent/abusive marriage.

No one wanted to listen, to understand. They wanted to know why I couldn't cope and why I didn't think about my two-and-a-half-year-old daughter when I overdosed. They didn't once think about me and that hurt, really hurt. There was one thing I needed at that time and that was for someone to think about me. Then you came along – a Home-Start volunteer. You really listened and understood what I was saying, you cared and you also seemed interested.

As each visit passed we seemed to be getting closer and I began to worry. I couldn't understand why you kept coming back. I wanted to trust you, to like you, but I was frightened about getting close to you because everyone I'd trusted or loved in the past had either gone away or hurt me.

I'd just found out I was pregnant for the fourth time when we met. The dilemma I had was deciding whether to keep the baby or not. This was heartbreaking. My husband wanted me to have an abortion and my heart was telling me to keep it. After a lot of soul-searching my heart won and my son Jamie was born.

The violence was now escalating in my marriage until I could take no more. As each day passed I became more and more depressed, no way out. I couldn't leave him and yet I couldn't stay. You tried so hard to help me to leave, but I kept on going back, thinking things would be better. You never once criticised my decision.

Three moves later and I'm trying hard to settle down in my new house. Things have been extremely hard for me and I still get down, but my life is slowly settling down with your help.

Helping in the office at Home-Start, something else you helped me to achieve, has given me my confidence back. I love being able to give something back to an organisation which befriended and supported me in my time of need.

Now, after completing the preparation course, I find that I am in a position to befriend and support a family who are finding it difficult. I only hope that I make as good a job as you did with me and my family.

From beneficiary to volunteer, Home Start

Give what you have. To someone, it may be better than you dare think.

Henry Wordsworth Longfellow (1807–1882)

'I was told, "You'll never walk or talk again." My next project is to walk 130 miles, fundraising for charity'

The unimaginable can happen. Andy Pascoe, at 44, was in the prime of life, loved his job as a marine engineer sailing around the world, and enjoyed his fast car when on dry land. After his latest stint on the ocean, Andy flew home from Hong Kong and the next morning went to retrieve something from his car. As he did so he was struck down by a stroke. 'My legs just went, and I lost my speech. I managed to get to my car phone and was just able to dial 999.'

The stroke was a major one. Andy was unconscious for a week in Battle Hospital, and on regaining consciousness moved to the rehabilitation ward to learn to use a wheelchair. 'I was told off for speeding in the ward,' he recalls now with a laugh. But at the time Andy was told that he would never walk or talk again. He had lost the use of the right side of his body.

Six months later, in April 1994, Andy and his wheelchair arrived home. He couldn't talk at all and slept downstairs. But, being a determined man, Andy decided he would walk and talk again, and started to teach himself; slowly, by sheer grit, he managed to circumnavigate the sitting room, then the house, and eventually he walked out into the garden. His burning aim was to cross the A4 to get down to the Thames, just to indulge his passion for boats and life on the river. 'But I couldn't cross the road. I wasn't ready. So I started to walk a mile a day. Today, I walk ten miles every day.'

While in hospital Andy saw an advertisement about John Grooms, an association that has been helping disabled people for the past 128 years, wanting to build a hospital for brain-damaged people. 'There's a shortage of such specialist units in this country. I've been there myself with my stroke. There were no instructions being sent from my brain to my body to work.' By Christmas 1994 Andy had learned more about John Grooms's work and decided to walk from London to Oxford to raise money both for their new brain injuries rehabilitation unit in Suffolk and for the Reading hospital that had treated him.

While training for the walk he bumped into Rufus, a part-labrador, stuck in the middle of the A4. 'No one was stopping and I realised that I had to get him out of the middle of the road before he was run over. It was an incentive to get the cars to stop, and I then took Rufus home.' When Andy met Rufus's owners he volunteered to take Rufus for his daily constitutional, which resulted in Rufus eventually accompanying Andy on his 100-odd-mile walk in January 1995, which raised more than £7,000. 'We walked 10 miles a day, and it took us about two weeks to complete. We stayed at B&Bs and in pubs. No one charged us, and instead donated money towards the walk.'

Next year the target is a 130-mile walk and although Andy's goal is to raise £50,000 he'd be very happy with £20,000. This time, however, Andy may have to find another canine companion since, sadly, Rufus has gone to meet his master.

'I just want to help those stuck in hospital, who won't be able to recover as well as me to walk and talk,' says Andy, who only managed to speak again about six months ago. 'It's still not 100 per cent, but it has improved. Before that, I could talk in my brain, but what was coming out was gibberish.' Andy's goal is to help to finance more hospitals to help others. Although he will never fully recover the use of the right side of his body, and accepts he'll never be able to drive again, Andy is slowly rebuilding old boats. 'Before, I had people working for me on ships, which I had to make sure were making profits. If something wasn't right, I would order people to put it right. I was the boss. I used to drive a fast car, and was a bit of a bastard with it.

'Now I have had a second life. Half of my body is finished, but I'm still very, very lucky and I believe in helping the less fortunate.'

Andy Pascoe for The John Grooms Association

We hold these truths to be sacred and undeniable; that all men are created equal and independent, that from that equal creation they derive rights inherent and alienable, amongst which are the preservation of life, and liberty, and the pursuit of happiness.
Thomas Jefferson, original draft for the Declaration of Independence

In 1986 SANE had a deficit of £70. Since that time Marjorie Wallace has raised £8.5 million

Passionate is a word many use of Marjorie Wallace and it's difficult to imagine her staying away from a cause that aroused her sense of injustice and compassion. As the director of SANE – a charity she swears she never meant to be involved in – she campaigns ceaselessly for the care of the mentally ill. She is high-profile, well-connected and bubbly. She loves champagne and glitzy parties where she makes contacts among the rich and famous who may support her cause. She established her reputation in the seventies when she interviewed thalidomide families as a journalist for the *Sunday Times*. She spent time with the families; staying with them so that she could write a three-dimensional story of their suffering. She wanted to find out exactly what it was like to care for a child with no arms or legs.

Her understanding of suffering and the compassion that she felt for it, changed her from a reporter to a campaigner, and when SANE (originally Schizophrenia: A National Emergency) ran into financial problems in the late eighties she was persuaded to become its chief executive.

Wallace is a shining example to all those who complain about the difficulty of fundraising for an invisible cause. People with mental illness don't necessarily look different, yet an estimated third of homeless people are mentally ill. She has denounced the implementation of Care in the Community which leaves the mentally ill to cope in the harsh outside world. While lesser mortals might hide, she has used her recent breast cancer to publicise the cause further: how she is coping, how she cannot give up, how she is still prepared to tackle a full workload, how she is too busy to worry about her illness.

When she joined SANE in 1986 there was a deficit of £70. Since that time she has raised £8.5 million to pay for an international research centre to be built in Oxford. She doesn't see schizophrenia as incurable. In the meanwhile Saneline is manned by 140 volunteers and takes 1,000 calls a week from people who have nowhere else to turn to.

Her achievements are remarkable, but then she is a remarkable woman. On fundraising for a difficult cause she merely says: 'If it were popular it wouldn't be so much fun. In context, our annual income is still no greater than some of the animal charities. People still prefer to give to animals and children.'

Marjorie Wallace, Director of Sane

All human beings are born free and equal in dignity and rights.
Universal Declaration of Human Rights

'Food is more than just filling your stomach. It is about human dignity, and those of us who have it, take it for granted.'

Ceri Sheppard, 27, came to London to look for work and found herself during Christmas 1993 doing a temporary job manning telephone lines at Crisis, a national charity for single homeless people. 'It was absolutely hectic answering all sorts of calls. Towards the end of the day shops, especially sandwich outlets, began calling to offer food.' Crisis, a fundraising charity, had no vehicles or resources to collect and distribute the food. 'We offered it to other homeless projects, but no one had the facilities. It was farcical. Here we were being offered food for the homeless and we couldn't do anything about it.'

Ceri put on her thinking cap, did a feasibility study and presented a business plan to Crisis. It looked neat on paper, but concerns were raised, especially the legal aspects of handling fresh food and the fear that it could end up in backstreet markets. Any charges of food poisoning would pose a legal minefield for Crisis. But Ceri was persuasive and answered all the concerns, she had researched and discussed the issue of food poisoning with environmental health officers. Just before Christmas 1994 the project, Fareshare, was launched. A refrigerated van was donated and two food retailers, Marks & Spencer and Prêt á Manger, a sandwich chain, agreed to support the project. 'Other retailers were cynical, saying that it would not work. The view was that since it had never been done before, it could not be done,' says Ceri.

Food wastage is a sensitive issue. Few food retailers want it known that they throw away high-quality produce when they have already priced in the cost of wastage. Some insist they have no wastage at all. Some supermarkets prefer to give the food to animal charities rather than humans; others spray the food with dye so that it is inedible. 'Getting the backing of Marks & Spencer was very important to the project. Smaller bakeries, too, support us because there is no bureaucracy. But supermarkets tend to be very defensive, though there are those who support us in principle.'

Now, daily, Ceri and her volunteer crew make an average of seven collections. These could range from 100 sandwiches, 100 loaves of bread, between 20 and 30 trays of food and vegetables, packed salads, ready meals, raw meat, hundreds of litres of soups to cakes. When the food arrives, it is thoroughly inspected, and computer-checked to match it with the needs of homeless shelters. 'At homeless projects for young people, ready meals are not popular. They want to be involved in the cooking and prefer fresh ingredients. At "wet shelters", for alcoholics, they love ready meals, since they can eat them whenever they are hungry.' Fareshare now provides 10,000 meals for homeless people each week.

Fareshare, which costs about £100,000 a year to run, has turned out to be a showpiece project for Crisis, and Ceri's initiative has made a positive addition to the welfare of homeless people. But the growing demands it makes on Crisis is always worrying for Ceri, who understands the pressure to spend that amount of money a year on other projects instead of Fareshare, the success of which is unquantifiable. 'Food,' argues Ceri, 'is more than just filling your stomach. It is about human dignity, and those of us who have it, take it for granted.' Moreover, the project also encourages people to use day centres, where they have access to advice on resettlement.

Ceri, understandably, is 'terribly proud' of Fareshare and its success so far. 'I could not have done it myself. It would have been very difficult without Crisis.' Ceri, who has an MA in human rights, never thought she would be working with homeless people or caring for their welfare. Now that she has stumbled into it, she says: 'I'm actually doing a job I love. The language of human rights is still not used very much in charities or the voluntary sector. People should have rights, even if they are homeless.'

Ceri Sheppard, founder of the Crisis Fareshare project

Anticipate charity by preventing poverty; assist the reduced fellow man, either by a considerable gift, or a sum of money, or by teaching him a trade, or by putting him in the way of business, so that he may earn an honest livelihood, and not be forced to the dreadful alternative of holding out his hand for charity. This is the highest step and the summit of charity's golden ladder.

Maimonides (Moses ben maimon)

'Now, I'm a sighted person who happens to be blind. I'm the same as everyone else'

The light went out in Ken Woodward's life when a chemical explosion at his workplace left him blind at the age of 45. 'It put me in a sense of fear for the future; I didn't know what life was going to be like.' It had changed dramatically, as it did for his family, but he wasn't aware of their pain. He realises now, with hindsight, that he was selfish then. 'I spun a cocoon around myself and had no idea how my family felt. It must have been devastating for them. My parents won't get over it, really, since I am their only child. It has taken a long time for them to treat me the old way. As for my four children, they have been very positive.'

From being independent, Ken was now dependent on a crutch and was taken everywhere on an arm. Months after his accident in November 1990, he went to the Royal National Institution for the Blind's adult training centre at Manor House in Torquay. Initially he visited for an assessment, but his retraining involved a six-month stay. There Ken found a new sense of purpose. 'The training I received gave me back my mobility, confidence and a future. Unless you have mobility you can't do anything, and the staff take the barriers down for you so much so that I even went abseiling. Now, I'm a sighted person who happens to be blind. I'm the same as everyone else, I just happen to be blind, like one without a limb, or one in a wheelchair.'

But Ken's life has really soared since he took up flying. 'It just came up one day. I was asked whether I wanted to go on a flying lesson, and I said "No fear."' So, flying out of Exeter Flying Club, Ken had co-piloted a two-seater plane for the first time by July 1995, becoming an immediate media celebrity. He is now on advanced training to fly round the world. 'As it stands, in 1996 we circle the UK, starting at Clacton-by-Sea in Norfolk. That will be the springboard for the round-the-world attempt. The experienced pilot sits next to me, but I handle all the controls. It is a joint effort, and we work well together.'

Ken went back to work in March 1995. 'It is lovely going back. It takes a good two to three years to understand blindness. There are a lot of hurdles; you take 12 paces forward, and get knocked back. You are forever chiselling away. But you carry on as you did before, or as best you can.'

Ken's round-the-world trip is aimed at raising funds for the RNIB. 'I owe so much to Manor House. The staff were so patient and caring. I want to make the flight because I want to give something back to those who helped me so much. Manor House can send you out with an aim if you want it. When I arrived there I was a gibbering wreck. Now I am happy, back at work and training as a pilot. It is a very special place, and I want others in my place to experience it.'

Ken Woodward, for the RNIB

8

Tax-Efficient Ways of Giving

If you are a UK resident taxpayer, wanting to give to charity, then it would be beneficial to the charities that you support if you contacted the Charities Aid Foundation (CAF).

The Charities Aid Foundation is itself a charity. It exists to enable individuals and organisations to improve the quality and value of their donations to charity. The Foundation also provides services to other charities to help them raise and manage their funds more effectively. For more than 150,000 private individuals and many of Britain's leading companies the Charities Aid Foundation is, simply, the best way to give.

CAF runs different schemes to suit everybody, from individuals who can give large amounts up front to those who prefer to give 'a little and often'. CAF acts as a banking service providing a charity cheque book and card for those who open an account with them. With these you are able to make donations to any charity or charitable organisation (recognised by the Inland Revenue), by post or simply over the telephone (0345-6266 55) and CAF will reclaim the tax that you have already paid on it. In this way your gift is increased by nearly a third at no extra cost to yourself.

Covenants
Pay a regular sum (minimum £10 per month or £120 per annum for four years) and again CAF will reclaim the tax already paid on it. Certain membership subscriptions can be paid for by a covenant if the charity agrees. This is not possible with any of the other schemes run by CAF. Taking out a covenant is better if you are prepared to make a four-year commitment but cannot put up the £250 in one go needed for Gift Aid.

Gift Aid
This is for those who are prepared to pay a lump sum of £250 or more into their CAF account. More donations can be made at any time. You are under no obligation to give on a regular basis but when you do the sum must be, again, of £250 or more for tax purposes.

Give as You Earn (GAYE)
This scheme allows individuals to give through deductions from their pay at source. *You don't have to have a Charity Account to be part of the GAYE scheme, but your employer has to be registered for GAYE.* You merely fill out a form and the charities of your choice will receive regular payments. Overseas payments are not permitted by the Inland Revenue. The contact address for GAYE is: Give As You Earn, Foundation House, Coach & Horses Passage, Tunbridge Wells, Kent TN2 5TZ, tel: 0891-4242 44

Legacy account
CAF's Legacy Management Centre is there to help people wanting to leave a charitable donation in their will. Legacy income forms a very substantial proportion of income for some charities. Taking out a legacy account ensures that the charities that you

care about will benefit when the time comes to deal with your estate. All you have to do in your will is name CAF as your charity beneficiary and whatever you have left as a donation will, in the event of your death, immediately be credited to your legacy account. CAF will then distribute the money to the charities that you have selected on the Legacy Distribution Form provided by them. The major benefit is that changing your mind doesn't involve changing your will and the money that you leave will be free of inheritance tax.

For example, a gift of £100 becomes £125 if covenanted (see Covenants), £250 becomes £325 if given by Gift Aid (see Gift Aid).

9
USEFUL ORGANISATIONS

Donations

Charities Aid Foundation
48 Pembury Road, Tonbridge, Kent TN9 2JD.
Tel: 01732-771 333

CAF exists to help you to give money to the charity or charities of your choice in the most tax-efficient way possible, whether you are an individual or a large company. They manage Covenants, Gift Aid and other Appeal Income (see Tax-Efficient Ways of Giving), increasing the flow of resources to charities. The Information Department has a Charity Search Facility for anyone looking to identify particular causes or organisations.

Information On Existing And New Charities

The Charity Commissioners (England and Wales)
St Alban's House, 57–60 Haymarket, London SW1Y 4QX.
Tel: 0171-210 4477

This is the regulatory body for all registered charities. (All English and Welsh charities with an income exceeding £1,000 must be registered with the Charity Commissioners in order to adopt the status of charity.) They give wide and varied advice on all aspects of setting up and running your own charity as well as providing guidelines in the form of literature for people to follow when doing so. In addition to this the public can check with them that a charity is registered or that someone is a known fundraiser.

The Scottish Council for Voluntary Organisations (SCVO)
18–19 Claremont Crescent, Edinburgh EH7 4QD.
Tel: 0131-556 3882

SCVO operates a charities' register of 24,000 charities, schools and friendly societies operating in Scotland.

Information On Volunteering In The UK

Charity Fair
Directory of Social Change, 24 Stephenson Way, NW1 2DP.
Tel: 0171-209 4949

Every March The Directory of Social Change runs this event at the Business Design Centre, London, which includes a Volunteer and Employment forum.

Community Service Volunteers (CSV)
237 Pentonville Road, London N1 9NJ. Tel: 0171-278 6601

The national volunteer agency creating opportunities for people to work as volunteers in their own community or further afield. Volunteers can be of any age, status or background as the CSV works with the belief that everyone has something to offer. CSV runs a wide variety of programmes for specific age groups with this in mind such as the CSV Retired Senior Volunteer Programme (RSVP) for the over-fifties, whether partly or fully retired.

They find work in schools, hospitals or museums, with jobs ranging from visiting the sick, to protecting the environment, to teaching in schools.

Councils for Voluntary Service
Check for your local branch in the telephone directory.

The Councils provide advice and information for volunteers with some opportunities for volunteers to work in their own offices, giving administrative support.

National Association of Citizens' Advice Bureaux
Check for your local branch in the telephone directory.

Citizens' Advice Bureaux train a wide cross-section of people, including young people, unemployed and ethnic minorities, to become advisers. There are 1,300 bureaux in the country, each with a 90 per cent voluntary workforce who give advice and support to the general public.

Retired Executives Action Clearing House (REACH)
89 Southwark Street, London SE1 OHD. Tel: 0171-928 0452

This is a free placement service for retired and early retired people looking for a second career – expenses are paid but only people with skills and experience are considered. They are placed with charities who need, but cannot afford, their particular experience.

Scottish Corps of Retired Executives (SCORE)
Scottish Business in the Community, Romano House, 43 Station Road, Edinburgh EH12 7AF. Tel: 0131-334 9876

A register for retired professionals. Contact them if you want to use your experience to help charities.

The Trustee Register
c/o Reed Charity Fund, 114 Peascod Street, Windsor SL4 1DN.

Contact them if you are a prospective trustee wanting to get hold of the appropriate charity.

The Volunteer Centre UK
29 Lower King's Road, Berkhamsted, Hertfordshire HP4 2AB.
Tel: 01442-886 051

The Volunteer Centre produce information leaflets on being a volunteer and their database lists current volunteering opportunities around the country. Print-outs of these lists are available to the public, upon request, for a small fee.

Volunteer Bureaux
Check for your local bureau in the telephone directory. Everyone is welcome to drop in.

Volunteer Bureaux act as central recruiting and interviewing agencies, introducing volunteers to organisations in need of their help. Contact them and tell them what you want to do in the voluntary sector. These organisations will try to match you with a position which is both relevant to your requirements and uses any skills you have to offer. There are often volunteering opportunities in the Bureaux themselves.

Working for a Charity (WFAC)
44–46 Caversham Road, London NW5 2DS.
Tel: 0171-911 0353

An organisation that runs three-month courses providing training and work experience in the form of voluntary placements. They help people to understand how the voluntary sector operates. The courses have to be paid for by those taking part, though it is a minimal amount.

Information On Volunteering Overseas

There are a variety of organisations that support charities or projects overseas. Some of these require you to raise the cost of your expenses before you go. Figures vary, depending largely on the destination, from a few hundred pounds to well over £2,000.

Overseas Development Administration (ODA)
Esso House, Victoria Street, London SW1E 5JL.
Tel: 0171-917 7000

This organisation supports four independent voluntary agencies sending suitably qualified, skilled volunteers to various countries:

Voluntary Service Overseas (VSO)
Arranges long-term (two years minimum) assignments for people overseas.

International Co-operation for Development (ICD)
Recruits volunteers, particularly for community projects for the poor.

Skillshare Africa
Sends skilled people to four Southern African Countries.

United Nations Association International Service (UNAIS)
Sends volunteers to agricultural, health and social development projects.

Gap Activity Projects

Gap House, 44 Queens Road, Reading RG1 4BB.
Tel: 01734-594 914

Gap organises project and work opportunities for young people. They operate in around 30 different countries worldwide and work periods are normally between six and nine months long.

Project Trust

The Hebridean Centre, Ballyhough, Isle of Coll, Argyll PA78 6TE. Tel: 0187 93444

Specialises in placing young people in overseas projects for a year between school and higher education.

Raleigh International

Raleigh House, 27 Parsons Green Lane, London SW6 4HS. Tel: 0171 371 8585

Gives a rare chance to make a valuable contribution in remote and unfamiliar parts of the world. Expeditions are ten and five weeks long. There are also opportunities to be one of the 350 recruited members of staff. They must be skilled (eg a medic or an engineer) and over 26. Staff are often sponsored by their employers in the UK.

10
CHARITY PROFILES

ANIMALS AND BIRDS

ANIMAL HEALTH TRUST

PO Box 5, Newmarket, Suffolk CB8 8JH
Tel: 01638-661 111 *Fax:* 01638-665 789
Charity Reg. No: 209642
Contact: **Johnny Fountain, Fundraising Manager**
Date established: **1942**
Annual income: **£6.46m (1995)**
Area covered: **National**

The Animal Health Trust is the only charity to investigate full-time the prevention, treatment and cure of disease and ill health in animals, particularly family pets. Through investigations and comparative clinical studies the Trust aims to improve the health care and welfare of all animals and to alleviate unnecessary pain and suffering. Under its Royal Charter it is dedicated to advancing the theory and practice of veterinary medicine. The Trust's discoveries are shared with veterinary practitioners and animal devotees worldwide, so the information can be used to achieve the goal: 'a healthy animal is a happy animal'.

Fundraising support is needed at events, sporting competitions and shows. Supporters may be required to assist with the organisation, hosting guests, selling merchandise, handing out literature, helping with collections or just being a general 'dogsbody'. Whatever your role you are a vital part of the success of the day. A membership scheme for individuals and clubs provides regular updates on activities, invitations to events and an opportunity to visit a Trust open day. In 1992 the Trust celebrated its 50th anniversary and, in commemoration, launched a redevelopment appeal to build a new hospital. This is now well under way but more funds are needed to equip them.

The Animal Health Trust encourages volunteers to join its existing network of fundraising committees and to form new ones where gaps exist. Each committee aims to raise money in support of the Trust's activities and introduce the Trust and its work to a wider audience. Committees organise a wide range of fundraising activities, from operas and parties to sponsored events and flag days. Some committees confine themselves to one big event a year, others hold a series of smaller ones. In every case, wherever possible, the Trust helps through support such as literature and advice.

BIRDLIFE INTERNATIONAL

Wellbrook Court, Girton Road, Cambridge CB3 ONA
Tel: **01223-277 318** *Fax:* **01223-277 200**
Charity Reg. No: **2985746**
Contact: **Judi James, Head of Marketing**
Date established: **1922 (as ICBP)**
Annual income: **£1.2m (1994)**
Area covered: **International**

BirdLife is the leading authority on the status of the world's birds and their habitats. Its aim is to prevent the extinction of birds in the wild and to identify, and secure conservation for, the world's critically important sites. BirdLife also promotes worldwide interest in bird conservation through its partners in over 100 countries. Committed, like-minded conservationists identify priorities through scientific research and provide practical solutions.

BirdLife works closely with the RSPB, its British partner, to achieve the same objectives, sharing resources and information. It greatly appreciates all the help from volunteers who work on BirdLife projects and it is through them that the charity can lobby governments for change.

BLUE CROSS

Shilton Road, Burford, Oxfordshire OX18 4PF
Tel: 01993-822 651 *Fax:* 01993-823 083
Charity Reg. No: 224392
Contact: Alice Burns, Marketing Director
Date established: 1897
Annual income: £6.6m (1994)
Area covered: National

The Blue Cross aims to foster the bonds of friendship between animals and people. Free veterinary care is provided at four animal hospitals, for animals whose owners cannot afford private veterinary fees. There is a network of 11 animal adoption centres which will take unwanted and abandoned animals (cats, dogs and horses), caring for them until new homes can be found.

Blue Cross needs volunteers for many aspects of its work. Its 11 animal adoption centres need volunteer helpers to help walk, groom and interact with animals in the kennels. Equine centres also need help from people with some equine experience. Volunteers have to be over 14 years old. The Blue Cross's pet fostering scheme (from 1996) needs people who can help pet owners by offering short-term assistance with animal care in their own homes. Volunteer fundraising groups are being established regionally, and enthusiastic animal lovers are welcome to take part in a range of activities.

In 1997, Blue Cross will be celebrating its centenary. There will be a number of events to mark this anniversary, and Blue Cross is looking for potential partners to promote special events.

British Union for the Abolition of Vivisection (BUAV)

16a Crane Grove, London N7 8LB
Tel: 0171-700 4888 *Fax:* 0171-700 0252
Company Reg. No: 243873
Contact: **Ms Lisa Wolfe, Fundraising Director**
Date established: **1898**
Annual income: **£1.5m (94/95)**
Area covered: **International**

The BUAV was founded in 1898 and today, nearly 100 years on, still leads the campaign to end animal experiments. The BUAV undertakes a whole range of activities to further its work on behalf of laboratory animals, including producing educational materials, political lobbying, conducting undercover investigations and working with the media. At all times the BUAV works strictly within the law.

The BUAV has a number of fundraising events throughout the year, including the Walk for Laboratory Animals, the National Prize Draw, street collections and appeals associated with specific campaigns. They will also have a number of special events during the 1998 centenary year. Please contact the office for any further information.

THE CATS PROTECTION LEAGUE

17 Kings Road, Horsham, West Sussex RH13 5PN
Tel: 01403-261 947 *Fax:* 01403-218 414
Charity Reg. No: 203644
Contact: **Brian L. Morris, Legacy Officer**
Date established: 1927
Annual income: £4.7m (1995)
Area covered: National

The CPL was founded in 1927 and is the oldest charity devoted solely to the welfare of cats. Its aims are: to rescue stray, unwanted and injured cats, rehabilitate and find new homes for them where possible; to provide information to the public on the care of cats; to encourage the neutering of all cats not required for breeding. The CPL is supported entirely by members' subscriptions, donations, legacies and bequests and its own fundraising events. It receives no help from Government or local authorities.

There are some 45,000 members on the roll at headquarters and several thousand others attached to the charity's branches. New members and helpers are always welcome; the annual subscription is modest and includes the League's journal, *The Cat*, published every month. Contact the charity for further information.

COMPASSION IN WORLD FARMING TRUST

Charles House, 5a Charles Street, Petersfield, Hants GU32 3EH
Tel: 01730-264 208 *Fax:* 01730-260 791
Charity Reg. No: 295126
Contact: **John Callaghan, Education Officer**
Date established: 1986
Annual income: £100,000 (94)
Area covered: National

Compassion in World Farming Trust is an educational charity promoting concern for the welfare of farm animals. The charity is the educational wing of Britain's leading farm animal welfare organisation, Compassion in World Farming. CIWF works at all levels of the education system to raise awareness of farm animal welfare, to promote serious debate of the issues and provide educational resources for students, teachers and lecturers. CIWF Trust is concerned about the intensive rearing of millions of farm animals in factory farms. Other priority areas for CIWF Trust are the long-distance transport of farm animals; markets; slaughter; and recent developments in genetic engineering.

CIWF Trust runs a network of voluntary speakers in Britain and Ireland (initial training is given to those who take part) to help give presentations about farm animal welfare in schools and colleges. There is an education catalogue targeted at schoolchildren that is available and, if you are interested in being on the charity's speaker training list, you should contact the Trust.

Volunteers from the Petersfield area are always needed to help with a range of administrative jobs in the office (contact the office manager for more details). Alternatively, you might persuade your local school or library to have a CIWF Trust exhibition.

CIWF Trust welcomes practical support for its fundraising activities. If you would like to organise a fundraising event for the Trust it would be happy to provide back-up for the purpose. CIWF Trust organises street collections throughout the UK and is always on the lookout for co-ordinators and collectors. If you know any individuals, schools or other groups who would like more information about CIWF Trust's work then send the details to CIWF who will send them the relevant information pack.

THE DOGS HOME BATTERSEA

4 Battersea Park Road, London SW8 4AA
Tel: 0171-622 3626 *Fax:* 0171-622 6451
Charity Reg. No: 206394
Contact: Shirley Piotrowski, P.A.
Date established: 1860
Annual income: £3.5m (95)
Area covered: Regional

The Home was founded in 1860 by Mrs Mary Tealby in Holloway. Eleven years later it moved to its current site in Battersea because the ever-increasing number of dogs had become too noisy. The Battersea site, which was non-residential and bordered by railway lines, proved ideal. The aims remain the same: to provide food and shelter for lost and stray dogs; to restore lost dogs to their owners; to find suitable homes for deserted or stray dogs, at a modest charge. The Home also takes in cats and has done since its Holloway days. In 1995 the Home took in 1,602 cats.

All injured or ill animals are treated immediately by a veterinary team of a surgeon and 12 nurses. On average, a dog spends 34 days in the care of the Home before a new and permanent home can be found for it. The Home is open seven days a week: Monday to Friday, 10.30 am to 4.15 pm; Saturdays and Sundays, 10.30 am to 3.15 pm.

THE DONKEY SANCTUARY

Sidmouth, Devon EX10 0NU
Tel: **01395-578 222** *Fax:* **01395-599 266**
Charity Reg. No: **243312**
Contact: **Dr Elisabeth Svendsen, Administrator**
Date established: **1969**
Annual income: **£6.6m (94)**
Area covered: **National**

The Sanctuary helps any donkey in trouble in the UK and Ireland, and those animals which are admitted to the Sanctuary are guaranteed the right of life, regardless of age or health, and to the best possible treatment, care and drugs to preserve their life to the maximum. The Charter grants permanent peace and freedom, the care and protection of the Sanctuary and the right to return if rehabilitated to a new home. When the time comes it grants a dignified, peaceful death, and this is induced only in the event of extreme suffering, and after the decision has been agreed by veterinary advisers and Sanctuary staff.

The Sanctuary has no membership scheme – any donation, no matter what the amount, is most gratefully received and as a result you will receive their spring and autumn newsletter and summer update. The Sanctuary's headquarters at Sidmouth, Devon, are open to the public. There is no admission charge. For families whose loved one made a bequest in their will or those who have donated a tree or bench in memory of a loved one, an annual Memorial Service is held on St Francis of Assisi Day.

Volunteers are needed to join the Friends Group to raise funds for the Donkey Sanctuary and its three sister charities (The International Donkey Protection Trust; The Slade Centre and The Elisabeth Svendsen Trust for Children and Donkeys). Volunteers are asked to give only as much time and effort as they want to give. Support and assistance are provided through Friends County Co-ordinators. Volunteers are also needed to assist in the riding sessions for children with special needs and disabilities at The Slade Centre, Sidmouth, Devon, and at The Elisabeth Svendsen Trust for Children and Donkeys, Sutton Park, Birmingham.

International League for the Protection of Horses

Anne Colvin House, Snetterton, Norfolk NR16 2LR
Tel: 01953-498682 *Fax:* 01953-498373
Charity Reg. No: 206658
Contact: S. L. Turner, Press Officer
Date established: 1927
Annual income: £2.549m (95)
Area covered: International

The International League for the Protection of Horses (ILPH) has operated as a charity since 1927, dedicated to preventing and alleviating the suffering of horses and other equines, wherever they are located and however humble their roles. Based in the United Kingdom, the ILPH has become the world's leading equine welfare charity, operating in over 20 countries. Its worldwide activities embrace rescue and rehabilitation, education and training, scientific research, and influencing political opinion and legislation.

In the UK the ILPH runs four farms dedicated to the rest and rehabilitation of horses: Hall Farm and Overa House Farm in Norfolk, Cherry Tree Farm in Surrey and Belwade Farm in Aberdeenshire. Visitors are welcome at any of these centres.

London Zoo (Zoological Society of London)

London Zoo Outer Circle, Regents Park, London NW1 4RY
Tel: 0171-449 6226 *Fax:* 0181-586 1412
Charity Reg. No: 208728
Contact: **Claire Knapton, Head of Development**
Date established: 1826
Annual income: **£8m (94/95)**
Area covered: **National/International**

London Zoo fights to conserve the natural world by breeding endangered animals and by inspiring commitment to the conservation of wildlife and threatened habitats. It participates in conservation action worldwide, acts as a centre for visitors, to educate and inform, and adds to the body of zoological knowledge by collaboration in scientific research.

London Zoo is fundraising to regenerate the zoo site and help inspire commitment to conservation through the creation of world class exhibits.

National Canine Defence League

17 Wakley Street, London EC1V 7LT
Tel: 0171-837 0006 *Fax:* 0171-833 2701
Charity Reg. No: 227523
Contact: **Mrs C. Baldwin, Chief Executive Director**
Date established: 1891
Annual income: **£5.5m (95)**
Area covered: **National – 15 centres**

The National Canine Defence League exists to protect and defend all dogs from abuse, cruelty, abandonment and any form of mistreatment, both in the UK and abroad, and is committed to the belief that no healthy dog should ever be destroyed, but cared for by responsible owners for life. The charity seeks to achieve this aim through the network of NCDL rescue centres, education and welfare campaigns.

The NCDL requires volunteers for varied works. Administrative duties can be carried out at its Head Office in central London, whilst dog walkers are also needed at its 15 rescue centres. In addition, the NCDL has a number of charity shops where help is needed in serving customers. Volunteers are also needed to transport dogs from centre to centre, as flag day collectors and to deliver leaflets to houses.

The NCDL has a number of local fundraising groups throughout the country. Activities range from street collections to sponsored walks. Further details can be obtained by writing to the Community Fundraising Manager at NCDL Head Office.

ST TIGGYWINKLES – THE WILDLIFE HOSPITAL TRUST

Aston Road, Haddenham, Aylesbury, Bucks HP17 8AF
Tel: 01844-292 292 *Fax:* 01844-292 640
Charity Reg. No: 286447
Contact: **Chris Patterson, PA to Sue Stocker**

Date established: **1983**
Annual income: **£350,000 (94)**
Area covered: **National**

Have you ever had that helpless feeling on seeing an injured wild bird or animal and not knowing who can help? St Tiggywinkles can. For 18 years the charity has been rescuing, treating and rehabilitating all sick, injured and orphaned British wildlife, including hedgehogs, badgers, deer and owls. They do not have a 'put down' policy and in most instances the casualties are returned to the wild when they are fit. In 1991 their purpose-built teaching hospital was opened by the charity's Patron, HRH The Princess Alexandra, and the charity now takes in between 15,000 and 20,000 patients each year and runs courses in wildlife care. St Tiggywinkles relies on the general public and caring companies such as British Telecom for funding their work. They also raise funds by having a membership system whereby people can join and receive news on the hospital's patients. An adoption scheme enables people to help pay towards the medical treatment and care of a casualty while it is being cared for.

Projects in the pipeline that need funding include the 'Back in Action' appeal to fund a specially designed unit where disabled children and adults in wheelchairs can help as part of their occupational therapy, particularly with hand-rearing orphans. Also an education unit is to be opened to schools and disadvantaged children to further environmental awareness. St Tiggywinkles relies almost totally on volunteer helpers who all receive specialist training. Volunteers are asked to make a regular commitment, ie Monday each week. This builds team spirit and is essential for the patients whose welfare depends on the reliability of their human carers.

Southern Marine Life Rescue (SMLR)

60 Braishfield Road, West Leigh, Havant, Hants PO9 2HS
Tel: 01705-552631 *Fax:* 01705-472151
Charity Reg. No: 1049571
Contact: **Andy Williams, Chairman/Rescue Co-ordinator**
Date established: **1993**
Annual income: **£10,000 (95)**
Area covered: **Regional**

Southern Marine Life Rescue aims to make provisions for the rescue, rehabilitation and welfare of marine mammals along the southern coast of Britain. SMLR's objectives include: to co-ordinate the rescue of sick, injured, stranded or orphaned marine mammals, and to provide immediate medical assistance to these animals where necessary; to give information, advice and support to related organisations; and to uphold the conservation ethic and provide education within its specialist field.

Southern Marine Life Rescue was formed in 1993 by individuals who had previously been working independently in the fields of marine biology, veterinary medicine, animal welfare and marine mammal rescue. SMLR is a non-political charity which has been used by the RSPCA to handle marine mammals. It is run by a committed team of volunteers with a breadth of relevant knowledge, expertise and skills. Every member of SMLR gives his or her time for nothing, and the charity does not employ any personnel. In this way all money goes directly towards all the facilities needed to ensure a successful rescue.

SMLR relies on public donations. Much of its financial support comes from sponsorship and collection boxes, from which the charity receives a small but steady income. SMLR is not a large charity and cannot afford a glossy fundraising campaign; however, the small contributions received make all the difference to its work. Previous donations have provided a communication system and supplied each of the rescue teams with a kit of essential equipment. The charity's longer-term aims are to procure and support a fully equipped marine mammal ambulance, and to provide all the facilities which are available on permanent standby.

UFAW
(UNIVERSITIES FEDERATION FOR ANIMAL WELFARE)

8 Hamilton Close, South Mimms, Potters Bar, Herts EN6 3QD
Tel: **01707-658 202** *Fax:* **01707-649 279**
Charity Reg. No: **207996**
Contact: **Victoria Taylor, Development Officer**
Date established: **1926**
Annual income: **£350,000 (94)**
Area covered: **National/International**

UFAW is a science-based animal welfare charity which has helped improve the lives of numerous farm, laboratory, zoo, wild and pet animals since 1926. UFAW funds research, holds meetings and workshops, and publishes books, leaflets and videos on animal care. UFAW also publishes *Animal Welfare*, the only technical journal which brings together information on how to improve conditions for animals. UFAW is an independent charity and does not receive income from universities, Government or commerce.

In 1996 UFAW celebrates its 70th birthday and needs more members to extend its influence. It seeks donations to support current work, and legacies to help secure future improvements in animal welfare. Membership is £10 per annum (£5 for students, retired or unwaged). Telephone or write for membership forms, publications lists, legacy leaflets and further information.

WILDFOWL & WETLANDS TRUST

Slimbridge, Gloucester GL2 7BT
Tel: 01453-890 333 *Fax:* 01453-890 827
Charity Reg. No: 1030884
Contact: **Kim Stiles, Head of Communications**
Date established: **1946**
Annual income: **£4.5m (94)**
Area covered: **National – HQ: Slimbridge**

The Wildfowl & Wetlands Trust was founded by the late Sir Peter Scott in 1946. It works to save the world's threatened wetlands for wildlife and people and has eight centres nationwide. These are important wetlands for wildlife, especially water birds, and wonderful places to visit – all are open all year round. WWT carries out extensive research and provides information and educational activities for all ages. It shares its expertise globally, to promote effective conservation practices for all wetlands.

The UK's only charity dedicated to wetland wildlife needs your support. Donations, legacies and company sponsorships are greatly appreciated; and WWT centres welcome volunteers. The WWT membership scheme provides free entrance to centres where there are special 50th birthday celebrations in 1996 – further details are available on request.

WOOD GREEN ANIMAL SHELTERS

Kings Bush Farm, London Road, Godmanchester, Cambs PE18 8LJ
Tel: 01480-830014 Fax: 01480-830566
Charity Reg. No: 298348
Contact: **David Goddard, Chief Executive**
Date established: **1924**
Annual income: **£2.9m (94/95)**
Area covered: **International**

Wood Green is considered to be the most progressive animal charity in Europe. Its aim is to lead internationally in all aspects of the welfare and environment of animals through education and example'. Founded in 1924, the Shelter now has three sites in the UK. Thirteen thousand domestic and wild animals are taken in each year and more than 82 per cent are found new homes. Others, particularly farm and exotic animals, become permanent residents.

Wood Green is wholly dependent on public support and has a network of volunteer fundraising support groups. New supporters are always welcome. The Shelter has a 50 acre visitor centre at Godmanchester in Cambridgeshire and welcome visitors 365 days of the year. Wood Green operates: Pet Alert Scheme (a free scheme to look after your pet in an emergency); and a junior supporters' club, The Critters' Club. Wood Green always has need for volunteers to help in a variety of ways: looking after the animals; walking dogs; helping Wood Green's riding for the disabled group; fundraising; assisting at events from bazaars to steam engine rallies.

SEE ALSO

Hearing Dogs for the Deaf
Royal Society for the Protection of Birds
Scottish Wildlife Trust

ARTS AND MUSEUMS

ARTSLINE

54 Charlton Street, London NW1 1HS
Tel: 0171-388 2227 *Fax:* 0171-383 2653
Charity Reg. No: 287988
Contact: R. Robinson, Director
Date established: 1981
Annual income: £290,132 (95/96)
Area covered: Regional

Artsline is London's only information and advice service for disabled people on Access to the arts and entertainment. It is a helpline for all disabled people, giving information on the accessibility of all of the capital's arts and entertainment venues; publishing Access Guides to venues, such as theatres, cinemas, galleries, major tourist attractions and music venues; encouraging disabled people to participate in the arts as audience or as performers. The charity offers Disability Equality Training to front-of-house staff at arts venues, as well as advice to MPs and Ministers on issues concerning access for disabled people. Core funding is obtained from the London Boroughs Grants Scheme, London Arts Board, some local authorities, appeals to trusts and companies, as well as fundraising events. Except for core funding, all monies go towards projects, access guides, leaflets, information packs.

The organisation has existed for 14 years, and is an efficient, free, unique service for disabled people. Artsline is, however, poorly funded with a need for greater support from corporate and trust sources. It started the only mobile library which is free to disabled people, containing 500 videos in major Asian languages; with funding this service will extend to all disabled people.

Artsline has a full-time staff of six. As a busy helpline taking over 6,000 enquiries a year from disabled Londoners, and from throughout the UK and overseas, Artsline welcomes the work of its regular volunteers. Each volunteer works on projects with a staff member. Volunteers are given induction training and participate in decision-making at staff conferences, and can attend all Management Committee meetings. Their importance is such that they have their own section in the Annual Report. Volunteers assist in undertaking surveys of venues to obtain access data; fundraising and administrative duties.

BRITISH MUSEUM

Great Russell Street, London WC1B 3DG
Tel: 0171-636 1555 *Fax:* 0171-323 8480
Charity Reg. No: Exempt Charity x23490
Contact: Frances Dunkels, Press and PR Officer
Date established: 1753
Annual income: £45.85m (94/95)
Area covered: National

The British Museum is one of the great museums of global culture, attracting over 6 million visitors a year. It displays the works of mankind from prehistory to the present day, and houses world-famous treasures such as the Parthenon Sculptures, Rosetta Stone and the Assyrian lionhunt reliefs.

Admission is free. The Museum's main functions are the care and preservation of the collections; making the collections available to the public through research, publication, exhibition and teaching; and the development of the collections by acquisition, excavation and fieldwork.

The British Museum Society, the Museum's 'Friends' organisation, funds purchases and projects for the Museum. Its members enjoy a variety of benefits, and have the opportunity to act as volunteer guides, help with special events and run the BMS membership desk. In 1994 the British Museum Development Trust was established to raise support for the Museum's £110 million development programme. One of its many fundraising projects is to increase voluntary donations from the public. Volunteers are sought to help with this initiative. Please contact the British Museum Society or the British Museum Development Trust at the following addresses: The British Museum Society, c/o British Museum, Great Russell Street, London WC1B 3DG (*Tel:* 0171-323 8605). Benefits include free entry to special exhibitions and evening openings, and a free subscription to the British Museum Magazine.

In 2003 the Museum will celebrate its 250th anniversary with the completion of a major development programme. The plans include new galleries, a Centre for Education and improved visitor services. The centrepiece is Sir Norman Foster's Great Court scheme, which will create London's first covered public square.

ARTS AND MUSEUMS

FRIENDS OF THE ROYAL ACADEMY

ROYAL ACADEMY OF ARTS

Royal Academy of Arts, Piccadilly, London W1V 0DS
Tel: 0171-439 7438 *Fax:* 0171-434 0837
Charity Reg. No: 212 798 (RA) 272926
Contact: Susie Dawson, Friends Co-ordinator
Date established: 1768/1977
Annual income: £2.5m (Friends 94)
Area covered: National

The Royal Academy of Arts is a major private institution which mounts a programme of international art exhibitions and an annual 'open' exhibition, the Summer Exhibition. Comprehensive educational programmes are arranged for all groups. The Academy also supports a postgraduate art school and maintains an archive on the history of British Art. The Friends of the Royal Academy (now 70,000 members) was formed in 1977 to support the Academy. The Academy also seeks corporate sponsorship.

Without direct public funding, the Academy is dependent upon corporate and individual support and sponsorship. Legacies and bequests contribute to the maintenance of a long tradition. The Royal Academy is open seven days a week (except Good Friday, Christmas Day, Boxing Day). Details of exhibitions are listed in the visual arts section of the national press, or contact 0171-439 4996/7.

Natural History Museum Development Trust

Cromwell Road, London SW7 5BD
Tel: 0171-938 8962 *Fax:* 0171-938 9002
Charity Reg. No: Exempt. Full charitable status for tax purposes
Contact: Andrew Craven, Development Director
Date established: 1987
Annual income: £939,844 (95)
Area covered: National/International

The Natural History Museum is a world leader in advancing the understanding of the natural world, offering lively and innovative exhibitions enjoyed by over 1.5 million visitors a year. In addition to being one of London's busiest attractions for schoolchildren, families and tourists, the Museum is also one of the world's leading research institutions, housing a collection of 68 million natural history specimens and employing over 300 scientists working in the Museum's five scientific departments (Botany, Entomology, Mineralogy, Palaeontology and Zoology). The Development Trust supports both the educational and scientific work of the Museum via an extensive fundraising and friend-raising programme.

The Trust has established a fundraising strategy which includes corporate sponsorship, a Patrons' programme and an extensive diary of events such as behind-the-scenes tours and the annual ball, held each November in the Museum's spectacular Central Hall. Each department has a range of projects for which it seeks support. Current priorities include the new Earth Galleries, the conservation of rare books and works of art in the library and the preservation of Charles Darwin's home in Kent.

Further details on projects and events are available on request. Opportunities for volunteers range from helping to guide visitors around the galleries to behind-the-scenes work in the scientific departments, assisting in the libraries to working on fundraising and marketing projects.

VICTORIA AND ALBERT MUSEUM

South Kensington, London SW7 2RL
Tel: 0171-938 8271 *Fax:* 0171-938 8272
Charity Reg. No: **Exempt. Full charitable status for tax purposes**
Contact: **Caroline Usher, Development Officer**
Date established: **1852**
Annual income: **£42.5m (94/95)**
Area covered: **National/International**

The V & A is Britain's National Museum of Art and Design. It is the custodian of the National Collections of sculpture, watercolours, portrait miniatures, graphic design, silver, photography and calligraphy. It also administers the Bethnal Green Museum of Childhood; the Theatre Museum, Covent Garden; the Wellington Museum at Apsley House and the National Art Library. The V & A aims to increase the understanding and enjoyment of art, craft and design through its collections and to make the objects in its care available to the widest audience through programmes of research, conservation and education for people of all ages and backgrounds.

You can support the V & A by visiting and making a donation or by leaving a legacy in your will. There are various membership schemes and opportunities for corporate sponsorship. Further details are available from the Development office. The cost of basic building maintenance and object conservation absorbs more than the annual Government funding. The V & A is looking towards the future and needs support for major projects including the 21st Century building and the redevelopment of the British Art and Design galleries. Volunteers are an important form of support for the museum. They are involved in many aspects and the museum is extremely grateful for the help provided. Further details are available upon request.

SEE ALSO

Age Exchange Theatre Trust

CARE AND COUNSELLING

apa COMMUNITY DRUG AND ALCOHOL INITIATIVES

67–69 Cowcross Street, London EC1M 6BP
Tel: 0171-251 5860 *Fax:* 0171-251 5890
Charity Reg. No: 1001957
Contact: Gill Astarita, Head of External Affairs
Date established: 1967
Annual income: c £3m (95)
Area covered: National

apa reduces the harm caused by drugs and alcohol to both individuals and communities. Its national fundraising operation helps to provide services, from residential rehabilitation homes to drop-in centres. apa educates the young on the dangers of drugs and alcohol and runs family support groups for those already affected. An information service is available, including a quarterly journal, *Focus*, costing £8 a year. apa campaigns relentlessly for more resources.

Volunteers are actively encouraged to participate, with training and support provided. Opportunities range from research, clerical and administration work to fundraising and PR assistance. Participants are paid expenses, so please come forward to help meet this growing need.

BRITISH RED CROSS

British Red Cross
Caring for people in crisis

9 Grosvenor Crescent, London SW1X 7EJ
Tel: 0171-235 5454 *Fax:* 0171-245 6315
Charity Reg. No: 220949
Contact: Mr John F. Gray, Director of Public Affairs
Date established: 1870
Annual income: £95.2m (95)
Area covered: National

The British Red Cross is part of the International Red Cross and Red Crescent Movement, which provides impartial care to people in crisis both at home and abroad, in peacetime and in war. The British Red Cross works without discrimination through a network of paid staff and volunteers, providing first aid and care services in the UK community and aid to communities overseas. UK services include the Home from Hospital and Medical Loan schemes, and Fire Victim Support vehicles.

Fundraising is vital for the future provision of the Society's services. Their main fundraising drive is for Red Cross Week each May, but there are many other opportunities to support the Society's work. A Corporate Patrons Scheme caters for companies giving over £50,000 a year, and a special 125 Society welcomes members who pledge to donate at least £1,000 annually to the British Red Cross. The British Red Cross is committed to helping vulnerable people whatever their background, race, religion or beliefs. Their extensive network of volunteers means that every pound donated can go further, and by working within the community they ensure that appropriate services are delivered to those who need them most.

The British Red Cross requires volunteers for all aspects of its UK work. The Society has a network of 300 charity shops around the United Kingdom, all of which need volunteers to help serve customers and prepare new donated stock for resale.

Volunteers also help to provide their essential community services, especially Emergency Response, the Home from Hospital scheme, and the Transport and Escort service. In May each year, hundreds of volunteers are required to help to sell lapel pins during Red Cross Week. Volunteers also support the Society by organising events and other activities in aid of the Society's work.

CANCER RELIEF MACMILLAN FUND

CANCER RELIEF Macmillan FUND
Fighting cancer with more than medicine

Anchor House, 15–19 Britten Street, London SW3 3TZ
Tel: 0171-351 7811 *Fax:* 0171-376 8098
Charity Reg. No: 261017
Contact: **John Abbott, Director of Fundraising**
Date established: **1911**
Annual income: **£37.6m (94)**
Area covered: **National**

Cancer Relief Macmillan Fund is a national charity devoted to improving the care available to people with cancer and their families. At the heart of its work are the Macmillan nurses, of whom there are now more than 1,400, but the charity has also established a whole network of cancer care services throughout the UK, all of which are available on the NHS. Almost 6,000 new cases of cancer are diagnosed each week and the need for specialist support continues to rise. The Macmillan Appeal aims to raise the funds needed to extend and develop Macmillan services to help ensure they reach everyone who needs them.

In addition to finding Macmillan nurses Cancer Relief Macmillan Fund builds day care centres for cancer sufferers, makes £4.5 million of grants per annum to cancer victims who are financially disadvantaged, funds some 100 doctors as cancer care teachers and supports specialist cancer care charities. Cancer Relief Macmillan Fund continues to need volunteers to help raise funds since no financial assistance is forthcoming from Government sources. Everyone can help, and with over 660 local committees and 125 local appeals running there is a need in virtually every town in the country. Or perhaps you would like to organise one of the highly successful Coffee Mornings. Volunteers are increasingly needed to work alongside the Macmillan nurses as the charity's carer schemes grow in numbers.

CARERS NATIONAL ASSOCIATION

Ruth Potter House, 20–25 Glasshouse Yard,
London EC1A 4JS
Tel: 0171-490 8818 *Fax:* 0171-490 8824
Charity Reg. No: 246329
Contact: **Jill Pitkeathley, Chief Executive**
Date established: **1988**
Annual income: **£2.3m (94/95)**
Area covered: **National**

There are nearly 7 million carers in the UK, of all ages, looking after a child, relative, neighbour or friend who cannot manage without help because of sickness, age or disability. In fact you can become a carer overnight. Carers National Association was formed to address the needs of carers, to support carers and enable them to speak with a stronger voice. The aims of Carers National Association are: to encourage carers to recognise their own needs; to develop appropriate support for carers; to provide information and advice for carers; to bring the needs of carers to the attention of Government and other policy makers.

There are many ways that you can help Carers National Association. You can give a donation; encourage your workmates to support their work and give through the Give As You Earn scheme; persuade your employers to support the Association; or leave them something in your will. The Association will be celebrating its 10th anniversary in 1998 and plans a special programme of events which will need your support.

Carers National Association has come a long way in 10 years and has had a great success with getting the Carers (Recognition and Services) Act through both Houses of Parliament and onto the Statute Book. However, much still needs to be done. By supporting Carers National Association, you will be helping carers now and in the future. Carers National says: 'We are keen to work with volunteers in many ways, including fund-raising and profile-raising activities. We understand volunteering is a two-way process, and the volunteer must benefit from the partnership as much as the charity.

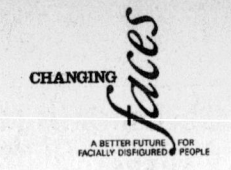

CHANGING FACES

1&2 Junction Mews, London W2 1PN
Tel: 0171-706 4232 *Fax:* 0171-706 4234
Charity Reg. No: 1011222
Contact: **James Partridge, Executive Director**
Date established: 1992
Annual income: £215,000 (94/95)
Area covered: National

Changing Faces promotes a better future for facially disfigured children and adults, whatever the cause of their disfigurement. The charity offers free help in the form of advice, information and training in communication skills, and supports the work of professionals in health and social services. Changing Faces recognises that those who meet a facially disfigured person may not find the experience an easy one. By working with schools, employers and the media, the charity addresses this unfamiliarity and the prejudices surrounding disfigurement.

A small, experienced team provides specialised help to about 1,000 facially disfigured people each year. The charity relies on public donations and grants to continue this neglected area of work. With a tiny fundraising team, Changing Faces is looking to you to take the initiative and raise money for the charity.

Crossroads (Caring for Carers)

CROSSROADS
CARING *for* CARERS

10 Regent Place, Rugby, Warks CV21 2PN
Tel: 01788-573 653 *Fax:* 01788-565 498
Charity Reg. No: 282102
Contact: Yvonne McCann, Information Officer
Date established: 1974
Annual income: £1.765m (95)
Area covered: National

Crossroads is the major UK charity providing practical help for carers. Through over 240 schemes across the country, the charity delivers more than 2 million hours of care to those people committed to the long-term care of loved ones. Carers are one of the fastest growing groups of people in Britain. Anyone can become a carer, at any time. Crossroads aims to relieve the stress upon carers of all ages through the provision of home-based respite care services.

By the end of the century, one in five of us will have to become a carer, and Crossroads must grow and develop its network of schemes in order to go on helping those whose lives are committed to looking after others. Please contact Crossroads if you would like to help further their work.

Cruse Bereavement Care

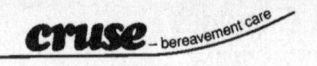

126 Sheen Road, Richmond, Surrey TW9 1UR
Tel: 0181-940 4818 *Fax:* 0181-940 7638

Charity Reg. No:	208078
Contact:	Wendy Wilson, Fundraising Manager
Date established:	1959
Annual income:	£1.7m (March 95)
Area covered:	National – 195 Branches

Cruse Bereavement Care offers help to all who are bereaved – young and old, men, women and children, wherever they live in the United Kingdom. The death of someone close can affect us in several different ways – emotionally, physically, socially and in many practical areas of our life. It can present us with one of the greatest challenges we shall ever have to face. Cruse offers free, personal and confidential help through counselling (the opportunity to talk through feelings with a trained counsellor), information on many aspects of bereavement, including financial and practical matters, and social support groups which offer companionship.

Cruse depends on voluntary contributions to continue and extend its work. Please consider giving a donation, becoming a Friend, taking out a covenant or remembering Cruse in your will. Funds are urgently needed to keep the UK Cruse Bereavement Line (0181-332 7227) open. Anyone can ring for direct personal and confidential help and advice. Cruse also needs support for its network of branches and to help open new ones. Branch membership is open to locals. Those without a branch nearby are offered national membership.

Cruse needs volunteers for all aspects of its work. There are over 4,000 bereavement counsellors and 2,000 people helping to run their local branch in other ways; for example, running social groups, acting as referral secretaries, branch organisers and fundraisers. All counsellors have thorough training and preparation and are given regular supervision and support. Training courses are run on local, regional and national bases.

Cruse's deployment of volunteers is a major channel for those who wish to involve themselves in caring for bereaved people. It encourages community care and neighbourhood support, it assists self-help and mutual support and encourages those who have been helped to help others in their turn.

DISABILITY NETWORK UK

8 Wolverhampton House, 123 Church Street, St Helens Merseyside WA10 1AJ
Tel: 01744-451 215 *Fax:* 01744-23427
Charity Reg. No: 511545
Contact: Paul Brennan, Director
Date established: 1981
Annual income: £200,000 (95/96)
Area covered: National

Disability Network is an independent charity which is run by people with disabilities. The charity aims to benefit all people with disabilities and promote their independence and their right to integration by: advising, supporting and representing disabled people and their families on issues which affect their lives; providing an advocacy and advice service, together with an extensive information service; recruiting and supporting volunteers interested in furthering equal opportunities for disabled people.

Every year the charity deals with over 20,000 enquiries from individuals seeking advice or support, and has helped many to claim benefits and allowances worth millions of pounds. To meet the ever-increasing demand for its services it needs to raise £350,000 every year – please help!

THE LEUKAEMIA CARE SOCIETY

Leukaemia CARE

14 Kingfisher Court, Pinhoe, Exeter, Devon EX4 8JN
Tel: 01392-464 848 *Fax:* 01392-460 331
Charity Reg. No: 259483
Contact: **Mrs Sandra Brown, Chief Administrative Officer**
Date established: 1967
Annual income: £192,231 (95)
Area covered: National

The Society was formed in 1967 by a small group of parents, all of whom had a child affected by leukaemia. All knew of the way in which serious illness can isolate patients and their families from the community, and were only too well aware of the feelings, including deep shock, anger, frustration, depression, loneliness and grief which often follow diagnosis, treatment and sometimes, death. The Society exists to support and help families in this position. Those suffering from allied blood disorders such as Hodgkin's Disease and Multiple Myeloma are also supported by a network of volunteers across the United Kingdom.

Another difficulty families often face concerns the financial implications of the illness. The Society is able to offer limited discretionary assistance. A holiday scheme allows families a short break away from prolonged treatment which can put enormous emotional strain on everyone. Holidays are offered in caravans at selected sites around Britain, at little or no cost.

Many of the Society's volunteers have experienced the illness personally or within their family but help is always welcome from anyone in sympathy with the charity's aims who can offer assistance in any way. There are voluntary support groups in many areas; someone who understands and cares is but a phone call away.

The charity is entirely self-funding and undertakes many fundraising activities including the sale of goods and Christmas cards, coffee mornings, sponsored events of all descriptions etc. Enquiries from individuals and companies regarding sponsorship of printing, postage, cost of holiday provision and publishing the newsletter are always welcome.

MARIE CURIE MEMORIAL FOUNDATION

28 Belgrave Square, London SW1X 8QG
Tel: 0171-235 3325 *Fax:* 0171-823 2380
Charity Reg. No: 207994
Contact: **Peter Jennings, Marketing and Fundraising Director**

Date established: **1948**
Annual income: **£41m (95)**
Area covered: **National**

Marie Curie Cancer Care provides free nursing and hospice care across the UK to thousands of people seriously ill with cancer, and carries out leading-edge research at The Marie Curie Research Institute into the causes, earlier detection and improved treatment of the disease. Patients or carers who need help from one of 6,000 Marie Curie Nurses nationwide are encouraged to contact the district nurse or GP for advice. Marie Curie Nurses give practical care overnight or throughout the day in the homes of people with cancer. Specialist medical and nursing care is offered at all Marie Curie Hospice Centres which provide the largest number of hospice beds outside the NHS and have day care, outpatient and education facilities.

Marie Curie relies on the help of thousands of volunteers but needs the support of thousands more. Can you spare some time to help on a weekly basis in one of their 125 charity shops, or spend an hour during the Marie Curie Daffodil Campaign in March, giving out their popular fabric daffodils in return for donations, or help behind the scenes? Could you display a box of fabric daffodils or delightful teddy badges and a collecting box in your workplace or offer to drive day patients to a Marie Curie Hospice? Perhaps you would prefer to organise a coffee morning or jumble sale or even run a marathon?

Each £7.50 you raise will enable a Marie Curie nurse to provide one hour of free care to someone with cancer. An hour of your time spent collecting during the Marie Curie spring Daffodil Campaign could fund the vital work of a Marie Curie nurse for a whole day or night. The Foundation will give you all the advice and support you need. If you'd like some more

details please ask for a leaflet on any of the following:
Volunteering; the Daffodil Campaign; Marie Curie Nurses;
Hospice Centres; Research Institute; Education for Health Care
Professionals; Tax-efficient Giving; or Cancer Prevention.
Helen Smith, supported by a nationwide network of fundraisers
and volunteers, looks forward to hearing from you.

NATIONAL FOSTER CARE ASSOCIATION

Leonard House, 5–7 Marshalsea Road, London SE1 1EP
Tel: 0171-828 6266 *Fax:* 0171-357 6668
Charity Reg. No: 280852
Contact: Ms Gerri McAndrew, Executive Director
Date established: 1974
Annual income: £1.3m (94/95)
Area covered: National

Since 1974, the National Foster Care Association (NFCA) has been working to improve the quality of life for all children in foster care. Fostering is a service to families in crisis. NFCA is there for all those involved – foster carers, social workers, parents and especially the children and young people themselves. Practical advice and guidance are provided through a helpline, face-to-face counselling, books, leaflets and an extensive conference and training programme. Through links with policy makers and a nationwide membership, NFCA promotes best practice in foster care and spearheads new initiatives.

NFCA is dependent on fundraising. Members of the public may like to take out membership and learn more about fostering or give a donation. The helpline is only open on four half-days per week and it is NFCA's dearest wish to offer a service every day to the hundreds of callers who need help. Membership brings a number of benefits, including a quarterly magazine *Foster Care*, containing up-to-date information on all aspects of fostering; discounts on all training courses, conferences and publications; free publications; a 24 hour legal advice service and legal costs insurance. Fostering is a difficult, demanding task as many children have been very hurt by their experiences, but it is also one that brings enormous rewards. Foster carers come from all sections of the community, their diversity reflecting that of the children and young people needing their support. A shortage of foster carers means that some children miss out on the help a foster family can provide. Each year Foster Care Week is held to give publicity to the need for more families.

PARENTLINE

Endway House, The Endway, Benfleet, Essex SS7 2AN
Tel: 01702-554782 *Fax:* 01702-554911
Charity Reg. No: 1043139
Contact: **Carole Baisden, Chief Executive**
Date established: **1979**
Annual income: **£155,000 (95)**
Area covered: **National**

PARENTLINE aims to promote, safeguard, protect and preserve good health, both mental and physical, of parents and children; and to prevent physical, emotional and sexual abuse of children and young people. The organisation provides a nationally networked telephone helpline service for parents or carers of children who are in need of support, information or guidance, and which is sensitive to a variety of family forms. Callers may also be helped to gain access to professional assistance when this is considered appropriate.

PARENTLINE UK is a national umbrella charity which provides support, training and advice to PARENTLINE Groups which are based in the UK and Ireland. Each PARENTLINE Group is managed and run by volunteers, all of whom have had parenting experience themselves and have successfully completed the PARENTLINE training course. To enable the helpline service to be as reliable and efficient as possible, training, support and supervision are continually provided. Volunteers are reimbursed for out of pocket expenses. Volunteers are needed not only for the helpline, but for the organisation of fundraising and publicity events. This activity is essential to PARENTLINE's objective of reaching out to as many families as possible.

Each PARENT Group is an independent registered charity and they are always in need of financial support for basic running costs. Some Groups also have 'Friends of PARENTLINE' members whose focus is to raise funds for the Group. In 1995 over 20,000 calls were received on a huge variety of family issues or problems. To find out more about your nearest PARENTLINE Group, look for a local number in the telephone directory or call the National Helpline for details.

THE SAMARITANS

10 The Grove, Slough, Berks SL1 1QP
Tel: 01753-532 713 *Fax:* 01753-819 004
Charity Reg. No: 219432
Contact: **Paul Farmer, Communications Manager**
Date established: 1953
Annual income: £5m (94/95) target: £6.5m
Area covered: National

The Samaritans is a nationwide charity, founded in 1953, which exists to provide confidential emotional support to any person, irrespective of race, creed, age or status, who is suicidal or despairing; and to increase public awareness of suicidal feelings. The Samaritans' service is provided 24 hours a day, 365 days a year, by trained volunteers, and needs over £6 million to maintain its work. You can contact the Samaritans by calling 0345-90 90 90 (for the cost of a local call), or one of the local branch numbers; by visiting them in person; via e-mail; and at events such as festivals.

The Samaritans relies on voluntary support to maintain and develop its service. Seven per cent of central income comes from the Government and over 90 per cent is in the form of public donations. Branches require volunteers to help their local fundraising activities.

Donation Line: 01753-819 009. For further information contact your local branch (under 'S' in the telephone directory) or ring 01753-532 713.

There are 22,500 volunteers located at over 200 branches across the UK and Ireland. Volunteers are thoroughly prepared by experienced training teams in each Branch, and are constantly supported by other volunteers whilst on duty. There are no formal qualifications, but you need to be a good listener, open-minded, and able to carry out a regular three- or four-hour shift. The Samaritans always need more listening and fundraising volunteers.

Turning Point

New Loom House, 101 Backchurch Lane, London E1 1LU
Tel: 0171-702 2300 *Fax:* 0171-702 1456
Charity Reg. No: 234887
Contact: **The Fundraising Director**
Date established: 1964
Annual income: £12.9m (94/95)
Area covered: National – (Eng., Scot.)

Turning Point exists to provide advice and social care, counselling and nursing to a wide variety of adults whom society classifies as 'difficult'. Across 60 projects in England and Scotland the charity offers: residential detox, rehabilitation, drop-ins and street-advice for drug users and problem drinkers; nursing care to chaotic drug users (some with AIDS); residential and day care for people with profound learning disabilities (ie mental handicap); social care, move-on accommodation and 'homes for life' for people coming out of psychiatric hospitals and regional secure units. Turning Point aims to enable people to achieve their maximum potential and independence by turning their lives around.

Turning Point holds fundraising events in Birmingham, Manchester and London from time to time (please join the mailing list) and actively seeks support through donations, covenants and legacies. With such a variety of centres, donors have plenty of choice in saying how they would like their donation used.

The charity does not have a formal network of volunteers, but asks for helpers, befrienders, escorts and can-shakers from time to time at specific centres. They also welcome people to undertake fundraising events on their behalf, support their fundraising committees in Birmingham and Manchester and help out with envelope-stuffing at head office.

For volunteering and fundraising in Scotland, please ring 0141-420 6777; in Northern England, 0161-832 3417; in central England, 0115-969 1263. Enquiries about Turning Point's centres are available on these numbers too.

WOMEN'S ROYAL VOLUNTARY SERVICE

234–244 Stockwell Road, London SW9 9SP
Tel: 0171-416 0146 *Fax:* 0171-416 0148
Charity Reg. No: 254891
Contact: **PR department**
Date established: 1938
Annual income: **Not stated**
Area covered: **National**

CARE AND COUNSELLING

The WRVS is the largest practical voluntary organisation in the UK, with 140,000 volunteers. One in 200 adults, from all walks of life, is a member of the WRVS, and 1 in 10 of these is a man. The WRVS achieves a great deal for the community through community services including Meals on Wheels, Books on Wheels, social clubs, contact centres, clothing shops and holidays for underprivileged children; hospital services such as tea bars, shops, ward services, and trolley shops, a retail service for patients; and emergency services providing administrative assistance to the blue-light services, comforting victims and providing general help and refreshments.

The members of the Women's Royal Voluntary Service, in partnership with the public and private sectors, are committed to being the premier providers of voluntary assistance to those in need of care within their local community. The WRVS aims to continue implementing new training programmes for its members; monitoring progress; expanding its services; and continuing to promote the WRVS and recruiting new volunteers.

The WRVS regularly raises funds for various projects and schemes in the community. In local hospitals, the WRVS runs retail projects, shops and tea bars, and raises funds to donate to the hospitals for their wage.

In 1995 the WRVS launched a new telephone linkline for people interested in finding out more about WRVS. The caller is immediately connected to the nearest WRVS Divisional Office and the call is charged at a local rate. The number to call is: 0345-595 555.

SEE ALSO

ASBAH
Barnardos
British Diabetic Association
British Liver Trust
Dyslexia Institute
Families Need Fathers
Family Service Units
John Grooms Association for Disabled People
Multiple Sclerosis Research Trust
National Association for Voluntary Hostels
National Stepfamily Association
Royal Air Force Benevolent Fund
St Christopher's Fellowship
Tenovus, The Cancer Charity
Terrence Higgins Trust Limited
Westminster Society
Youth with a Mission

CHILDREN AND YOUTH

BARNARDOS

Tanners Lane, Barkingside, Ilford, Essex IG4 1QG
Tel: 0181-550 8822 *Fax:* 0181-551 6870
Charity Reg. No: 216250
Contact: **Charles Holden, Director of Fundraising**
Date established: 1866
Annual income: £76.261m (95)
Area covered: **National**

Barnardos works with disadvantaged and challenging children and young people, offering support relevant to their individual needs, and giving them a chance through a wide variety of activities such as fostering or adoption. There are family support services in areas of particular deprivation, likewise youth and community work, and residential services for disabled children and behaviourally challenging children.

Barnardos aims have not changed significantly over the years but the ways in which they are met have. Barnardos works with children and young people in the context of today's society, although very much in keeping with the spirit of its founder, Dr Thomas Barnardo. However, there are now no orphanages. Alongside its mainstream objectives, Barnardos is pioneering work in the areas of sexual abuse, homelessness and the impact of the HIV virus on children's lives.

Without the wide and varied support of volunteers Barnardos would not achieve much of what it does. The charity enjoys support in its projects through volunteer carers – some as young as their mid-teens; support in the shops, where volunteers bring skills to the charity's retail activities and enjoy the regular companionship of working in a team; and support in raising funds through organising events or making collections. There are many skills from which Barnardos can benefit through volunteers, just as there is much that a volunteer can gain from supporting Barnardos – it is a partnership that is much appreciated and greatly valued.

Barnardos is at the forefront of child care service provision in the UK, yet it could do so much more. Barnardos needs £1.4 million a week to do its current work. Your help, in whatever way, will be very welcome.

Boys' and Girls' Welfare Society

Central Offices, Schools Hill, Cheadle, Cheshire SK8 1JE
Tel: **0161-428 5256** *Fax:* **0161-491 5056**
Charity Reg. No: **209782**
Contact: **Andy Haines, Chief Executive**
Date established: **1870**
Annual income: **£4.6m (94/95)**
Area covered: **National**

The objectives of the Boys' and Girls' Welfare Society (BGWS) are: to give aid, assistance and care to needy, sick or disabled children and young persons; to promote the education, training and advancement in life of children and young persons; to provide or assist in providing religious instruction for children and young persons in its care, according to the religious beliefs and traditions of Christian denominations or non-Christian faiths as may be applicable in each case.

Formed in 1870, BGWS now annually provides some 23 different services for over 1,000 children, young people and their families from all over the north-west. Through its residential centres, special schools, specialist contract services and training activities, BGWS works in partnership with 22 local authorities and many other voluntary agencies.

CHILD POVERTY ACTION GROUP

1–5 Bath Street, London EC1V 9PY
Tel: 0171-253 3406 *Fax:* 0171-490 0561
Charity Reg. No: 294841
Contact: **David Privett, Fundraising Director**
Date established: **1965**
Annual income: **£1.25m**
Area covered: **National**

CPAG promotes action for the relief, directly or indirectly, of poverty among children and families with children. The charity works to ensure that those on low incomes receive their full entitlement to welfare benefits. In their campaigning and information work they seek to improve benefits and policies for low income families. CPAG uses legal test cases as a tool for promoting social justice and bringing about much needed changes.

CPAG centrally, and through its local branches, gathers information on the real effects of changes in the benefit system.

CPAG's telephone advice line and advice publications are used by thousands of professionals and volunteers in the welfare rights field. For further information or details of how to become a member, please write to CPAG (Dept. CW) at the above address.

THE CHILDREN'S TRUST

Tadworth Court, Tadworth, Surrey KT20 5RU
Tel: 01737-357 171 *Fax:* 01737-370 118
Charity Reg. No: 288018
Contact: **Sarah Watts, Communications Manager**
Date established: **1984**
Annual income: **£5.4m (94/95)**
Area covered: **National/Regional**

The Children's Trust (formerly Tadworth Court Children's Hospital) is devoted to giving children with profound disabilities the best possible quality of life. The Trust has three principal services: a rehabilitation unit for children with head injuries (mainly caused by road traffic accidents); a special residential school, St Margaret's, for children with profound learning difficulties; a residential care unit for disabled children who need more intensive nursing and medical support. The Trust also provides Outreach services within the child's own home, and hospice care. The Children's Trust aims to provide a safe, happy atmosphere suitable to the lives of children with disabilities.

The Trust relies on fundraising for purchasing medical equipment, vehicles, special toys, and to build on or improve its current facilities. Without fundraising The Children's Trust would not be here today. Covenants, legacies, corporate gifts and single donations are some of the many ways in which thousands of people choose to support the charity every year. The Children's Trust is genuinely unique. There is no other facility nationwide that can offer the same variety of services to children who are so profoundly disabled. The Trust's philosophy is, 'they are a child first, their disability comes second', and children's care is always considered carefully in relation to the whole family.

There are currently more than 160 people who work as volunteers for The Children's Trust at Tadworth Court, a beautiful site with 22 acres of open woodland in Surrey. Volunteers never take the place of the highly skilled and trained professionals who work directly with the children, but they can add valuable 'extra pairs of hands'. Fundraising events, administration work, driving buses on excursions, helping to decorate living accommodation – these are just some of the ways in which volunteers help the Trust every single day. The Trust's Volunteers Organiser is always happy to discuss ways in which students, unemployed and retired people can help.

CRUSADERS

2 Romeland Hill, St Albans, Herts AL3 4ET
Tel: 01727-855 422 Fax: 01727-848 518
Charity Reg. No: 223798
Contact: **Dr Alan Kerbey, General Director**
Date established: 1906
Annual income: £1.5m (94)
Area covered: National

Crusaders is a dynamic youth organisation committed to providing Christian teaching on life issues in lively and relevant ways for children and young people aged 4 to 18. The backbone of the work is conducted through a network of weekly youth groups, many based in deprived inner city and rural communities. This is backed up by an exciting programme of activities including low-cost holidays, multi-activity camping weekends, roadshows and sports competitions. For those aged over 16, there are opportunities to get involved in short-term service projects in Third World countries. The organisation is currently serving 20,000 young people, many of whom are disadvantaged, in over 500 groups.

Crusader groups are run by volunteers: committed Christians who have both an ability to relate to young people and a desire to see them reach their full potential. They come from many different denominations and walks of life. Crusader leaders are provided with training, and a wide range of other resources including active teaching programmes. Volunteers are required for one to two weeks during the summer to act as leaders on Crusader holidays. No specialist skills are required, but experience of first-aid, catering or life-saving is particularly useful.

In recent years, Crusaders has demonstrated its ability to make relevant contemporary responses to the needs of a wide range of young people. It is supported in this work by an Advisory Council of more than 100 leading figures, in addition to 100 patrons for projects with disadvantaged young people. These patrons include two senior cabinet ministers: the Rt Hon Tony Blair MP; the Rt Hon Alan Beith MP; and five other MPs.

Funding is required in order to provide: continuing support for a national team of youth workers whose role is to start new Crusader groups and provide support for existing ones; a multimedia roadshow in 1996–97 which will present relevant social issues for young people aged 13 to 19; subsidies for disadvantaged young people to go on Crusader holidays.

FAMILIES NEED FATHERS

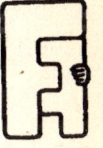

134 Curtain Road, London EC2A 3AR
Tel: 0171-613 5060 *Fax:* 0171-613 5060
Charity Reg. No: 276899
Contact: **Bruce Lidington, National Chairman**
Date established: 1974
Annual income: £37,000 (94)
Area covered: **National**

Families Need Fathers addresses the problem of parent loss in divorce (for which the UK has the highest rate in the world). The charity offers advice and support to parents (particularly non-custodials) in maintaining a sound parent/child relationship during and after divorce or separation. Its lengthy experience in this field means that it is regularly invited by Government, academia and policy-making bodies to make formal representations as the most balanced and authoritative voice for non-custodial parents and their children.

The charity gives direct service to separating parents and their children through a nationwide network of local branch advice venues. Appeals for funds and voluntary help are regularly made to expand this network.

FARMS FOR CITY CHILDREN

Nethercott House, Iddesleigh, Winkleigh, Devon EX19 8BG
Tel: **01837-810 573** *Fax:* **01837-810 866**
Charity Reg. No: **325120R**
Contact: **Clare Morpurgo, Secretary**
Date established: **1972**
Annual income: **£336,000 (95)**
Area covered: **National**

Farms for City Children has welcomed children from disadvantaged areas for over 20 years. During their stay on a farm the children take responsibility for as much of the farmwork as they can safely do. In this way they learn to work together and experience the satisfaction of doing a job to the best of their ability. It has been said that a child can learn more in a week on the farm than in a year in the classroom.

To enable the most deprived children to benefit from this positive experience the place for every child is subsidised by the charity. Any help is greatly appreciated and always acknowledged. Supporters receive a yearly newsletter and information about farm open days.

GREAT ORMOND STREET CHILDREN'S HOSPITAL FUND

40–41 Queen Square, London WC1N 3AJ
Tel: **0171-916 5678** *Fax:* **0171-831 1938**
Charity Reg. No: **235825**

CHILDREN AND YOUTH

Contact: **Joan Kearns, Fundraising Dep.**
Date established: **1852**
Annual income: **£10m (94/95)**
Area covered: **National**

Great Ormond Street Children's Hospital aims to offer hope to children often suffering from the rarest, most life-threatening and complex conditions and also to give the opportunity of a healthy future for them and generations to come. While the NHS pays for the day-to-day running of the hospital, the special trustees aim to raise an additional £10 million each year for providing family support services, buying new equipment and funding vital research.

With 32 specialities, Great Ormond Street offers the widest range of paediatric expertise under one roof in Britain today, welcoming more than 18,800 children as inpatients and seeing over 66,000 outpatients every year. Children are referred from all around the country and from overseas. Volunteers are always needed. Please call!

I CAN (INVALID CHILDREN'S AID NATIONWIDE)

Barbican City Gate, 1–3 Dufferin Street, London EC1Y 8NA
Tel: 0171-374 4422 *Fax:* 0171-374 2762
Charity Reg. No: **210031**
Contact: **Brian Jones, Chief Executive**
Date established: **1888**
Annual income: **£5m (94/95)**
Area covered: **National**

I CAN works with children who have speech and language difficulties, through three schools and a network of nurseries. I CAN is also establishing a network of secondary-level language units in existing mainstream schools. The charity offers short courses to parents and professionals in this field and has a range of teaching materials. I CAN also operates the UK's only school for children with asthma, eczema and related conditions.

I CAN offers membership to parents and professionals at special rates. It also welcomes as members anyone with an interest in the education of children with special educational needs, and encourages people to support the charity through Give As You Earn schemes and deeds of covenant.

I CAN welcomes volunteers in a number of capacities. Some are able to be involved in its schools as governors, or as helpers in a number of areas of the charity's work; others are actively involved in a range of fundraising activities within their local areas, supporting the work of a particular unit or contributing to development work through central funds. I CAN would be delighted to speak to anyone who has any ideas for fundraising.

Each year I CAN organises a number of children's parties in the London area. In 1995 the charity benefited from the fundraising of a marathon runner and a 14-year-old who cycled the length of the country. I CAN also organises a range of local events linked to schools and nurseries, and encourages business support, organising fun-days, golf days and inter-firm challenges.

CHILDREN AND YOUTH

Kids' Clubs Network

Bellerive House, 3 Muirfield Crescent, London E14 9SZ
Tel: 0171-512 2112 *Fax:* 0171-512 2010
Charity Reg. No: 288285
Contact: **Anne Longfield, Director**
Date established: **1981**
Annual income: **£2.5m (94)**
Area covered: **National**

Kids' Clubs Network is the national organisation promoting and supporting school-age childcare. The membership organisation numbers over 3,000 local kids' clubs, providing places for over 100,000 children aged from 4 to 12 before and after school during term time and all day during school holidays. The clubs offer safe and enjoyable play opportunities for children, and peace of mind for parents. By creating awareness of the needs of children, parents and employers, through information services, training courses and publications, Kids' Clubs Network aims to have a kids' club in every neighbourhood, accessible to all local children, and to promote and support quality childcare that is safe, rewarding and affordable.

Kids' Clubs Network provides a wide range of publications on every aspect of out-of-school childcare, backed up with training courses and an information and advice line. In addition, members can take advantage of preferential insurance rates, frequent special offers and Kids' Clubs Network's bi-monthly magazine, *School's Out*. With over 3,000 clubs across the country, volunteers are always needed on a local basis to serve on local club management committees or to help with fundraising at a local level.

National Kids' Clubs Day is held every year to promote awareness of kids' clubs and the need for more funding.

KIDS

80 Waynflete Square, London W10 6UD
Tel: 0181-969 2817 *Fax:* 0181-969 4550
Charity Reg. No: 275936
Contact: John Mulcahy, Founder
Date established: 1970
Annual income: £1.18m (95/96)
Area covered: National

KIDS responds to the needs of children with disabilities and their families through services which include integrated nurseries and holiday play schemes, respite care, home-based learning and developmental-structured play sessions. KIDS provides support through family centres in Birmingham, Camden, Fareham and Gosport, Hull and North Kensington. It intends to develop services and open new centres to help more children and their families.

KIDS believes children and their families should have access to a full range of the highest quality services, offering choice and diversity, and that families should share equally in decision making about their children. KIDS has just celebrated its 25th Anniversary.

CHILDREN AND YOUTH

LIFE EDUCATION CENTRES

20 Long Lane, London EC1A 9HL
Tel: 0171-600 6969 *Fax:* 0171-600 6979
Charity Reg. No: 800727
Contact: **Michael Roberts MBE, National Director**
Date established: 1986
Annual income: £391,690 (95)
Area covered: **National**

Life Education Centres aim to provide children (aged 3 to 15 years) with the knowledge and skills necessary, through positive and innovative health-based education, to keep them free from the abuse of drugs and other harmful substances. The charity's programmes are delivered nationwide, through the use of specially equipped mobile teaching classrooms, working in communities with trained 'educators', and involving parents and other community members. They set out to capture the child's imagination as to the wonders of the human body using discussion, role-play, puppetry, interactive audiovisuals, song and dance plus follow-up resources for use in the classroom and at home.

There are currently 26 mobile classrooms operating in the UK, seeing over 360,000 children every year, with over 50 community-based initiatives working towards their own mobile classrooms. The charity is part of Life Education International which represents other Life Education programmes around the world, currently seeing over 3 million children every year.

Committed volunteers are always welcome at Centres, on both a national and local basis. The national office in London always needs assistance with special projects, events, office administration and fundraising, as do all the local committees around the country. Locally, help is also always needed with the existing mobile classrooms (locations can be obtained from the national office), as well as fundraising to purchase new ones.

The national office fundraises to meet development demands and to expand the programme. Fundraising is conducted through a mix of sponsorship, appeals, donations and special events. Locals raise money to purchase mobile classrooms and to support running costs. The charity is constantly in need of support in this area of its work.

THE MALCOLM SARGENT CANCER FUND FOR CHILDREN

14 Abingdon Road, London W8 6AF
Tel: 0171-937 4548 *Fax:* 0171-937 2315
Charity Reg. No: **256435**
Contact: **Sylvia Darley, President**
Date established: **1968**
Annual income: **£2.5m (95)**
Area covered: **National & Australia**

The Malcolm Sargent Cancer Fund for Children was founded in 1968 as a practical and lasting memorial to the life and work of the great British conductor. The purpose of the Fund is to provide financial support and practical help to children and young people under the age of 21 (and their families) suffering from any form of cancer, including leukaemia and Hodgkin's Disease. There are 47 Malcolm Sargent Social Workers throughout the UK, working at the main cancer centres, and two holiday houses are provided to help with convalescence.

Fundraising support is needed in the form of sponsorship for the Hospitals' Christmas Carol Concerts in London (The Royal Festival Hall), Cardiff (St David's Hall), Manchester and Birmingham. Details of December and January concerts are available by telephoning 0171-937 5740. The Fund relies heavily on legacy income which is completely tax free. Your first thought should be for your family, dependants and friends, but you may wish to help people in great need, especially children, by remembering charities such as the Malcolm Sargent Cancer Fund for Children in your will. In 1994, 60 people kindly volunteered to run in the London Marathon and, as a result, £28,000 was raised. In future years, it is hoped that even more runners will come forward to wear the colours of the Malcolm Sargent Cancer Fund for Children. Further information is obtainable from the fundraising department on 0171-937 4405 or 01781-795 6550.

The Malcolm Sargent Festival Choir is drawn from members of choirs from every part of England. The Choir performs voluntarily and new members are always welcome. Further details are obtainable from the Fund Office on 0181-699 3309.

NATIONAL DEAF CHILDREN'S SOCIETY

15 Dufferin Street, London EC1 8PD
Tel: 0171-250 0123 *Fax:* 0171-251 5020
Charity Reg. No: 1016532
Contact: **Mark Astarita, Director of Public Affairs**

Date established: **1944**
Annual income: **£1.3m (95)**
Area covered: **National**

Imagine how you would cope if you were deaf as a child. Not to be able to hear your favourite bedtime story, share a joke with your friends or enjoy your favourite television programme without special equipment? The National Deaf Children's Society helps 65,000 deaf children and their families in the UK confront the daily challenge of childhood deafness and plan confidently for the future. The Society exists to enable deaf children to maximise their skills and abilities, providing a range of support and information services to families and carers through its network of regional and local representatives and 120 parent groups.

The Society relies on the generosity of donations from the public to continue its work. Legacies are important with approximately 50 per cent of the Society's annual income coming from people who leave money to deaf children in their will. Individual donations, large and small, all make a big difference to the lives of deaf children. Support is often needed for local events organised by the Society's 120 parent groups.

The National Deaf Children's Society welcomes volunteers throughout the organisation. Support is particularly helpful in the fundraising and public affairs department where volunteers may be asked to help process large appeals and mailings or update database records. The Society is occasionally able to offer short work experience placements across different departments for students from a variety of disciplines. Often additional administration support is called for by the directorate and a willing pair of hands is always welcome for street collections or at busy events.

National Playing Fields Association (NPFA)

25 Ovington Square, London SW3 1LQ
Tel: 0171-584 6445 *Fax:* 0171-581 2402
Charity Reg. No: 306070
Contact: Elsa Davies, Director
Date established: 1925
Annual income: £600,000 (95)
Area covered: National

'Play and sports for all' is the prime purpose of the National Playing Fields Association (NPFA). Founded in 1925, the NPFA works hard to provide the best in healthy recreation for everyone, especially children of all abilities. A leading UK authority on play safety, the NPFA promotes high standards in play and sports facilities. Its work is essential at a time when so many youngsters are attracted to sedentary pastimes such as computers and video games.

An independent charity, the NPFA's work relies on donations from the public and its supporters. Often called 'the national trust of recreation space', the NPFA currently protects over 2,000 sports fields and playgrounds in perpetuity for local communities. It produces an Inheritance Guide describing how recreational land can be protected.

National Stepfamily Association

Chapel House, 18 Hatton Place, London EC1N 8RU
Tel: 0171-209 2460 *Fax:* 0171-209 2461
Charity Reg. No: 1005351
Contact: Erica De'Ath, Chief Executive
Date established: 1983
Annual income: £161,570 (94/95)
Area covered: National

Every day 600 children experience their parents separating or divorcing. Five years later, half of those parents will have remarried. For some, conflicts may continue, causing further distress as step-parents may be unclear of their role, step- and half-siblings may be resented. The National Stepfamily Association provides a counselling Helpline for all generations; a children's newsletter called Stepladder; and information and advice on stepmothering, stepfathering, a new baby in a stepfamily, making a will, financial planning, weddings and step-parent adoption.

Stepfamilies have a higher risk of divorce than first families – a second disruption for stepchildren and a first for the new children. The National Stepfamily Association needs qualified volunteer counsellors to give six hours monthly on their Helpline (they run short courses and give support). Please help by sponsoring a counsellor or an edition of the Association's children's newsletter.

CHILDREN AND YOUTH

NCH Action for Children

85 Highbury Park, London N5 1UD
Tel: 0171-226 2033 *Fax:* 0171-226 2537
Charity Reg. No: 215301
Contact: Tony Manwaring, Director of Fundraising
Date established: 1869
Annual income: £48.1m (94/95)
Area covered: National

NCH Action for Children has had one aim for 126 years: to bring a better quality of life to Britain's most vulnerable children, young people, and their families. The charity began with just one home; now it offers many different services to help children who are at risk from abuse, poverty, homelessness, who have a disability or simply have nobody to turn to. It runs community, family and respite care centres; provides short-term accommodation for the homeless; runs community-based projects for young offenders; child sexual abuse treatment centres; residential homes and schools for children with severe disabilities; and home-finding services that match children who have special needs with adoptive and foster parents.

NCH Action for Children is growing. The number of projects to help children, young people and their families has grown to over 235 and the project work has developed and expanded too. The charity hopes to provide more services to ensure that vulnerable children, young people and their families are not treated unfairly. By supporting them, you will enable even more children to enjoy their right to a loving, caring and safe environment. If you are interested in helping NCH Action for Children with their important work by volunteering to help in one of their shops, helping with a house-to-house collection or joining a support group, please contact Patty Baxter on 0171-226 2033.

NCH Action for Children is also developing links with businesses. 'Taking the Charity Challenge not only helped NCH Action for Children but also greatly benefited our company and our people,' said Glenn F. Tilton of Texaco Ltd, describing his company's relationship with the charity. For further information on NCH Action for Children's work with businesses please contact Sarah Carnaby, Head of Corporate Fundraising, on 0171-226 2033.

SAVE THE CHILDREN FUND

17 Grove Lane, Camberwell, London SE5 8RD
Tel: 0171-703 5400 *Fax:* 0171-703 2278
Charity Reg. No: 213890
Contact: **Regional Fundraising Help Desk**
Date established: **1919**
Annual income: **£92m (94/95)**
Area covered: **International**

Save the Children works in the UK and in more than 50 countries overseas to achieve lasting benefits for children. It works with communities to ensure that children's rights – to health, food, shelter, safety, and a secure family life – are respected and promoted. In addition to providing emergency relief, Save the Children's work ranges from reuniting children with their families in former Yugoslavia and Rwanda, to supporting working children in Brazil and young people leaving care in the UK – where, after years in children's homes or foster care, young people can suddenly be without a support network.

A network of fundraising staff across the country helps to develop fundraising initiatives, provides information on Save the Children's work, gives talks to schools, groups and companies.

Save the Children enjoys the support of businesses, both locally and nationally, and aims to deliver commercial benefits in return for companies' fundraising efforts. The charity runs a number of special schemes including project support, covenants and pre-tax payroll giving where donors can support the charity's work through regular giving. Supporters can also make a gift through remembering Save the Children in their will. Save the Children also produces a gift catalogue.

Volunteers raise money for the charity's work at home and abroad. There are 150 shops, staffed entirely by volunteers as well as local fundraising events organised by the 700 branches, ranging from coffee mornings and jumble sales to tennis tournaments, dragon boat races and celebrity auctions. Other volunteers help Save the Children at specific times of the year – for example, collecting donations outside supermarkets during Save the Children Week.

SOS – Children's Villages UK

32a Bridge Street, Cambridge CB2 1UJ
Tel: 01223-365 589   Fax: 01223-322 613
Charity Reg. No: **255271**
Contact: **Daniel Fox, Director**
Date established: **1968**
Annual income: **£662,758 (95)**
Area covered: **International**

SOS – Children's Villages UK raises funds to support the worldwide work of SOS Children's Villages, giving orphaned and abandoned children in over 120 countries a mother, a family, a home and an education. An SOS mother cares for six to eight children, who grow up together like brothers and sisters in a family home in the SOS village. As well as 15 to 20 family houses, an SOS village will have a kindergarten and other facilities, as required, including schools and vocational training, to enable the children to achieve independence.

SOS – Children's Villages UK needs sponsors for the children and the villages. Sponsors correspond with 'their' child or village and receive regular reports on how their contribution is helping . All sponsorship money is sent, without deduction, to the sponsored project.

ST CHRISTOPHER'S FELLOWSHIP

217 Kingston Road, Wimbledon, London SW19 3NL
Tel: 0181-543 3619 Fax: 0181-544 1633
Charity Reg. No: 207782
Contact: **Ann Hithersay, Director**
Date established: 1870
Annual income: **£3m (94)**
Area covered: **Regional – London**

St Christopher's Fellowship provides supported housing, with care, for more than 200 young people sponsored by the housing corporation and local authorities, and a night shelter for those sleeping rough. It offers children and young people without stable families a secure base, providing for basic human needs, and conducive to physical, emotional and spiritual growth. The Fellowship helps them develop their personalities, learning to respect themselves and others, to control themselves and to develop skills. The Fellowship runs three registered children's homes; two for adolescents leaving care, and one for severely abused children who receive, in addition to residential care, a psychodynamic therapeutic treatment programme.

St Christopher's Fellowship was formed in 1968 by the amalgamation of Homes for Working Boys (1870) and Fellowship of St Christopher (1929). The Fellowship registered as a Housing Association in 1976 and employs 140 staff.

The Fellowship depends on volunteers to support staff working with homeless young people in the night shelter and in a number of supported housing projects. Volunteers are welcome additions to the appeals and public relations departments as well. The Fellowship receives students on placement from universities and offers work experience in social work/housing management/voluntary sector to such students. The Fellowship also provides accommodation to selected volunteers who live in its hostels and support young tenants, helping them prepare for full independence.

The Fellowship relies on fundraising income to supplement fees for therapeutic programmes for abused children, as well as for the development of innovative ways to provide care for children and young people to help them develop independence.

WHIZZ-KIDZ (MOVEMENT FOR NON MOBILE CHILDREN)

215 Vauxhall Bridge Road, London SW1V 1EN
Tel: 0171-233 6600 *Fax:* 0171-233 6611
Charity Reg. No: 802872
Contact: **Head of Fundraising**
Date established: 1990
Annual income: £1.1m (95/96)
Area covered: National

Imagine you have to sit where you're put and watch when your friends run after a ball, and you'll begin to see how crucial wheels are to disabled children who can't get around. Whizz-Kidz exists to provide mobility aids – mainly sports, lightweight and hi-tech powered wheelchairs – to disabled children. By giving them the freedom of wheels the charity enables them to live fuller and more independent lives, go to the same school as their friends and take part in sport. The increase in their confidence and self-esteem is immediate and remarkable.

Whizz-Kidz is a national but local charity which helps children whatever their disability. The charity believes every child has the right to live a life which is as independent as possible, and encourages mobility in very young children so that they never develop a 'disabled mentality'. A wheelchair costs between £1,000 and £10,000 and is a bit like a pair of shoes; it may need replacing as the child grows or simply become worn out. Demand far outstrips the charity's ability to supply, so it needs volunteers to talk to schools, collect cheques and fundraise around the country. The charity will always try to 'match' you with a child on its waiting list for whom it has carried out the proper medical assessments to select the best possible chair. In this way you will know how the money raised is being spent.

Whizz-Kidz receives no Government funding, so is dependent on the efforts of the public for much of its fundraising. Whether you wish to run a marathon (the charity will pay for flights to New York when you raise enough), organise a carol service or a karaoke evening Whizz-Kidz would be delighted to hear from you.

SEE ALSO

ASBAH
Cystic Fibrosis Research Trust
Changing Faces
Dyslexia Institute
Foundation for the Study of Infant Deaths
HYPED
Inter-Action Trust
MENCAP
The Motivation Charitable Trust
National Foster Care Association
Royal Air Force Benevolent Fund
Treloar Trust
Westminster Society

CIVIL LIBERTIES, HUMAN RIGHTS AND SOCIAL WELFARE

CSV (COMMUNITY SERVICE VOLUNTEERS)

237 Pentonville Road, London N1 9NJ
Tel: 0171-278 6601 *Fax:* 0171-837 9621
Charity Reg. No: 281222
Contact: Stephen Burke, External Relations Manager
Date established: 1962
Annual income: £19.9m (95)
Area covered: National

CSV creates opportunities for people to play an active part in the life of their community through volunteering, training, education, the environment and the media. At the heart of our work is a belief that everyone has something to give. Each year CSV works with over 3,000 full-time volunteers, 30,000 part-time volunteers, 3,500 employment trainees and in partnership with 3,000 schools and 1,000 radio and TV stations through seven nationwide programmes – CSV Volunteer Programme; CSV Education; CSV Innovations; CSV Media; RSVP (Retired and Senior Volunteer Programme); CSV Training and Enterprise and CSV Environment.

For further details about CSV and its work, including a copy of our annual review and the latest edition of our newsletter ACTION, please call 0171-278 6601.

CRISIS

7 Whitechapel Road, London E1 1DU
Tel: 0171-377 0489 *Fax:* 0171-247 1525
Charity Reg. No: 1036533
Contact: **Mark Scothern, Director**
Date established: 1967
Annual income: £3.5m (94/95)
Area covered: National

Crisis is the national charity for single, homeless people – those with no statutory rights to housing. Crisis researches, develops and funds schemes to provide help where it is most needed, at whatever stage of homelessness, from emergency help on the streets, through to hostel accommodation, permanent housing and resettlement support. Established in 1967, Crisis has operated and supported hundreds of innovative and valued services, such as the Open Christmas shelters in London, the Furnished Homes Partnership in the north-west and the nationwide WinterWatch emergency shelter programme.

Crisis relies on the financial support of individuals to carry out vital work for homeless people across the UK. A fundraising pack, advice and literature are available for anyone wishing to hold a fundraising event or collection for Crisis, together with information on a wide variety of ways to support their work all year round. Crisis needs volunteers for a variety of tasks, which can include helping at the Open Christmas, doing anything from peeling potatoes to washing hair. Crisis also supports regional Open Christmases and is able to refer volunteers to where help is needed. Volunteers are needed to assist at the offices in London and Manchester, where tasks can range from general admin, stuffing envelopes, computer data input to helping out with specific tasks. They are also able to refer people wanting to volunteer at local hostels and day centres.

Crisis manages a range of fundraising activities each year, including the Square Mile Run, The Crisis Challenge – a 60-mile walk from Canterbury to London – the Crisis Messiah and many more. Crisis always needs volunteers to help out at these events, to take part in a variety of activities such as marshalling, serving refreshments and preparing food.

FAIRBRIDGE

1 Westminster Bridge Road, London SE1 7PL
Tel: 0171-928 1704 Fax: 0171-928 6016
Charity Reg. No: 119251 & Scotland: SC021126
Contact: Andrew Page, Director of Fundraising
Date established: 1909
Annual income: £2.6m (95)
Area covered: National – 12 Centres

Fairbridge works exclusively with young people at risk, aged 14 to 25, in 10 of the UK's most deprived inner cities. The majority of these young people are deemed to be at risk as a result of unemployment, homelessness, drug and alcohol abuse, or criminal activity. Fairbridge delivers a progressive personal development programme, which is in three parts: 'One day Induction'; 'Eight-day Basic Course'; and 'Follow Through' which lasts as long as individual needs require. The programme supports young people to believe in themselves, set their own goals and despite their circumstances, overcome the barriers to achieving them.

Fairbridge has centres in Glasgow, Edinburgh, Newcastle, Middlesborough, Liverpool, Salford, London, Bristol, Cardiff and Chatham.

Fairbridge also operates 'The Spirit of Scotland', a 90 foot gaff-rigged training schooner, and a residential development training centre at Applecross, Scotland.

Fairbridge receives funding from Government, trusts, grant-making bodies and the corporate sector as well as private donations. £500 will ensure that a young person at risk can complete the Fairbridge Induction and Basic courses; £2,500 will support five Basic Course places; and £5,000 will provide 10 Basic Course places. A £10,000 'Lifestart Bursary' will ensure that 10 people will complete the entire programme.

Each year over 17,000 young people participate in the Fairbridge programme, of whom 60 per cent go on to employment, return to education, enter training schemes or join community projects.

There is some scope for volunteers who have the right experience, maturity and aptitude to become involved in Fairbridge's programme of follow-on support. Depending on local requirements, this could involve developing links with other specialist local youth agencies, mentoring or assisting with the personal skills courses.

CIVIL LIBERTIES, HUMAN RIGHTS AND SOCIAL WELFARE

Family Service Units

207 Old Marylebone Road, London NW1 5QP
Tel: 0171-402 5175 *Fax:* 0171-724 1829
Charity Reg. No: 212114
Contact: **Mike Briggs, Head of Fundraising**
Date established: 1948
Annual income: £5.9m (95)
Area covered: National

Operating in the country's most deprived areas, Family Service Units provide support to families under pressure. Support is provided through counselling for children and adults facing family breakdown; therapeutic work with families where children experience or are at risk of physical, emotional or sexual abuse; play schemes, holidays, educational projects, 'drop-in' services and groups where people combat isolation and help each other; programmes that teach parents to develop their skills in caring for their children and that offer advice on welfare benefits etc.

Family Service Units is heavily reliant on voluntary contributions to continue with its work. Volunteering opportunities arise within units and occasionally at the national office. The charity has a long history of innovation and is in the vanguard of developments in services for people from black and ethnic minorities; young carers; anti-bullying work and projects for refugees.

HOME-START UK

2 Salisbury Road, Leicester LE1 7QR
Tel: 0116-233 9955 *Fax:* 0116-233 0232
Charity Reg. No: 326148
Contact: **Margaret Harrison, Director**
Date established: 1981
Annual income: £0.68m (94/95)
Area covered: National

Home-Start is a voluntary organisation in which volunteers offer regular support, friendship, and practical help to young families under stress at home, helping to prevent family crisis and breakdown. Home-Start is a charitable trust committed to promoting the welfare of children and parents by providing effective training, information, guidance and support to each existing and potential local Home-Start scheme.

A hundred and eighty-one independent schemes give support to families throughout the UK, each run by at least one paid organiser and staffed by fully trained volunteers, many of whom have themselves received help from the Home-Start service.

In 1995–6, over 4,500 trained Home-Start volunteers helped more than 27,000 children and their parents during times of stress. Home-Start volunteers, who are themselves parents, offer support, friendship and practical assistance to the families, helping to increase their confidence and independence. Volunteers reassure parents that difficulties with bringing up children are not unusual, by encouraging the parents' strengths and emotional wellbeing. Volunteers help to develop relationships with a family in which time can be shared; the approach is flexible, to take account of different needs. There are many volunteers who choose to assist Home-Start by fundraising, and this work is invaluable if Home-Start's vital support is to continue.

Volunteers may fundraise either for Home-Start UK or for their local scheme. In addition, Home-Start welcomes cash donations including those by covenant, and for £20 a year, supporters can become a Friend of Home-Start UK. For details of your nearest Home-Start scheme, or if you would like more information about the work of Home-Start, please contact Home-Start UK in Leicester on 0116-233 9955.

NATIONAL ASSOCIATION FOR VOLUNTARY HOSTELS

8A The Parade, Beynon Road, Carshalton, Surrey SM5 3RL
Tel: 0181-286 2200 *Fax:* 0181-286 2727
Charity Reg. No: 271136
Contact: **Hazel Bonham, Director**
Date established: **1962**
Annual income: **£123,000 (94/95)**
Area covered: **National**

Some charities work better if they remain low-key and acknowledge that the areas in which they work require sensitivity and confidentiality. National Association for Voluntary Hostels is such an organisation. Founded in 1962, it operates on behalf of people who are single and homeless or suffering from psychological and physical infirmity who find themselves in need of assistance to find a settled way of life. NAVH supports those who make provision for such people.

What does NAVH need? Charitable donations (direct or covenants); volunteers to fill important caring roles; Personal, Corporate and Association Members.

THE NEW BRIDGE

27a Medway Street, London SW1P 2BD
Tel: 0171-976 0779 Fax: 0171-976 0767
Charity Reg. No: **53 BEN**
Contact: **Mr E McGraw, Director**
Date established: **1974**
Annual income: **£291,000 (95)**
Area covered: **National**

The New Bridge recruits and trains volunteers to write to, visit and befriend prisoners, and provides an employment service for ex-offenders. Many prisoners never receive letters or visits, yet everyone needs someone to be interested in them whom they can trust. New Bridge volunteers give this friendship and support. As a volunteer you may be taking the first steps in crime prevention, lessening the number of future victims.

Volunteers (aged 18 or over) are welcomed from all backgrounds, cultures and age groups. They undergo a short training course and expenses are paid. Sensible, sociable people are needed who are prepared to share experiences and time, offering patience, dependability and understanding. The New Bridge has offices in London, Dorset, Durham and Manchester.

CIVIL LIBERTIES, HUMAN RIGHTS AND SOCIAL WELFARE

Prison Reform Trust

prison Reform trust

15 Northburgh Street, London EC1V 0AH
Tel: 0171-251 5070 Fax: 0171-251 5076
Charity Reg. No: 1035525
Contact: Nick Flynn, Deputy Director
Date established: 1981
Annual income: £221,201 (95)
Area covered: National

The Prison Reform Trust works with, monitors and comments upon prisons and young offender institutions throughout Britain. Many prisons are overcrowded and prisoners receive little help to go straight. Within two years of release, the majority have committed more crimes. The work of the Prison Reform Trust is aimed at creating a just, humane and effective penal system. It achieves this by inquiring into the workings of the system; informing prisoners, staff and the wider public; and by influencing Parliament, Government and officials towards reform.

There are three main ways to support the work of the Prison Reform Trust. First, the quarterly magazine, *Prison Report*, presents news and features on the prison system and is available on subscription. (PRT also publishes a comprehensive list of reports, briefing papers and books.) Second, many prisoners have lost contact with their families and friends and so the Trust invites people to write to prisoners. More than a thousand people participate currently in the PRT Penfriend Scheme. Finally, a small number of volunteers undertake research for PRT and help out with general office duties.

You can make donations to the Prison Reform Trust through Give as You Earn, Deed of Covenant and Gift Aid and can also become a 'Friend of PRT' by making an annual gift of either £100, £250 or £1,000 a year. Friends receive regular bulletins and copies of *Prison Report* and are invited to all PRT events. The Trust works closely with the Prison Service to produce the *Prisoners' Information Book*, distributed to all prisoners free of charge. The Trust advises and helps hundreds of prisoners and their families each year. The annual PRT Essay Competition encourages new writing and research on penal policy.

ROYAL NATIONAL LIFEBOAT INSTITUTION

West Quay Road, Poole, Dorset BH15 1HZ
Tel: 01202-671 133 *Fax:* 01202-669 680
Charity Reg. No: 209603
Contact: **Ian Ventham, Head of Fundraising**
Date established: **1824**
Annual income: **£64.6m (94)**
Area covered: **National/Regional**

The Royal National Lifeboat Institution is a registered charity which exists to save life at sea. It provides, on call, the 24-hour service necessary to cover search and rescue requirements to 50 miles out from the coast of the United Kingdom and the Republic of Ireland. In addition the RNLI is engaged in a Sea Safety Initiative with other marine and safety agencies to try to prevent accidents from occurring.

CIVIL LIBERTIES, HUMAN RIGHTS AND SOCIAL WELFARE

The RNLI is a voluntary body in every sense. Its 4,000 volunteer lifeboatmen and women are available to go to sea at a moment's notice to rescue others. Volunteers manage each of the 215 lifeboat stations around the coast. Volunteer shore helpers help with the launch and recovery of all lifeboats. Every penny of the £62 million needed to run the service comes from voluntary sources, nothing from the Government. One of the biggest sources of income is that generated by the thousands of volunteer fundraisers in nearly 2,000 branches and guilds up and down these islands.

Professional fundraisers back up the work of the volunteers. Legacies, including pecuniary and residuary bequests, bring in more than £30 million each year. Regional fundraising, by dedicated groups of volunteers, generates over £10 million per year and the RNLI also receives sums from grant-making trusts and businesses. The RNLI's Shoreline Members, Governors and Donors contribute about £8 million each year.

There are 126 active all-weather lifeboats, 163 inshore, and a reserve of just over 100. The RNLI has saved 126,000 lives with an average in 1994 of one launch every two hours and four lives saved each day. Under way is a capital expenditure programme on new boats and stations which will total £120,000 million over the next 10 years.

THE SCOTTISH COUNCIL ON ALCOHOL

166 Buchanan Street, Glasgow G1 2NH
Tel: **0141-333 9677** *Fax:* **0141-333 1606**
Charity Reg. No: **SCO09538**

Contact:	**Mrs Ann Furst, PR and Appeals Director**
Date established:	1973
Annual income:	£464,100 (94/95)
Area covered:	Scotland

The Scottish Council on Alcohol is Scotland's national alcohol charity, which aims to reduce the level of alcohol misuse and to promote the adoption of healthier, safer, more sensible drinking styles. The SCA co-ordinates a unique network of 28 local agencies who, through the commitment of SCA-trained volunteers, help over 4,000 families annually to overcome alcohol-related problems. The SCA aims to educate young people and, through its National Information Resource Centre, responds to over 3,000 requests annually.

Volunteers are the backbone of this charity. Anyone can apply for selection to go on a training course and many more volunteers are needed. It now costs £600 to train one volunteer; please help us to help families in distress by supporting the training of at least 10 volunteers in 1996, and so help an additional 100 families.

SHELTER – NATIONAL CAMPAIGN FOR HOMELESS PEOPLE

88 Old Street, London EC1V 9HU
Tel: 0171-205 2000 Fax: 0171-505 2169
Charity Reg. No:	263710
Contact:	**John Trampleasure, Director of Fundraising**
Date established:	1966

Annual income: **£11.2m (94/95)**
Area covered: **National**

Shelter is dedicated to alleviating suffering caused by bad housing and homelessness in Britain by meeting immediate needs and working to find long-term solutions. In 1994–5 Shelter responded to calls for help from 76,000 people by providing free, professional and impartial help and advice through a national network of Housing Aid Centres. Shelter also works with fellow charity Crisis in the provision of winter shelters across the country.

December 1996 marks the beginning of Shelter's 30th anniversary year in which the public, businesses, churches and schools will be encouraged to join Shelter in a variety of events and fundraising campaigns. The year will be dedicated to ensuring homeless and badly housed people continue to get the help they need and are given real hope of having a home of their own.

Shelter is able to help thousands of desperate people each week because of the support it enjoys from individuals, churches, businesses, schools and local/national government. Shelter has a network of 66 shops and 48 Housing Aid Centres in England, Scotland and Wales and there is a variety of London-based projects. Volunteers are needed to serve in shops and to help in the smooth running of the Centres and projects. At Shelter's London headquarters there are additional volunteering opportunities in areas such as fundraising, accounts and personnel.

TERRENCE HIGGINS TRUST LTD

The Terrence Higgins Trust

52-54 Gray's Inn Road, London WC1X 8JU
Tel: 0171-831 0330 *Fax:* 0171-242 0121
Charity Reg. No: 288527
Contact: **David Richards, Director, Marketing**
Date established: **1983**
Annual income: **£3.5m (94/95)**
Area covered: **National**

The Terrence Higgins Trust is Europe's leading charity working to combat the effects of HIV and AIDS and is able to offer assistance to anyone whose life is touched by the virus. The Trust is able to offer extensive services, information, and advice. The services include counselling; legal help; advice on welfare rights; housing and health promotion; 'Buddying'; a year-round confidential helpline; and practical support. The helpline telephone number is 0171-242 1010 (12 noon to 10pm daily).

The Trust relies on the dedication and support of 1,300 volunteers to provide many of the services. Volunteers are still needed in the Greater London area. For further information, please contact the Volunteer Office. The Trust also depends on the generosity of individuals for funds. For further information about giving, please contact the Fundraising Department.

CIVIL LIBERTIES, HUMAN RIGHTS AND SOCIAL WELFARE

SEE ALSO

British Red Cross
Carers National Association
Child Poverty Action Group
Crossroads (Caring for Carers)
Cystic Fibrosis Research Trust
Families Need Fathers
HYPED
Kids' Club Network
MENCAP
Ockenden venture
Parentline
Rural Housing Trust
Save the Children Fund
Women's Royal Voluntary Service

CONSERVATION, HERITAGE AND ENVIRONMENT

COUNCIL FOR THE PROTECTION OF RURAL ENGLAND

Warwick House, 25 Buckingham Palace Road,
London SW1W 0PP
Tel: 0171-976 6433 Fax: 0171-976 6373
Charity Reg. No: 233179
Contact: John Morris, Fundraising Officer
Date established: 1926
Annual income: £2m (94)
Area covered: Regional

CPRE is the only independent environmental charity working for the whole countryside, making decisions from its Westminster office and the local branches in every county in England. CPRE aims: to improve and encourage the protection of the English countryside, its towns and villages; to stimulate public awareness and enjoyment of the countryside; to advise and inform on the planning , improvement and protection of the countryside; to undertake and commission research to enable a better understanding of countryside issues; and to campaign for firm planning laws, Green Belts, National Parks, woodland/hedgerow protection, benign agricultural, forestry and water policies. Its business is effective lobbying and exerting influence.

CPRE branches rely on the work of over 1,500 volunteers, with a broad range of skills and interests. CPRE's volunteers work on anything from preparing a technical response to a draft local plan, to arranging a coffee morning; from dealing with the press to stuffing envelopes.

For information on membership, contact Emma Kerby; on branch volunteering, contact Joanne Cross who will put you in contact with your local CPRE branch. You can contact Emma and Joanne at the national office, address above.

THE GAME CONSERVANCY TRUST

Burgate Manor, Fordingbridge, Hants SP6 1EF
Tel: 01425-652 381 *Fax:* 01425-655 848
Charity Reg. No: 279968
Contact: David Bird, Development Manager
Date established: 1969
Annual income: £2m (95)
Area covered: National

Pheasant, partridge, grouse and trout, once so abundant, are now in serious decline. Their habitats are disappearing and their predators are rife. The Game Conservancy Trust is working to address these problems and to restore these game species to their former glory. The backbone of the Trust's work is research, concentrating on practical projects, each designed to help the Trust to manage the countryside in the best interests of game. Advice based on this research is crucial to farmers, gamekeepers and to everyone concerned about wildlife and the environment.

The Game Conservancy Trust's research and educational work is carried out by professional ecologists and staff. There are, however, important ways in which volunteers can help. The Trust has a countrywide network of voluntary County Committees, drawn from local members of the Trust, who run social and educational events of all types in order to raise funds. Members also help to man stands at game fairs and country shows throughout the summer. Occasionally, there is also scope for students trained in ecology to help with the research fieldwork on a voluntary basis.

During 1996, national fundraising events included: The Game Conservancy Ball, a Sporting Auction and a Good Game Dinner. There were also over 150 regional events for members and friends. The Trust's Scottish branch runs a Grouse Ball and The Scottish Game Conservancy Scottish Fair. The Game Conservancy Trust can succeed only with the help of its members, sponsors and friends. If you have an interest in game and the countryside and would like to help, please contact the above address. The Trust will be delighted to hear from you.

THE NATIONAL TRUST FOR SCOTLAND

❦ The National Trust for Scotland

5 Charlotte Square, Edinburgh, Scotland EH2 4DH
Tel: 0131-226 5922 *Fax:* 0131-243 9501
Charity Reg. No: SC007410
Contact: **Mr Julian Birchall, Controller – External Funding**
Date established: 1931
Annual income: £30m (95)
Area covered: Scotland

CONSERVATION, HERITAGE AND ENVIRONMENT

The National Trust for Scotland is an independent charity responsible for over 100 properties throughout Scotland. Its affairs are governed by an elected Council. It is Scotland's leading conservation organisation with a duty to preserve places of outstanding beauty or historic interest for future generations to enjoy. The Trust has 23,000 members and administers an annual budget of some £15 million. Over 300 full-time members of staff are assisted by hundreds of volunteers who undertake a wide variety of conservation tasks, both in the countryside and in historic buildings. More volunteers are always needed, as are donations and legacies, so that Scotland's heritage can be secured for the future.

The Trust has a staff of four looking after fundraising from individuals, companies and charitable trusts. In addition, 28 autonomous Members' Groups run a variety of fundraising events – walks, films, lectures, outings, plant sales, etc.

The Trust is Scotland's largest conservation charity. It is separate from, but has excellent relations with, the National Trust for England, Wales and Northern Ireland. The Trust is responsible for castles and historic houses, mountains, coastline and islands, wild countryside, battlefields and historic sites.

Volunteers are used in a wide variety of capacities: on Council and all Committees of the Trust; as Guides at several properties; undertaking conservation work in the countryside; restoring needlework; running fundraising events; using specialist and professional skills for the benefit of the Trust.

Although the Trust has 350 full-time employees it is still assisted by many hundreds of volunteers who give willingly, year after year, for a cause which they love.

Royal Society for the Protection of Birds

The Lodge, Sandy, Bedfordshire, SG19 2DL
Tel: 01767-680 551 *Fax:* 01767-692 365
Charity Reg. No: 207076
Contact: **Frances Hurst, Director, Marketing**
Date established: 1889
Annual income: £38.8m (95)
Area covered: **National**

The Royal Society for the Protection of Birds takes action for the conservation of wild birds and the environment. It researches threats and proposes solutions to environmental problems; buys land and creates new nature reserves to protect wildlife; advises landowners and planners by sharing knowledge and experience; and helps conservation organisations overseas. It strives to inform and involve the public, runs educational programmes for the young, and has a 140,000-strong junior section, the YOC. With 925,000 members, the RSPB is Europe's largest wildlife conservation charity. It is the UK partner of BirdLife International, a global partnership of bird and habitat conservation organisations.

The RSPB relies almost entirely on the support of its membership to finance its conservation work. In 1994–5, subscriptions generated £11 million, legacies £9.3 million and other forms of fundraising (much of it by volunteers' efforts) almost £7 million, representing 80 per cent of the year's income. The balance came largely from business support, charitable trusts and grants.

RSPB members can learn about birds and conservation as they support the Society's important conservation work. There are various categories of membership (from £22 for adults in 1996), giving members free access to more than 115 nature reserves. RSPB members receive the Society's award-winning magazine *Birds* quarterly, and YOC members the bi-monthly *Bird Life*.

Volunteers play a vital role in the RSPB's work. Every year some 7,000 volunteers of all ages undertake a wide range of activities. On reserves, they give more than 20,000 days work a year. Assistance comes in many forms – from artists creating displays to electricians carrying out safety checks. At headquarters and regional offices around the UK the expertise of translators assists the RSPB's international work, while those with clerical skills provide much-needed support. All members' and YOC groups are run by volunteers. There are hundreds of ways that volunteers can help the RSPB, and more are always needed.

SCOTTISH WILDLIFE TRUST

Cramond House, Cramond Glebe Road,
Edinburgh EH4 6NS
Tel: 0131-312 7765 *Fax:* 0131-312 8705
Charity Reg. No: SC005792
Contact: David Hughes Hallett, Director
Date established: 1964
Annual income: £3m (96)
Area covered: Regional

Scottish Wildlife Trust is Scotland's leading voluntary organisation for the conservation of all forms of wildlife and their habitats and is committed to conserving Scotland's wildlife for future generations. The Trust owns or manages over 107 wildlife reserves, covering approximately 18,500 hectares of Scotland's finest countryside, and is currently supported by 15,000 members, a permanent staff of 103, and a strong network of volunteers covering all of Scotland. SWT works in four areas: conservation; education; its training work is supported by Forward Scotland.

SWT is also involved in education through the junior wing, Scottish Wildlife Watch (there is a special service for schools, Watch Education Service (WES)), campaigning and training through the Forward Scotland Initiative. Through the Initiative, the Trust operates an extensive programme of training in environmental conservation with around 400 trainees in place at any one time.

Sustrans National Network

sustrans
PATHS FOR PEOPLE

35 King Street, Bristol BS1 4DZ
Tel: 0117-926 8893 *Fax:* 0117-929 4173
Charity Reg. No: 326550
Contact: **Carol Freeman, Development Director**
Date established: 1983
Annual income: £1.5m (95)
Area covered: National

Sustrans stands for Sustainable Transport. It is a practical charity which designs and builds traffic-free routes for cyclists, walkers and wheelchair users. Sustrans is the designer and promoter of the 6,500 mile National Cycle Network, which is planned to pass through most major towns and cities in the UK, within 2 miles of over 20 million people. The National Cycle Network has been chosen as a millennium project, with 2,500 miles scheduled for completion by the year 2000. Sustrans also promotes Safe Routes to School and other projects.

The National Cycle Network is dependent on public support and Sustrans welcomes donations and volunteers. Supporters receive a newsletter and information about routes nearby. Please write for details.

TIDY BRITAIN GROUP

The Pier, Wigan WN3 4EX
Tel: 01942-824 620 *Fax:* 01942-824 778
Charity Reg. No: 1018496
Contact: **Barbara Sinker, Executive Director**
Date established: **1955**
Annual income: **£4.3m (94/95)**
Area covered: **National – 5 regional offices**

Tidy Britain Group is an independent charity working for the improvement of local environments. TBG has a specific brief as the National Litter Abatement Agency, for which it is part funded through the Department of the Environment. TBG aims to encourage individual, corporate and community responsibility for the care of the environment through a variety of programmes.

Sponsorship is invited for events, campaigns, educational packs and promotional materials. Donations towards general funds are also welcomed. In particular, funding is sought for an advertising campaign and a regular newsletter.

Community-based litter abatement programmes and projects are a consistent part of TBG's strategy, as are campaigns to emphasise individual responsibility for litter and refuse. A free information service is provided. Regional offices are in Scotland, Northern Ireland and Wales.

There are opportunities for everyone to get involved in the National Spring Clean which takes place during April each year. There are also administrative work opportunities at any of TBG's offices

THE WOODLAND TRUST

Autumn Park, Dysart Road, Grantham, Lincolnshire NG31 6LL
Tel: 01476-74297 Fax: 01476-590 808
Charity Reg. No:	294344
Contact:	Hilary Allison, Public Affairs Manager
Date established:	1972
Annual income:	£7.4m (94)
Area covered:	National

The Woodland Trust is Britain's largest conservation organisation dedicated solely to the protection of the country's heritage of native and broad-leaved trees and woods. The Trust achieves this through the acquisition of existing woods and land for planting, and through its subsequent care and management of the woods for public access and enjoyment, their enhancement of the landscape and value to wildlife. Virtually all the Trust's woods are open to the public, be they remnants of spectacular ancient woodland which are living links with the past, or newly planted woods on the edges of villages and towns – the mature woods of the future.

There are a variety of ways in which people can support the Trust's work, including taking part in tree planting schemes, dedicating trees to an individual or organisation to mark special events, and taking part in commemorative projects to adopt areas of existing woodland. Business sponsorships, grants, donated land and legacies are actively welcomed. The Trust organises events throughout the year to encourage people to visit its woods.

The Trust offers specific volunteer opportunities, such as becoming a voluntary speaker or photographer. Other volunteer opportunities tend to be concerned with specific sites, such as fundraising to allow the Trust to purchase a wood with the support of local people, and becoming involved with practical aspects of woodland care and management. For further details of opportunities, please write to the Woodland Trust's Grantham office.

SEE ALSO

Birdlife International
Camphill Village Trust
Country Trust
Inter-Action Trust
National Playing Fields Association
Victoria & Albert Museum
Wildfowl & Wetlands

DISABILITY

ACTION FOR BLIND PEOPLE

action for blind people

14-16 Verney Road, Bermondsey, London SE16 3DZ
Tel: 0171-732 8771   Fax: 0171-639 0948
Charity Reg. No: 205913
Contact: **Barbara Ormston, Publicity Officer**
Date established: **1857**
Annual income: **£8.03m (94/95)**
Area covered: **National**

There are an estimated 1 million visually impaired people in the UK. If you know anyone with troubled eyesight, Action for Blind People can help. The charity provides an information, advice and grants service; holiday hotels by the sea; residential and nursing homes; independent and supported accommodation; employment training; sheltered workshops and business support for the self-employed. Action for Blind People's aim is simple: to enable visually impaired people to enjoy equal rights and opportunities in every aspect of their lives.

To find out more about these services, to make a donation, or for more information on sight loss contact Action for Blind People at the above address and telephone number.
Employment training is available in London, Preston, Liverpool and Carlisle.

DISABILITY

ASBAH

42 Park Road, Peterborough PE1 2UQ
Tel: 01733-555 988 Fax: 01733-555 985
Charity Reg. No: 249338
Contact: John Williams, Senior Appeals Manager
Date established: 1966
Annual income: £1.84m (94)
Area covered: National

ASBAH exists to care for everyone who has spina bifida and hydrocephalus in England, Wales and Northern Ireland. Until recently, children with these conditions died while quite young. Advances in medical care have transformed the picture; with help people can overcome problems and fulfil their potential. Through its network of dedicated fieldworkers and specialist advisers ASBAH supports thousands of babies, children and young adults, helping them gain confidence, build up self-esteem and prepare for a more satisfactory and rewarding future.

ASBAH celebrates its 30th anniversary in 1996. The charity still needs to extend its fieldwork service, as emergency cover only is available in some areas. To do this it must increase its income. This vital care is made possible only by voluntary contributions, including covenants and legacy donations. Please help ASBAH to achieve this aim.

British Sports Association for the Disabled (BSAD)

Solecast House, 13–27 Brunswick Place, London N1 6DX
Tel: 0171-490 4919 *Fax:* 0171-490 4914
Charity Reg. No: 297035
Contact: Gordon Neale, Marketing Manager
Date established: 1961
Annual income: £1m (94)
Area covered: National

The British Sports Association for the Disabled provides a wide range of sporting and recreational opportunities for disabled people of all ages. Programmes offer award schemes, regional and national championships, and training opportunities. Other areas include an information and advice service and campaigns to increase awareness of the needs and achievements of disabled people in sport. BSAD also works in partnership with several agencies, including the Sports Council and the British Paralympic Association. Founded in 1961, BSAD is a national organisation with 10 regional branches incorporating 550 clubs, schools, and associations. BSAD has contact with other sports organisations around the world.

Opportunities exist for commercial companies, clubs and individuals to assist BSAD with their work programme. A detailed list is available from Head Office. The Association receives funding from various sources, including the Sports Council, governing bodies, charitable trusts, commercial sponsorship and private donations. Support in this area is always welcome. The Annual Report, Year Book, Policy Charter, leaflets, posters and other information are available on request from Head Office.

There are 21 full-time and 5 part-time staff presently employed by BSAD. Annual recruitment varies and occurs in the areas of administration, fundraising, development and events. Volunteers are the charity's lifeblood and are required throughout the organisation. They facilitate the Regional Executive Committees, manage local clubs, organise regional events, provide administrative support, assist in fundraising and conduct research in partnership with staff and trustees. No minimum time commitment is required. Enquiries are welcomed and should be directed initially to Head Office.

BRITISH WIRELESS FOR THE BLIND FUND

34 New Road, Chatham, Kent ME4 4QR
Tel: **01634-832 501** *Fax:* **01634-817 485**
Charity Reg. No: **211849**
Contact: **Mrs M R Grainger, Chief Executive**
Date established: **1929**
Annual income: **£1m (94)**
Area covered: **National**

The British Wireless for the Blind Fund was founded in 1929 to help ease part of the hardship of blindness. Because many blind people live on a very limited income, our aim is to supply radios or radio/cassette recorders to all those in need over the age of eight. Since 1929 we have supplied over half a million sets. We are a totally independent charity relying solely on voluntary contributions, donations and legacies.

THE CAMPHILL VILLAGE TRUST

19 South Road, Stourbridge, West Midlands DY8 3YA
Tel: 01384-372 122 *Fax:* 01384-372 122
Charity Reg. No: 232402
Contact: **Mr Vivian Griffiths, PR Secretary**
Date established: 1954
Annual income: £7.2m (95)
Area covered: **National**

The Camphill Village Trust's first village community for people with special needs is Botton Village, founded in 1955. From the CVT 1995 Annual Review: '. . . Botton Village is a busy and dynamic place and the rugged Yorkshire landscape lends something to this energy. The physical manifestation of this is revealed in the farms, gardens, workshops, the community centre, the village college and the new award-winning and beautiful church. But what gives life to the 25 extended families where people with special needs share the house communities in a unique and integrated way, is the spirit of Community which is almost as tangible as the landscape and buildings themselves . . .'

Living in the extended household of a Camphill adult community is a surprising experience for both short- and long-stay co-workers. The interaction between workers and residents, and learning about the cultural, social and working life of the community make this a unique experience. There are also less dramatic, but no less helpful, ways of offering support, by joining Camphill Village Trust Friends Group. A list is available from the address above.

As all monies are pooled, with budgets to cover all the main expenditures, no salaries are paid to people residing in CVT communities. This year direct support goes to the work and to the important areas of development, such as a new village store near the Royal Deeside Road into Aberdeen at the Newton Dee Village Community.

To find out more about Botton Village and the work of the nine other Camphill Village Trust communities, each uniquely involved in their work, their locality and their challenges and development, please write to the address above. CVT welcomes enquiries from those interested in spending either a long or short stay as a co-worker in one of its centres.

THE CARE FUND

9 Weir Road, Kibworth, Leicestershire LE8 0LQ
Tel: 0116-279 3225 *Fax:* 0116-279 6384
Charity Reg. No: 261774
Contact: **Janet Wickens, Director of Fundraising**
Date established: 1970
Annual income: £1,024,000m (95/96)
Area covered: **National**

The Care Fund builds and equips communities for people with a learning disability (mental handicap), offering a home, training, work and long-term security. Its aim is to enable residents to lead a useful and interesting life, leading to maturity, security and a sense of personal value.
Communities are now in Devon, Kent, Lancashire, Leicestershire, Northumberland, Shropshire, West Sussex and Wiltshire.

The Care Fund seeks funds from trusts, companies and individuals, relying on the generosity of others to maintain its building and development plans as well as replace vital equipment and tools in residential accommodation and workshops.

DOWN'S SYNDROME ASSOCIATION (DSA)

155 Mitcham Road, London SW17 9PG
Tel: 0181-682 4001 Fax: 0181-682 4012
Charity Reg. No: 265812
Contact: Anna Khan, Director
Date established: 1970
Annual income: £812,600 (94/95)
Area covered: National (Eng., Wales, N.I.)

Down's syndrome is a genetic condition resulting in slower development and learning abilities. However, most children with Down's syndrome today will walk, talk, read, write, go to school and lead a semi-independent adult life. Down's syndrome is not an illness. People with Down's syndrome do not 'suffer' as a result of the condition.

The Down's Syndrome Association is the only national charity working exclusively with people who have Down's syndrome. It exists to provide them, their families and carers with support, information, advice and counselling. The Association funds research aiming to enhance the lives of people with Down's syndrome.

One of the Association's main aims is to educate the public in all aspects of Down's syndrome and enable people with the condition to fulfil their potential. To this end the Association works hard to challenge public opinion and to present a balanced, positive image of the condition, largely through a wide range of information leaflets.

The Association has a small staff and relies heavily on a network of volunteer, parent-led branches and groups throughout England, Wales and Northern Ireland. It offers important support to new and expectant parents of a child with Down's syndrome. It is always looking for volunteers to help with the organisation and administration of its special events, and branches may require assistance with local activities. The Down's Syndrome Association celebrated its 25th anniversary in 1995 and during 1996 there is a celebrity cricket match planned and a national raffle which will take place between April and October. Volunteers help to ensure that people with Down's syndrome get as much as possible out of life.

The DSA needs support for its fundraising activities and constantly asks companies, charitable trusts and individuals to support its work. It relies almost entirely on voluntary donations to continue with its work; every contribution is put immediately to good use and really does make an enormous difference.

THE ENHAM TRUST

Enham Place, Enham Alamein, Andover, Hants SP11 6JS
Tel: 01264-345800 *Fax:* 01264-335 108
Charity Reg. No: 211235
Contact: **Denise Gabriel, Head of Appeals and PR**
Date established: 1917
Annual income: £5m (94/95)
Area covered: **Regional**

The Enham Trust, set in a Hampshire village, is a pioneer in providing the best opportunities for people with disabilities to achieve their full potential. Through Enham, those who previously had little hope of work can find a route to rewarding employment, while those who have always lived in care have the opportunity of independent living within a supportive community. Assessment and training are provided to enable people to recognise their potential and develop new skills. Some then live in the village and work in one of the Trust's business operations; others take their new skills back to their own communities.

Enham does its best to stand on its own feet but could not maintain its pioneering work without charitable appeals. The superb Resource Centre was achieved only through donations. Now Enham's priority is Cedar Park, a project to transform the residential care home into an innovative new concept in community care. To appreciate fully the true magic of Enham you need to visit the village, which is just north of Andover on the A343. The Trust would be delighted to welcome you and to show you what makes this unique community tick. Please contact The Enham Trust Appeals Office for further information.

In addition to its governing body, Enham has the enthusiastic support of volunteers known as the Friends of Enham who give their time to help the charity in many ways. They perform an invaluable service in supporting the staff of the Resource Centre in encouraging activities that foster personal development, such as the acquisition of literacy, business skills, an enjoyment of the arts and many others. Further volunteers are now urgently needed nationwide to hold events and help raise over £4 million for Enham's vitally important care home appeal, Cedar Park. This project will represent a flagship in the provision of care services to people living in independent accommodation.

THE GENERAL WELFARE OF THE BLIND

37-55 Ashburton Grove, London N7 7DW
Tel: 0171-609 0206 Fax: 0171-607 4425
Charity Reg. No: 210794
Contact: **Brigitte Philippe, Fundraising Manager**
Date established: 1854
Annual income: £8.5m (94)
Area covered: National

General Welfare of the Blind exists solely to create improved opportunities and lifestyles for people who are blind or partially sighted. Its founder, Elizabeth Gilbert, herself blind, set up a handicraft workshop for a group of blind men, and today the original aims of GWB remain unchanged. Three out of four blind people cannot find a regular job and over the years the charity has built up a business that offers these people full employment with a pension scheme and information on the welfare services available. The charity believes that this fundamental right to work is the key to leading a satisfying life.

GWB provides some of its employees with accommodation, special training and instruction courses. It organises social events and visits pensioners but this aspect of its work relies upon public support – donations and legacies – so that it may continue to provide its services. Any donation will be greatly appreciated.

General Welfare of the Blind is involved in the manufacture of household and toiletry products. Some of its products, manufactured under its own brand name, are sold door to door. The others are manufactured under contract for retailers. Due to the nature of the General Welfare of the Blind, it does not have full-time volunteers as such, but relies on the generosity of the local community.

THE GUIDE DOGS FOR THE BLIND ASSOCIATION

Hillfields, Burghfield, Reading, Berks RG7 3YG
Tel: **0118-983 5555** *Fax:* **0118-983 5433**
Charity Reg. No: **209617**
Contact: **Alison Radevsky, PR & Marketing Manager**
Date established: **1931**
Annual income: **£31.7m (94)**
Area covered: **National**

The Association is responsible for breeding, training and providing guide dogs in the UK, and training visually impaired people to use them safely. There is a nominal charge of just 50p for the guide dog plus £1 per week board and lodging during a residential training course of up to four weeks. The Association pays a feeding allowance for the dog and meets vets' bills. In addition, the Association offers other services to help improve the quality of life for people with visual impairment, and sponsors ophthalmic research and canine veterinary studies. The charity receives no money from the Government.

In the first week of October each year, Guide Dog Week celebrates the time when the first four guide dogs qualified with their owners in 1931. The Week acts as a focus for the Association's fundraising efforts.

The Association thanks its supporters with a framed and suitably inscribed guide dog photograph when they achieve specific fundraising targets. An 'in memory' scheme allows donors to name a guide dog in memory of a loved one. Names may also be submitted for a future guide dog to meet the request in a will.

The Association welcomes volunteers who can help in a variety of ways. Fundraisers can undertake projects on their own or can join one of over 450 local voluntary fundraising branches. Volunteer puppy walkers (in certain parts of the country only) take a six-week-old puppy into their homes for around a year until it returns for professional training. This is a vital part of a future guide dog's development. The Association's Holidays Group organises holidays and activities for visually impaired people, and always needs volunteers to act as sighted guides.

HAMPSHIRE AUTISTIC SOCIETY

59 The Avenue, Southampton SO17 1XS
Tel: 01703-220 825 *Fax:* 01703-220 832
Charity Reg. No: 288141
Contact: **Ann Jarman, PR/Fundraising Director**
Date established: **1969**
Annual income: **£1.8m (95)**
Area covered: **Regional**

The Hampshire Autistic Society is dedicated to improving the quality of life for people within the autistic spectrum. The Society is an independent charity providing specialised facilities for people with autism, a school for 46 pupils, a training centre and 3 group homes for a total of 25 adults. A resource centre based at Head Office is available to parents, carers and professionals providing books and other information on help available in the area.

Autism affects 120,000 people in the UK; it is an invisible, lifelong disability affecting all forms of communication. The degree of independent living enjoyed by someone with autism depends on the availability of appropriate facilities. Provision of those facilities depends heavily on voluntary donations – please help autism by supporting The Hampshire Autistic Society.

DISABILITY

Hearing Dogs for the Deaf

HEARING DOGS FOR THE DEAF

The Training Centre, London Road, Lewknor, Oxon OX9 5RY
Tel: 01844-353 898 *Fax:* 01844-353 099
Charity Reg. No: 293358
Contact: Mrs Christine Green
Date established: 1986
Annual income: £1.1m (April 95)
Area covered: National

Hearing Dogs for the Deaf aims to provide deaf people with greater independence, confidence and awareness to sounds through the careful selection, training and placement of a hearing dog. Most dogs are selected from rescue centres, thus helping to give an unwanted dog a useful life, to the benefit of a deaf person. A hearing dog provides practical help, alerting the recipient to specific sounds, using a paw to gain attention and then leading to the sound source. The dog also has considerable therapeutic value, lending a positive focus to the invisible disability of deafness, providing invaluable and unconditional companionship and helping the recipient feel more secure.

Hearing Dogs for the Deaf requires volunteers in *all* aspects of the charity's work. Some of the key areas are: puppy socialising – volunteers play a vital role in the socialisation and training of puppies and young dogs for periods of two to eight months; charity shops – Hearing Dogs for the Deaf opened their first charity shop, 'Wags to Riches', in 1995, and hopes to establish a network of charity shops throughout the UK for which they require premises and volunteers; branches – many volunteers have joined together to form a fundraising branch (minimum of three persons). Between them, branches help raise awareness and the much-needed funding for the day-to-day operation of the charity.

Your fundraising support can directly help provide a trained dog for a deaf person. If you would like a list of fundraising and sponsorship targets please contact Head Office.

You can visit the centres in Lewknor, Oxfordshire, or Selby, North Yorkshire on Thursdays at 2pm (prior booking only); collect used postage stamps. Send *stamps only* to: Used Stamps, HDFD, PO Box 1, Chesham, Bucks. HP5 2YJ; make a donation by CAF card, Gift Aid or Deed of Covenant; make a bequest in your will.

HOME FARM TRUST

Merchants House North, Wapping Road, Bristol, BS1 4RW
Tel: **01179-273 746** *Fax:* **01179-225 938**
Charity Reg. No: **313069**
Contact: **Jasper Dorgan, Director**
Date established: **1962**
Annual income: **£12m (94)**
Area covered: **National**

Home Farm Trust aims to provide and manage residential homes and development care services for people with learning disabilities. Over 80 houses in 13 schemes throughout England provide individual care for over 530 disabled people and the Trust has recently developed new day care services so that even more people can benefit. The Trust's core philosophy is the desire for residents to achieve their fullest potential and develop their skills. For some this may mean learning the basic life skills, for others it might mean looking towards more independent living and paid employment.

While 80 per cent of the Trust's income is through statutory grants, it relies upon the 20 per cent of voluntary income to support the highest levels of quality care provision and to support the development of new homes and services. The Home Farm Trust is a highly professional and efficient charity with a leading and proven expertise in the field of learning disability care.

Whatever the disability, HFT believes it can help, and the high-quality care service, together with the creation of a friendly home environment, ensures a more rewarding life for its residents.

JOHN GROOMS ASSOCIATION FOR DISABLED PEOPLE

50 Scrutton Street, London EC2A 4PH
Tel: 0171-452 2000 *Fax:* 0171-452 2001
Charity Reg. No: 212463
Contact: **Keith Wenden, Director of Fundraising**
Date established: 1866
Annual income: £7.6m (94)
Area covered: **National**

John Grooms, a Christian-based organisation, has worked in partnership with disabled people for over 130 years, encouraging greater quality of life, independence and integration. Across all its diverse projects the charity's underlying conviction is that disabled people are people first. The charity provides nursing, residential and domiciliary care, including a forthcoming day care rehabilitation centre for people with brain injuries. John Grooms builds wheelchair-standard housing for disabled people and their families and offers a range of accessible holiday accommodation, as well as employment and training opportunities. Overseas, practical help is given to disabled people in Kenya and Bangladesh.

Volunteers, a vital part of the charity's community fundraising, help in many ways. 'Friends' and Volunteer Support Groups based near the Association's projects in North London, Essex, Norfolk, Suffolk, the Midlands, North and South Wales provide help, while other supporters are involved in specific sponsored events. Some fundraising initiatives are organised through company partnerships and the companies' employees can take part in these. Giving children and young people the opportunity to fundraise is an important part of an expanding programme, as is the charity's desire to educate and inform about disability. Three Regional Co-ordinators around the country are able to support individual or group efforts with fundraising materials and ideas.

You can also become a Friend in Deed, by taking out a standing order or by giving a covenant. Much of the Association's work is also made possible through legacies. Should you wish further information on any of these ways of giving, John Grooms would be happy to supply them.

In 1996 Grooms celebrates its 130th birthday. Additional events will be taking place, including a central London street party, a Gala Dinner at St James's Palace, a Lambeth Palace garden party, a House of Lords Reception for the Bangladeshi community and a Christian concert at Wembley.

JUBILEE SAILING TRUST LTD

Test Road, Eastern Docks, Southampton SO14 3GG
Tel: 01703-631 388 *Fax:* 01703-638 625
Charity Reg. No: 277810
Contact: **Lindsey Neve, Director**
Date established: 1978
Annual income: £1.2m (94/95)
Area covered: National

The Jubilee Sailing Trust was set up in 1978 to promote integration between able-bodied and physically disabled people. This is achieved through the means of tall ship sailing on board the Trust's square-rigged ship, STS *Lord Nelson*. The successful formula of giving people of mixed ages (from 16 to over 70) and abilities the opportunity of working together at sea has changed many people's lives, and demand has led to the need for a second ship. The three-year construction of the JST's new ship commenced in 1996. The professional shipbuilding crew will be assisted by able-bodied and physically disabled people, thus bringing the aims of integration ashore for a completely different shared challenge.

The Jubilee Sailing Trust has a network of 52 branches around the United Kingdom. These are run entirely by volunteers, donating their time to raise funds and create awareness of the

Trust's work. Funds raised go towards maintenance of the *Lord Nelson* and help with the task of fundraising to build a second ship. Branches also raise funds to send both able-bodied and physically disabled people from their local area on board STS *Lord Nelson*. The Trust attends many events and boat shows throughout the country to promote its work, and volunteers make a major contribution by helping to man stands etc.

Adventure sailing holidays, lasting from 5 to 11 days, are available for both able-bodied and physically disabled people on board STS *Lord Nelson* in the UK, Northern Europe and Canary Islands throughout the year. One- or two-week working holidays called Shorewatch holidays are being launched in 1996 to coincide with the construction of the JST's second ship.

Funds for the work of the Trust are raised from various sources including membership, legacies, charitable trusts, individuals and companies. The Trust enjoys support from Rotary and other service groups. In addition, people may donate items that are required for the *Lord Nelson*, for the Trust's second ship, or for the office.

THE LEONARD CHESHIRE FOUNDATION

Leonard Cheshire House, 26-29 Maunsel Street, London SW1P 2QN
Tel: 0171-828 1822 *Fax:* 0171-976 5704
Charity Reg. No: 218186
Contact: **Neil Byrne, Press and PR Officer**
Date established: 1948

Annual income: **£12m (95)**
Area covered: **International**

The Leonard Cheshire Foundation aims to provide real choice and opportunity to people with disabilities. The Foundation provides a range of services for people with physical and learning disabilities and people with mental health problems, and support for their carers, both in the UK and throughout the world. Services include residential, nursing and care-at-home services; independent and semi-independent housing schemes; respite care and day care; assessment and rehabilitation; and counselling and training.

MENCAP

mencap
making the most of life

123 Golden Lane, London EC1Y ...
Tel: 0171-454 0454 *Fax:* 0171-608 3254
Charity Reg. No: 222377
Contact: **David Scott-Ralphs, Director of Fundraising**
Date established: 1946
Annual income: **£69m (94/95)**
Area covered: **National**

MENCAP is the UK's leading charity for people with a learning disability. The charity works to give people with a learning disability and their families a better life and to ensure that they have the same rights and opportunities as everyone else. MENCAP's direct services cover housing, education, employment and leisure. Advice, support and information are provided through MENCAP fieldworkers and the charity's 450 affiliated groups. Over 700 Gateway Clubs provide personal development opportunities and a chance for people with learning disabilities to express their views.

MENCAP requires volunteers for all aspects of its work. Befriending, visiting and other support schemes are run across the country, and more are needed. Local groups need help in providing a range of services, to work in the Gateway Clubs and with fundraising. The MENCAP Holiday Service relies heavily on volunteers who receive appropriate training. MENCAP's National Centre in London and its seven divisional offices provide volunteering opportunities for fundraising and in other areas. MENCAP places increasing emphasis upon training for volunteers.

MENCAP celebrates its 50th birthday in 1996. In commemoration, the charity is launching a national fundraising drive to increase the support services it provides, especially to young families. Fundraising events, commercial promotions and merchandise sales will be much in evidence and MENCAP is seeking to involve all parts of the community for local benefit.

MENCAP benefits from an affinity Visa credit card issued through Halifax Building Society, which has raised over £1.5 million for the charity since its launch in 1988. This is an ideal supplementary way for people to support MENCAP at no additional cost to themselves, and details can be obtained from any Halifax branch.

MULTIPLE SCLEROSIS RESEARCH TRUST

Spirella Building, Letchworth, Herts SG6 4ET
Tel: 01462 675613 *Fax:* 01727-854 424
Charity Reg. No: 1026971
Contact: **Mrs Jill Holt**
Date established: 1993
Annual income: £70,000 (94)
Area covered: **National**

The MS Trust focuses upon and supports those people already diagnosed as having MS. The Trust funds research projects which help people manage their disease – a seriously underfunded area – and provides constructive and positive information about MS. Trust information packs are found in hospitals and general practices, and are available direct from the Trust on 01462-675 613. All help is greatly appreciated, so please contact the Trust at the above address and number.

The Trust's five trustees are all closely involved with MS. They include two leading UK figures in rehabilitation and research into MS: Dr Rosie Jones who runs the MS Research and Resources Unit at Bristol Royal Infirmary, and Michael Barnes, Professor of Neurological Rehabilitation at the University of Newcastle upon Tyne.

THE NATIONAL AUTISTIC SOCIETY

276 Willesden Lane, London NW2 5RB
Tel: 0181-451 1114 *Fax:* 0181-451 5865
Charity Reg. No: 269425
Contact: **Ann Stirling, Press and PR Manager**
Date established: **1962**
Annual income: **£13.9m (95)**
Area covered: **National**

Autism is a disability which disrupts the way a person communicates with and relates to other people. There is, at present, no cure for autism which is believed to be caused by an impairment to the way the brain functions. People with autism often need specialist help to cope with the demands of everyday life – without this help their world is like a jigsaw where pieces do not fit.

The National Autistic Society aims to ensure that by its 50th anniversary in the year 2012 all those in the UK whose lives are affected by autism receive services and support appropriate to their needs. Acting as an umbrella organisation the NAS works with more than 70 local societies and branches, raising awareness of autism and providing services such as schools, training, diagnosis, employment programmes as well as residential and day care programmes for adults.

ROYAL NATIONAL INSTITUTE FOR THE BLIND

RNIB
challenging blindness

224 Great Portland Street, London W1N 6AA
Tel: 0171-388 1266 *Fax:* 0171-388 2034
Charity Reg. No: 226227
Contact: **Mike Lancaster, Director of External Relations**
Date established: 1868
Annual income: **£46m (94/95)**
Area covered: **National**

The Royal National Institute for the Blind (RNIB) is the leading charity working for blind and partially sighted people throughout the UK. RNIB wants a world in which blind and partially sighted people enjoy the same rights, freedoms and responsibilities and quality of life as people who are fully sighted. Their task is to challenge blindness. They challenge the disabling effects of blindness by providing more than 60 services to help people determine their own lives. They challenge the underlying causes of blindness by helping to prevent, cure or alleviate them.

Major fundraising events in 1996 include RNIB week in September. During this week Ken Woodward, a blind pilot, will be flying a plane around Britain to raise money and awareness of RNIB. There will be lots of fundraising events and house-to-house collections throughout the country to support the week. A covenant makes your donation worth 33 per cent more to the charity, as does the Gift Aid scheme for single large donations of £250 or more. You can become a Friend of RNIB and be kept informed of their work through newsletters and other updates. A legacy to RNIB can reduce inheritance tax –

RNIB's Wills and Legacies Advisory Service provides free information and advice on all aspects of will-making.

Volunteers who require work placements, or would simply like to help, are welcomed in all of RNIB's 40 establishments. In addition, RNIB's Express Reading Service and Cassette Library needs good readers to record information on a wide range of subjects onto tape. Volunteers who have technical qualifications can help by setting up RNIB's Talking Books players for new listeners, demonstrate how they work and service the players when necessary. Much-needed income is raised by volunteers who help organise fundraising events and collections.

ROYAL NATIONAL INSTITUTE FOR DEAF PEOPLE

19–23 Featherstone Street, London EC1Y 8SL
Tel: 0171-387 8033 *Fax:* 0171-296 8199
Charity Reg. No: 207720
Contact: **Debbie Reynolds, Head of Campaigns & PR**
Date established: 1911
Annual income: £22m (94)
Area covered: National

The RNID's vision is for deaf people to have the right to realise their full potential as individuals and to fully participate in the social, political and economic structures of society. The RNID holds these to be the rights to full citizenship to be exercised by deaf people using the communication of their choice. The RNID provides quality services for the 8.4 million deaf and hard of hearing people in the UK.

The RNID runs six care services: Typetalk (the national telephone relay service between hearing and deaf people); Sound Advantage (provides advice on assistive devices); Information; Deaf Awareness Training; residential centres and Communication Support Units (providing sign language interpreters and speech text translators).

SPINAL INJURIES ASSOCIATION

Newpoint House, 76 St James's Lane, Muswell Hill, London N10 3DF
Tel: 0181-444 2121 *Fax:* 0181-444 3761
Charity Reg. No: 267935
Contact: Mary Anne Tyrell, Administrator
Date established: 1974
Annual income: £815,658
Area covered: National

The Association's aim is to enable spinal cord injured people to achieve their goals. It supports all who are affected by paralysis, including family and friends of the disabled person. It achieves its goals by the provision of quality services, publications, information and support. The Association promotes research into the development of equipment which will improve the quality of life for spinal cord injured people and raises awareness among the general public of paraplegia and tetraplegia and its causes and consequences.

The Association seeks volunteers and support from the public with fundraising events, the annual Awareness Day and through membership of the Association. It produces a catalogue of gifts and cards, and welcomes the support of individuals and corporate sponsors who can make general donations to its work or who will sponsor specific projects.

TALKING NEWSPAPER ASSOCIATION

National Recording Centre, 10 Browning Road, Heathfield, Sussex TN21 8DB
Tel: 01435-866 102 *Fax:* 01435-865 422
Charity Reg. No: 293656
Contact: **Ms Suzanne Campbell, Director**
Date established: **1974**
Annual income: **£448,000 (95)**
Area covered: **National**

The Talking Newspaper Association provides tapes as an alternative to printed material for the 1.7 million blind or partially sighted people in Britain who cannot read such material. The Association currently records more than 180 national newspapers and magazines and is the umbrella organisation for over 500 Talking Newspaper groups across the UK which record local news for the benefit of the community. The Association gladly welcomes volunteers to become part of its production and editorial teams or to help with fundraising events.

The Association is dependent on voluntary donations and proceeds from its events to pay towards the general operating costs and maintenance of the specialised equipment. The work enables over 150,000 people to lead fuller, more interesting lives, keeping them in touch with new trends and opinions. Please help the Association to spread the word.

DISABILITY

UNITED RESPONSE

113-123 **Upper Richmond Road, Putney, London SW15 2TL**
Tel: 0181-780 9686 *Fax:* 0181-780 9538
Charity Reg. No: 265249
Contact: **Debbie Lyne, Head of Appeals & Publicity**
Date established: **1973**
Annual income: **£18.5m (95/96)**
Area covered: **National**

United Response helps adults and young people with learning disabilities – also known as mental handicap – or those with mental health problems, to lead dignified, fulfilled lives within the community. It does this by providing a wide variety of services, including small residential-care homes, training and employment schemes, outreach support, advocacy and family placement services. United Response was founded in 1973 with just one house in West Sussex. Today it works in 70 locations across the country, supporting almost a thousand people. Some of the people United Response cares for have very profound disabilities; others just need a few hours' support a week in order to live independently in their own homes.

United Response wants to help people, including those with profound disabilities, to live ordinary lives as fully integrated members of their local communities. It concentrates on the positive things that can be achieved once people have the support they need. Most importantly, it looks at people as individuals, tailoring services to fit the needs of each person it supports.

The charity works in close partnership with others to ensure that opportunities are available to everyone it supports. It needs the help of donors to enable it to develop its work – for new employment and training initiatives, some residential services and for special items of equipment.

United Response greatly appreciates the work of its volunteers who help in so many ways. Some people like to assist with local fundraising schemes while others prefer to befriend individuals or to help support people in the charity's employment programmes. Please contact United Response to find out more about what the charity is doing in your locality.

WESTMINSTER SOCIETY

16a Croxley Road, London W1 3HL
Tel: 0181-968 7376 *Fax:* 0181-968 9165
Charity Reg. No: 801081
Contact: Dr. Roger Foggitt, Director
Date established: 1962
Annual income: £3m (94/95)
Area covered: Regional

The Westminster Society is one of London's foremost providers of care and support for people with learning disabilities and their families. Activities include a specialist day nursery, a respite care home, holiday play schemes, youth activities and clubs and housing for adults who have either been resettled from long-stay hospital or have left the family home. The Society emphasises ability rather than disability and, as far as possible, promotes independence of living.

Volunteers are gladly welcomed from all walks of life to join the Society's befriending scheme or just to help at one of its fundraising events. Proceeds from fundraising activities, along with donations, legacies and covenants, provide support for the families caring for a child at home.

WINGED FELLOWSHIP TRUST

Angel House, 20-32 Pentonville Road, London N1 9XD
Tel: 0171-833 2594 *Fax:* 0171-278 0370
Charity Reg. No: 295072
Contact: **Marcella McEvoy, Communications Officer**
Date established: 1963
Annual income: £1,209m (95)
Area covered: **National**

Winged Fellowship provides respite for carers and quality holidays for people with severe physical disabilities, at five fully equipped centres in the UK and also abroad. Twenty-four-hour full care is provided by professional staff supplemented by volunteers. Daily trips out and entertainments are offered and special-interest weeks (eg Youth, 30s–45s and Alzheimer's Disease Week) are also provided. Volunteers who come for a week or two need no experience and their travel expenses and board and lodging are paid.

Help with fundraising is always appreciated, whatever it might be, on a regular basis or as a one-off. Join the mailing list to be sent details of forthcoming events, or take out membership . Free information packs on respite breaks and volunteering are available.

SEE ALSO

Artsline
Barnardos
Boys and Girls Welfare Society
British Diabetic Association
British Lung Foundation
Children's Trust
Changing Faces
Crossroads (Caring for Carers)
KIDS
The Motivation Charitable Trust
Muscular Dystrophy Group of Gt Britain & N. Ireland
National Deaf Children's Society
National Playing Fields Association (NPFA)
National Star Centre College
Treloar Trust
Whizz-Kidz

EDUCATION

THE COUNTRY TRUST

Stratford Grange, Stratford St Andrew, Saxmundham, Suffolk IP17 1LF
Tel: 01728-604 818 *Fax:* 01728-602 233
Charity Reg. No: 275429
Contact: **Mrs Louisa Thorp, Office Manager**
Date established: 1978
Annual income: £97,873 (95)
Area covered: **National**

The Country Trust is a national educational charity that organises and conducts day-long and week-long educational expeditions for urban children, particularly for classes of children with their teachers from deprived inner city areas, to farms, estates, woods and rural businesses etc not normally open to the public, to see the English country, to learn at first hand from those who live and work in it, and to see how it is managed and maintained.

Visits can be fitted around the national curriculum and can generate a large amount of work to follow up in class. They are conducted by Country Trust representatives throughout the year, except in August, and no charge is made. The Trust often subsidises the cost of the children's transport. It exists solely on donations.

DYSLEXIA INSTITUTE

THE DYSLEXIA INSTITUTE

133 Gresham Road, Staines, Middlesex TW18 2AJ
Tel: 01784-463 851 *Fax:* 01784-460 747
Charity Reg. No: 268502
Contact: **Michael Nation, Head of Public Affairs**
Date established: **1972**
Annual income: **£3.5m (94)**
Area covered: **National – 23 centres**

The Dyslexia Institute aims to prevent educational failure by identifying, teaching and supporting people of all ages with dyslexia. It is a national authority on assessment and teaching methods and provides educational services throughout the UK, including a wide range of courses at all levels for over a thousand teachers a year. The DI's Friends network provides information on all activities, including ways in which volunteers might help, and *The Dyslexia Review* is published termly for Guild members. The Guild is a professional body with open membership for those with a special interest or professional training in the area of dyslexia – for example teachers and psychotherapists. Membership is £35 p.a.

The money raised by the Institute is used to provide subsidised teaching for families who can neither get help at school nor afford the specialist teaching their children urgently need, and to develop and offer training and resources for parents and teachers. Events in 1996 include the 'Last Night of the Kenwood Proms'.

EDUCATION

INTER-ACTION TRUST

**HMS President (1918), Victoria Embankment,
nr Blackfriars Bridge, London EC4Y 0HJ**
Tel: 0171-583 2652 *Fax:* 0171-583 2840
Charity Reg. No: 267043
Contact: **ED Berman MBE, Director**
Date established: **1968**
Annual income: **£1.1m (94)**
Area covered: **National**

'Inter-Action's imaginative and refreshingly simple schemes are exactly the sort of thing we aim to encourage', said HRH The Prince of Wales.

Inter-Action is an innovative educational charity, developing new learning projects for disadvantaged children, young people and families. The charity's main target groups are: homeless, unemployed and at risk young people; babies/toddlers and mothers; women returning to work and unemployed adults. Deloitte Touche have said in a report for the Corporation of the City of London: 'We have been unable to identify any other organisation with such a successful history of education, arts, employment and environmental projects.' Inter-Action's major successes have been achieved on a project-by-project basis. Inter-Action identifies needs inadequately met by statutory or voluntary provision.

Because Inter-Action's centre is a historic landmark ship, it provides unique fundraising opportunities: setting up and running events on board to generate funding, such as St Valentine's Day, New Year's Eve and Guy Fawkes Night celebrations, private and corporate functions, clubs, etc. Advisers/Patrons include: Sir Christopher Chataway, Sir Peter Parker, Eric Reynolds, Richard

Briers, Sir Hugh Casson, Bob Hoskins, Glenda Jackson MP, Sir Yehudi Menuhin, Michael Palin, Dame Diana Rigg, Prunella Scales. The trustees are: Sir John Banham, JEM Miller, Sir Peter Newsam, Roy Shaw OBE, Henry Stage. The auditors/bankers are KPMG/Coutts and Co.

Inter-Action needs volunteers at all levels to help the national work done from its centre, HMS *President* (1918), in the City of London. Volunteers are given 'social contracts' which embody growth and development opportunities for them. Volunteers are needed in the following areas: PR (press/media agents); marketing; publishing (from proofreading to placing new titles); co-ordinators working to CEO to develop major new projects; word processing help for CEO (evenings and weekends); part-time receptionists; and events working groups. All profits from events/venue hire on board go to Inter-Action which helps 250,000 disadvantaged children and young people annually.

NATIONAL STAR CENTRE

Ullenwood, Cheltenham, Gloucestershire GL53 9QU
Tel: 01242-524 478 *Fax:* 01242-222 234
Charity Reg. No: 220239
Contact: **Thomas Harlend, Director of Appeals**
Date established: **1967**
Annual income: **£2.6m (94/95)**
Area covered: **National**

The National Star Centre is a specialist College of Further Education for students with physical or sensory disabilities. The emphasis is on maximising students' abilities and helping them develop their full potential. By placing emphasis on vocational studies alongside independence training, the College increases students' prospects of gaining employment or going on to higher education. The College relies on voluntary contributions to continue its important work and provide for specialised equipment and facilities for its students.

The Appeals Office depends on volunteers to co-ordinate collecting tins, run stalls at local events and to make and sell greetings cards. They are looking to set up a local fundraising group and anyone who is interested in joining should contact the Appeals Office.

TRELOAR TRUST

Alton, Hants GU34 4JX
Tel: 01420-22442 *Fax:* 01420-23957
Charity Reg. No: 307103
Contact: **Robin Radley, Appeals Director**
Date established: **1908**
Annual income: **£750,000 (94/95)**
Area covered: **National**

Nearly 90 years ago Sir William Treloar, Lord Mayor of London, decided to provide disabled children, often from very poor conditions, with the chance to enjoy better health, and the education and training to seek independence later in life. His vision founded a school and college where today 270 students, who might otherwise have been condemned to empty, frustrated lives, are given the inspiration and skills which drive many of them on to enjoy full and successful lives.

Students come from all over Britain. Former students have won Oxbridge places and national and international sporting records as well as built successful business careers. The Trust is currently raising £2.6 million for a new ground floor student house for younger children, 80 per cent of whom are in wheelchairs. Help is still wanted.

SEE ALSO

Boys and Girls Welfare Society
British Liver Trust
Compassion in World Farming
Enham Trust
Farms for City Children
Feed The Minds
Hampshire Autistic Society
KIDS
Life Education Centres
Marie Curie Memorial Foundation
National Autistic Society
National Deaf Children's Society
Scottish Wildlife Trust
UFAW (Universities Federation for Animal Welfare)

ELDERLY

THE ABBEYFIELD SOCIETY

53 Victoria Street, St. Albans, Herts AL1 3UW
Tel: 01727-857 536 *Fax:* 01727-846 168
Charity Reg. No: 200719
Contact: Mrs. A. Whitcher, Head of Information
Date established: 1956
Annual income: £1,107,023 (95/96)
Area covered: National

Abbeyfield provides sheltered housing for 9,000 older people within their local communities throughout the UK. The housing is for people who are no longer willing or able to live alone. Residents live in small family groups, usually 10 to 12 people. Each house is different; some are purpose-built, others specially converted. All are part of the local community and involve large numbers of volunteers who add the special Abbeyfield touch. Residents have both company and privacy. Single rooms, often with en suite facilities, are furnished by themselves with treasured possessions. A resident housekeeper makes two meals a day, with volunteers ensuring that there is a wide range of optional activities in the house and garden.

Abbeyfield dedicates its resources to providing an independent lifestyle with the companionship of others in a secure and friendly environment. Abbeyfield actively involves around 15,000 volunteers at all levels throughout the movement. Volunteers undertake a wide range of activities, calling for differing levels of time and commitment, and all achieve the satisfaction of knowing that their contribution is helping to improve the quality of life for Abbeyfield's residents.

Abbeyfield is dependent on charitable donations to upgrade, extend and develop new accommodation. Fundraising will be a theme increasingly important as Abbeyfield strives to meet the needs of a rapidly growing population of older people.

AGE CONCERN

1268 London Road, Norbury, London SW16 4ER
Tel: **0181-679 8000** *Fax:* **0181-679 6069**
Charity Reg. No: **261794**
Contact: **Sally Greengross, Director General**
Date established: **1940**
Annual income: **£17.9m (95/96)**
Area covered: **National**

The National Council on Ageing works to improve the quality of life for the country's 12 million-plus older people, providing opportunities for the active and able, as well as help for the frail and vulnerable. It is the centre of a network of 1,100 local organisations and 180,000 volunteers, offering a wide range of community-based services, including day centres, lunch clubs, home visiting and transport. Age Concern supports this work through the provision of information and advice, policy analysis, publications, grants, training to improve the quality of services to older people, and campaigns.

Age Concern works closely with partner organisations in the UK, Europe and internationally, and is committed to teaching

ELDERLY

and research through the Age Concern Institute of Gerontology at King's College, London. Age Concern is dependent on public support. Donations, covenants and legacies are always urgently needed.

AGE EXCHANGE THEATRE TRUST

The Reminiscence Centre, 11 Blackheath Village, London SE3 9LA
Tel: 0181-318 9105 *Fax:* 0181-318 0060
Charity Reg. No: 326899
Contact: **Bernie Arigho, Reminiscence co-ordinator**
Date established: 1983
Annual income: **£363,000 (94/95)**
Area covered: **National**

Age Exchange aims to improve the quality of life of older people by emphasising the value of their memories. The Reminiscence Centre in London acts as a public museum of memorabilia, a training and resource centre, a publishing house for relevant books, and the home of the country's leading reminiscence theatre company.

Volunteers are needed to welcome visitors to the Centre, and also to help regular staff in the office. There are also opportunities to take part in creative art groups, theatre productions and school projects. Sponsorship is welcomed to promote the Trust's work and so support special projects.

CONTACT THE ELDERLY

Contact the Elderly

15 Henrietta Street, London WC2E 8QH
Tel: 0171-240 0630 *Fax:* 0171-379 5781
Charity Reg. No: 244681
Contact: Jane McVigh, Director
Date established: 1965
Annual income: £115,000 (94/95)
Area covered: National

Sundays can be lonely. Can you help drive away loneliness? Can you spare one Sunday afternoon a month? Do you have a car? Could you collect a local elderly person and take him or her to visit someone's home? Could you help as a relief driver on a less regular basis? Can you spare one Sunday afternoon a year? Could a Contact the Elderly group visit your home for afternoon tea once, perhaps twice a year? Just a few hours can make all the difference to the life of an elderly person.

One Sunday afternoon a month Contact the Elderly volunteers provide companionship for elderly people living alone who are unable to get out without help, and have limited contact with family and friends. Throughout the UK, over 160 small groups of volunteer drivers take elderly people on regular monthly visits to hosts' homes. Groups visit a different home each month throughout the year and spend a few hours in the company of friends, old and new.

One and a half million elderly people over 75 feel especially lonely at the weekends and 10 per cent have not been out at all in the previous 7 days. Donations help Contact the Elderly to set up new groups across the UK so that they can provide a vital link to normal living for thousands of elderly people. If you can spare a few hours by helping to Contact the Elderly, write to the charity for more information or ring them on 0800-716 543.

HELP THE AGED

St James's Walk, London EC1R 0BE
Tel: 0171-253 0253 *Fax:* 0171-895 1407
Charity Reg. No: 272786
Contact: **Janet South, Executive Director of Fundraising**
Date established: **1976**
Annual income: **£40.09m (95)**
Area covered: **International**

Help the Aged works to improve the quality of life of elderly people in the UK and other parts of the world, particularly those who are frail, isolated or poor, by identifying their needs and raising public awareness through effective fundraising. Help the Aged promotes and develops aid programmes of high standards which are practical and innovative. Seniorline is one example: the only free telephone helpline for elderly people and their carers; accommodation fitted with alarms is another. As a result of Help the Aged's work, elderly people can live independently, with peace of mind, enjoying active social lives, with help, such as minibuses, purchased through Help the Aged grants.

The charity needs volunteers to help raise funds by working in its high street shops; helping with door-to-door collections; providing administrative and clerical help for full-time fundraisers; assisting with sports and social events; or through playing an active role on any of its county committees. Administrative and clerical help are also required in the charity's offices in London, Leeds, Edinburgh and Belfast.

Cash raised for overseas work helps provide a lifeline for elderly refugees from Bosnia and Rwanda. Cataract operations bring sight to thousands in Asia and Africa whilst projects in developing countries help countless elderly people survive the hardships of extreme poverty.

Help the Aged runs a programme of widely varied events throughout the UK. Special events in London include the Golden Awards (outstanding achievement in the over 65s) and a garden at the Chelsea Flower Show. Local sporting events include running, mountain biking, aerobics, abseiling and many others. Social events include fashion shows, art exhibitions and concerts.

HILL HOMES

21 North Hill, London N6 4BS
Tel: 0181-340 5140 *Fax:* 0181-348 8618
Charity Reg. No: 12687r/x71708
Contact: **Veronica Lawlor, Appeals Director**
Date established: **1944**
Annual income: **£2.5m (94/95)**
Area covered: **Regional**

Hill Homes is a charity which was founded in 1944 by local people to care for homeless elderly people displaced by war. Today, in five homes in the Highgate area, the charity cares for elderly people suffering from dementia and those who are physically dependent. Some residential care is also offered. There are over 160 residents, three-quarters of them funded by DSS or local authorities. Hill Homes aims to offer a home and care to an increasing number of seriously dependent older people who have limited resources. By 2005, numbers should increase to 275. The charity also aims to rebuild all its homes in that time-scale.

In 1996–97 Hill Homes will build a new home for 50 residents in Islington. Residents will be of mixed physical and mental dependency, cared for in small groups. The likely capital cost is £3 million, of which Hill Homes will fund £2 million. An appeal has been launched for £1 million. Associate members of Hill Homes support this work through their donations, many of them under Deed of Covenant. In return, they receive regular news about the homes and current developments.

Today's Management Committee is still made up of committed volunteers. There are also about 50 other local volunteers and clergy, visiting and helping in the homes and the sheltered housing unit. The Director and all nursing staff are paid professionals. Hill Homes have appointed a full-time Appeals Director and Secretary to plan and implement a long-term fundraising programme. Local volunteers will also be involved.

RESEARCH INTO AGEING

Baird House 15/17 St Cross Street, London EC1N 8UN
Tel: 0171-404 6878 Fax: 0171-404 6816
Charity Reg. No: 277468

Contact: **Elizabeth Mills, Director**
Date established: **1976**
Annual income: **£688,000 (94)**
Area covered: **National**

Research into Ageing aims to keep more older people fitter, healthier and independent for longer so that they and their families can enjoy the retirement years to the full. They fund medical research projects at hospitals and universities around the UK into, for example, Alzheimer's disease, blindness, mobility and exercise, osteoporosis, incontinence and the ageing process itself. They identify causes, pinpoint risk factors, improve current treatments and aim, ultimately, to eliminate the diseases and disabilities so common in old age. They aim to provide information on specific diseases and issues surrounding ageing and health to the medical and caring professions and to the general public.

In 1997 Research into Ageing celebrates its 21st birthday. Its aim is to raise £1 million to fund its new Queen Elizabeth The Queen Mother Research Fellowship Awards, supporting the best young British scientists in the field of ageing research. Help is needed with a variety of national and local fundraising events. If you are energetic, enthusiastic and recognise the long-term importance of their work, Research into Ageing would love to hear from you. From research results already available, Research into Ageing knows that with enough money to fund enough basic research into the common health problems of older individuals, it will be possible for everyone to enjoy a healthy old age. Briefings, workshops, conferences are held regularly and a wide range of publications is available.

Volunteers willing to give freely of their time and expertise are needed to support Head Office and regional teams in a variety of ways. You may like to take part in one of the research projects around the country investigating, for example, exercise or nutritional needs. At Head Office administrative assistance is always welcome, as is help with mailing leaflets and booklets to existing and new supporters. Around the country there are 13 county groups, each with their own administrative and fundraising teams, who always need help.

SEE ALSO

British Lung Foundation
King George's Fund for Sailors
Rural Housing Trust
Talking Newspaper Association

FUNDRAISING

ALEXANDRA ROSE DAY

2A Ferry Road, Barnes, London SW13 9RX
Tel: 0181-748 4824 *Fax:* 0181-748 3188
Charity Reg. No: 211535
Contact: **Mrs Gillian Greenwood, National Director**
Date established: 1912
Annual income: £500,000 (95)
Area covered: **National**

Founded in 1912 as the nation's first Flag Day, this much-loved charity continues today, as it began, to enable other 'people-caring' charities within the United Kingdom to raise funds for themselves by participating in Alexandra Rose Day and benefiting from 80 per cent of the funds that they raise. Alexandra Rose Day also provides a much-needed and informed 'voice' for the growing number of small charities and local branches of larger organisations that come under its umbrella.

In addition to the Children's Hospice 'Kit Appeal' and a Summer Camp for underprivileged children, Alexandra Rose Day operates a Fund set up to provide emergency help to 'people-caring' charities participating in Rose Day and facing financial crisis. Funding comes from social events, individual donations, and a percentage of the return from the Flag Day.

HOUSING

DISABLED HOUSING TRUST

Norfolk Lodge, Oakenfield, Burgess Hill,
W. Sussex RH15 8SJ
Tel: 01444-239 123   Fax: 01444-244 978
Charity Reg. No: 800797
Contact: Norman Thody, Chief Executive
Date established: 1989
Annual income: £1.9m (95)
Area covered: National

The Disabled Housing Trust provides sheltered housing for people with severe physical disabilities. It aims to create an environment which provides the most modern and progressive facilities, but in a homely and caring setting. The Trust actively encourages development of an independent lifestyle and promotes integration with the local community. The hallmarks of the Trust's services are care and respect for each individual and a belief in their having real choice. The Trust also operates a sister charity, the Brain Injury Rehabilitation Trust, to help the increasing number of clients whose disability was acquired as a result of a serious head injury. Services offered include assessment, social rehabilitation, training and in some cases long-term care.

Introduction of the Community Care Act has seen, in many cases, the transfer of residential and domiciliary services from local authorities to voluntary and independent sector providers. This means that organisations like the Disabled Housing Trust are needed by local authorities to run services for them. The

Trust aims to rise to these challenges and provide high-quality care in residential settings up and down the country. Volunteers are welcome, especially to organise fundraising activities.

A team of fundraisers is employed by the Disabled Housing Trust which is a not-for-profit charity. Funds are raised either generally or for specific units. This can be for refurbishment of an existing unit which includes fundraising for specific equipment or for new units, where funds are raised to build the property as well as to furnish it.

HYPED

353 Ashley Road, Parkstone, Poole, Dorset, BH14 0AR
Tel: 01202-779 010 *Fax:* 01202-779 011

Charity Reg. No:	1053090
Contact:	**Mike Kearley, Financial administrator**
Date established:	**1990**
Annual income:	**£259,100 (96)**
Area covered:	**Regional – Dorset**

Hyped was created to provide accommodation, support, advocacy, and reintegration for vulnerable, young (16–25 years) single homeless people in the eastern half of Dorset. Out of a population of 518,000 in the area, up to 1,800 people are homeless. Hyped provides 33 bed spaces in 4 houses locally – one is for 14 of the very vulnerable 16 and 17 year olds. These houses provide a mixture of independence, along with a strong sense of community. Accommodation is the basic need Hyped fulfils, but they believe that the experience and support that residents receive whilst with them can be fundamental to beginning the process of healing and reassessing their relationships with themselves, society, and their past.

The Directors (The executive committee) consists of 12 volunteers. The present fundraising campaign is operated by a further 10 volunteers. Five volunteers assist at the house for 16 and 17 year olds, teaching cooking and other life skills, counselling and sometimes just talking.

The main Government support is via Dorset Social Services and the Housing Corporation (Special needs Management Allowance). The main source of fundraising is via the many national and local charitable trusts – supported by local fundraising events, and approaching local churches, organisations, business and individuals.

Forty per cent of the residents have been in care, of the remainder a high proportion come from backgrounds which include physical, mental and sexual abuse. Residence with Hyped is often their first experience of a stable, functional and caring environment.

RURAL HOUSING TRUST

THE RURAL HOUSING TRUST

Prince Consort House, 27–29 Albert Embankment, London SE1 7TJ
Tel: 0171-793 8114
Charity Reg. No: 270213
Contact: **Janet Hart, Fundraising & Publicity**
Date established: 1976
Annual income: £1,189,289m (95)
Area covered: National

The Rural Housing Trust works with rural communities to find solutions to the housing needs of local people who cannot afford to buy a house in their village. Through regional field staff, the Trust works in close partnership with parish councils and rural housing associations to provide new houses for rent and shared-ownership sale at affordable prices. The schemes are designed to meet the housing needs of current and future generations of local people.

The Trust relies on donations from charitable sources to enable it to carry out the extensive fieldwork that is necessary for small and scattered rural developments. It welcomes donations of all sizes, especially those made by Deed of Covenant, and seeks volunteers to help with fundraising events; in particular, it would like to hear from marathon runners.

SEE ALSO

Enham Trust
National Association for Voluntary Hostels
Shelter – National Campaign for Homeless People
St Christopher's Fellowship
United Response

MEDICINE AND MEDICAL RESEARCH

ASH

Devon House, 12–15 Dartmouth Street, London SW1H 9BL
Tel: 0171-314 1360 *Fax:* 0171-222 4343
Charity Reg. No: 262067
Contact: **Linda Keuning, Supporter Services Officer**
Date established: 1971
Annual income: £616,000 (94/95)
Area covered: National

ASH works to eliminate the single largest preventable cause of death and disease within the UK, by influencing policy and public opinion on tobacco use. It aims to reduce smoking prevalence and consumption and to relieve the pressure on people to take up smoking. ASH seeks to educate people about the health risks of tobacco use, trying to achieve a smoke-free environment as the norm. ASH works to protect everyone, especially vulnerable groups like children and people with respiratory difficulties, such as asthma, from environmental tobacco smoke. ASH aims to publicise the commercial tactics of the tobacco industry.

The charity needs voluntary donations and legacies to maintain its independence and to fight the might of the tobacco industry's promotion of their products. ASH believes that, pound for pound, they can save more lives by their work to discourage people from smoking, and thus reduce the incidence of smoking-related diseases, than by spending in any other direction. It is children who take up smoking, rarely ever adults; therefore, a lot of ASH's campaigning and research work is designed to help prevent children from starting to smoke, and thus becoming addicted. ASH is not anti-smoking but is on the side of smokers, most of whom regret their addiction.

ASH needs volunteers to support its small staff in London and at regional level, with professional expertise, with time to give to campaigning, and able to offer clerical support for fundraising and campaigning. ASH runs a Supporters' Scheme, with an annual subscription of £15 (£7.50 for the unwaged). It also publishes *Burning Issues*, which helps people keep in touch with national and local activity and the latest tobacco-related news and information. Volunteers can act individually or form/join a local branch that acts in co-ordination with Central Office. ASH celebrates its 25th anniversary in 1996, with events planned nationwide. For further information contact Linda Keuning, ASH Supporter Services.

BRITISH DIABETIC ASSOCIATION

10 Queen Anne Street, London W1M 0BD
Tel: 0171-323 1531 *Fax:* 0171-636 3096
Charity Reg. No: 215199
Contact: **Vanessa Hebditch, PR Officer**
Date established: **1934**
Annual income: **£9.7m (94)**
Area covered: **National**

The British Diabetic Association has helped and supported diabetes research for over 60 years. Its careline offers advice on diabetes, providing a confidential service from health-care professionals for anyone affected directly or indirectly by diabetes. Last year the BDA helped over a thousand sufferers and covered topics from care of your diabetes to driving and insurance.

Youth and Family Services organise holidays for children, enabling them to meet others with diabetes and become more independent, and also run a Tadpole Club for children with diabetes, their brothers, sisters and friends. The BDA funds research into the possible causes, prevention, treatment and cure of diabetes.

There are an estimated 1.4 million people in the UK with diabetes and it is believed that many are as yet undiagnosed. As the 'voice of people with diabetes' the BDA works to influence Government policy and campaigns continually for the best care, best quality of life and an end to unfair discrimination. The BDA has an extensive network of voluntary groups and branches who fulfil a vital role, both on a local and a national scale. Groups vary in their activities; for some it is a chance for people with diabetes and their families to chat and share experiences, other groups will be actively fundraising for research. Volunteers are always welcome to help promote public awareness. Local groups can help monitor and improve their local diabetes services. Many health authorities now have local Diabetes Services Advisory Groups, containing one or more patients' representatives who are often drawn from the BDA voluntary groups section.

Volunteers carry out fundraising for the BDA in two main areas – with a local branch, or in National Diabetes Week, which is in June each year. Diabetes 2001 is a major scheme to fund research. The BDA holds two major lotteries a year.

British Heart Foundation

British Heart Foundation
The heart research charity

14 Fitzhardinge Street, London W1H 4DH
Tel: 0171-935 0185 *Fax:* 0171-486 5820

Charity Reg. No:	225971
Contact:	Mandy Ford, Director of Fundraising
Date established:	1961
Annual income:	£40.263m (94/95)
Area covered:	National

The British Heart Foundation raises money for research into the causes, prevention, diagnosis and treatment of heart disease – the UK's number one killer. BHF is the largest funder of heart research in the UK. At present, BHF funds around 850 research projects looking at differing aspects of heart disease. The Foundation also plays a major role in educating and influencing people – from encouraging the general public to reduce their own risk of heart disease to informing health professionals of the latest advances in heart care and research. BHF also provides support and information to heart patients.

Major fundraising events in 1996 include the London to Brighton Bike Ride (June), Israel bike rides (April and November) and a national series of walks in September. Children and youth events include Jump Rope for Heart, Keep the Beat and National Schools Golf. Our awareness-raising British Heart Week is held in June. BHF relies entirely on public generosity for its income which includes donations, legacies, covenants and company sponsorship. BHF provides a wide variety of educational material to assist heart patients and their families, as well as information to help people reduce their risk of heart disease.

BHF welcomes volunteers to help with many aspects of its work, and offers a wide variety of opportunities to people with varying skill levels. Their greatest areas of need are within their national network of 460 branches and over 270 shops. Volunteers are also needed to assist with basic office duties at both the London headquarters and regional offices.

BRITISH LIVER TRUST

Central House, Central Avenue, Ransomes Europark, Ipswich, Suffolk IP3 9QG
Tel: 01473-276 326 *Fax:* 01473-276 327
Charity Reg. No: 298858
Contact: Alison Rogers, Director
Date established: 1988
Annual income: £366,000 (95)
Area covered: National

The British Liver Trust helps people with liver disease. It provides information and advice via a full-time trained ex-transplant nurse (Information Line: 01473-276 328) and via its growing network of voluntary self-help support groups. It produces publications about liver disease for patients, families and medical practitioners, and runs conferences and meetings to ensure that the medical profession is up to date in its knowledge of liver disease. It also funds research to benefit current and potential future patients.

Funds are very tight so the charity actively encourages volunteers to help by working in the office, running support groups, talking to others with liver disease and fundraising. The Trust is always keen to hear from people with innovative ideas, especially anything which generates publicity or funds, or allows the charity to deliver a better quality of service to people with liver disease.

BRITISH LUNG FOUNDATION

78 Hatton Garden, London EC1N 8JR
Tel: 0171-831 5831 *Fax:* 0171-831 5832
Charity Reg. No: 326730
Contact: **Ian Govendir, Chief Executive**
Date established: **1985**
Annual income: **£1.3m (95)**
Area covered: **National**

The British Lung Foundation works throughout the UK to raise money for research into the prevention, diagnosis and treatment of all lung conditions, including asthma, lung cancer, emphysema, pneumonia, tuberculosis and chronic bronchitis. It aims to inform people about the benefits of good lung health and about specific lung diseases through a series of helpful and easily understood leaflets and fact sheets. As part of its commitment to people living with lung disease the British Lung Foundation runs the Breathe Easy Club which offers support and advice at over 40 groups nationwide.

The Breathe Easy Club is for anyone living with or affected by a lung condition and is free. Supporters receive a regular magazine and have access to information leaflets on specific lung conditions. Additional information is available about leaving a legacy or taking out a covenant.

The British Lung Foundation needs volunteers to help with all aspects of its work. Volunteers can help with a wide variety of tasks in the London office and the five regional offices in Bristol, Birmingham, Liverpool, Newcastle and Glasgow. Opportunities vary from sending out information leaflets to promoting the Breathe Easy Club in a region or assisting with special fundraising events locally. As a growing charity, the Foundation has an increasing need for volunteers and would welcome people who can give help regularly, if only for a few hours a week. In return, the charity can offer a stimulating and lively environment.

In 1996 The Breathe Easy Club is celebrating its fifth birthday. A number of promotions are planned, including the Breathe Easy 5 Challenge. The same year also sees the culmination of the British Lung Foundation's Sew a Little Hope programme with the exhibition and auction of up to 20 embroidered quilts depicting the wishes of people with a lung condition.

CANCER RESEARCH CAMPAIGN

10 Cambridge Terrace, London NW1 4JL
Tel: 0171-224 1333 *Fax:* 0171-487 4310
Charity Reg. No: 255838
Contact: Mrs Jackie McDougall, Appeals Director
Date established: 1923
Annual income: £45m (94)
Area covered: National

For over 70 years the Cancer Research Campaign has been fighting cancer on all fronts. They are the European leader in the development of new anti-cancer drugs and are responsible for one-third of all cancer research in the UK, and 65 per cent of all cancer research in Scotland. With an ongoing programme of 700 projects, supported by spending of around £43 million, the Campaign funds research into every aspect of the disease, from the causes to the cures. Their aim is to look for better and more effective ways to prevent and treat cancer and to reduce the suffering this disease can cause.

The 1996 national events schedule includes a Walk Week, Raffle, In-Line Skating, Bridge-a-Thon, and various bike rides and running marathons, and for the more adventurous, parachuting, sky diving and rally driving. Alternatively, if you would like to help, why not set up your own fundraising committee? Contact your local Area Appeals Organiser for more information.

All the money raised comes from the public: the Campaign receives no Government support. For information on supporting the charity through a legacy, by Deed of Covenant, Gift Aid, or Payroll Giving, or simply by purchasing the charity's Christmas cards, contact them on the above telephone number. If you would like to volunteer in a Cancer Research Campaign shop there are over 230 in the country and they need your help. The charity asks for just four hours a week as a minimum to help serve customers and prepare donated stock for resale. Local committees and fundraising groups organise a wide variety of events and functions and always welcome new volunteers. Your can also join in celebrating CRC Day on May 23 each year. If you would like to arrange your own events the Area Appeals Organiser for your area can provide help and support.

MEDICINE AND MEDICAL RESEARCH

CANCERLINK

CancerLink

17 Britannia Street, London WC1X 9JN
Tel: 0171-833 2818 *Fax:* 0171-833 4963
     0131-228 5567   0131-228 8956
Charity Reg. No: 1750782
Contact: **Angela Hayes, Director**
Date established: 1982
Annual income: £1.3m (94)
Area covered: National

Cancerlink is the national cancer charity which supports all people by promoting self-help, providing emotional support and information. Experienced staff provide free and confidential information by telephone, post and through audio and video tapes and publications. Materials are available in various languages. Cancerlink gives details of local self-help groups and individual supporters. It also offers consultancy services, training courses and other assistance for people affected by cancer; self-help groups; and one-to-one supporters.

CHILDREN NATIONWIDE MEDICAL RESEARCH FUND

Nicholas House, 181 Union Street, London SE1 0LN
Tel: 0171-928 2425 *Fax:* 0171-928 0154
Charity Reg. No: 289600
Contact: **Ms Francesca MacArthur, Director**
Date established: 1977
Annual income: £1m
Area covered: National

Children Nationwide is a national charity funding medical research into a wide range of serious childhood conditions such as cancer, kidney and liver disease, asthma, sickle-cell anaemia, growth problems and prematurity in newborn babies.

The fact that the charity looks after so many conditions means that it is not well known by the public. This makes it more difficult for it to raise money than the better known charities. Donations are therefore always welcome, but if you are not able to contribute in this way you may like to help in a more practical way by doing your own fundraising for the charity eg organising an event or doing a sponsored slim, walk, etc or by coming and working as a volunteer in the office.

CYSTIC FIBROSIS RESEARCH TRUST

Alexandra House, 5 Blyth Road, Bromley, Kent BR1 3RS
Tel: 0181-464 7211 *Fax:* 0181-313 0472
Charity Reg. No: 281287
Contact: Ian Thorn, PR Director
Date established: 1964
Annual income: £3.6m (94/95)
Area covered: National

The Cystic Fibrosis Trust works to educate people about CF and to provide advice and support to those with the disease and their families. The CF Trust has also funded more than £15 million-worth of vital research in hospitals and universities – all paid for by public donations. The aim of this research is to improve detection and treatment of CF and eventually to find a cure. The CF Trust has also established and continues to support an expanding network of hospital clinics which specialise in treating Cystic Fibrosis. The CF Trust produces a quarterly magazine, *CF News*, and an extensive range of informative booklets to keep readers up to date with current developments, fundraising activities and advances in treatment.

Cystic Fibrosis is caused by a single defective gene and results in a thick sticky mucus which clogs the lungs and gut, making it difficult to breathe and digest food. This mucus may also damage other major organs such as the pancreas and liver. There is currently no cure for CF. It claims the lives of some three people a week in the UK. The Cystic Fibrosis Trust has over 300 voluntary branches and groups throughout the country and a network of volunteers providing support and raising money. Support volunteers are co-ordinated by the CF Trust's Family and Adult Support Services (FASS) department, based at the Kent headquarters.

The Trust's fundraising department co-ordinates everything from national flag days to mountain climbing! They rely on volunteers to organise and take part in sponsored events, car boot sales, raffles and fetes. There are 90 branch secretaries who run the CF Trust's voluntary branches, masterminding lots of their own events and encouraging others to support them or join in.

Foundation for the Study of Infant Deaths

14 Halkin Street, London SW1X 7DP
Tel: 0171-235 0965 *Fax:* 0171-823 1986
Charity Reg. No: 262191
Contact: **Mrs Joyce Epstein, Secretary General**
Date established: **1971**
Annual income: **£1.1m (95)**
Area covered: **National**

Every week in the UK 10 apparently healthy babies die suddenly, silently, unexpectedly. The FSID funds research into the causes and prevention of these terrible tragedies, supports bereaved families, and promotes information about cot death amongst health professionals and the general public. Following the charity's launch in 1991 of the UK's first national campaign to 'Reduce the Risk' of cot deaths (made possible largely as a result of the FSID's research) the number of cot deaths fell by over 50 per cent. But it remains the largest cause of death in babies over a month old. The FSID's priority now is to spread the 'Reduce the Risk' message to all parents.

The FSID needs volunteers to help out in the London headquarters with all aspects of office work. The charity also needs people throughout the country to become 'Befrienders' for bereaved parents: 'Befrienders' need not have suffered a cot death themselves but they must have an interest in listening to and helping others, and must undergo the FSID's preparation programme.

The FSID celebrates its Silver Anniversary in 1996. There will be 'silver-themed' events throughout the country, and help is needed to reach the fundraising target of £2.5 million. There will be sports events, opera, an outdoor family day, bazaar, greyhound races, Gala Ball, and many more such events.

IRIS FUND FOR PREVENTION OF BLINDNESS

York House, 199 Westminster Bridge Road, London SE1 7UT
Tel: 0171-928 7743 Fax: 0171-928 7919
Charity Reg. No: 293204
Contact: Mrs Vanessa Wride, Executive Director
Date established: 1965
Annual Income: £837,848 (95)
Area covered: National

The Iris Fund funds research to alleviate, cure and prevent blindness and serious eye disorders, and provide new equipment nationwide. Research findings have already resulted in radical improvements in diagnostic and surgical techniques. Eye disorders will affect most of us at some stage in our life, from infections resulting from contact lens use, to cataracts or glaucoma. The Iris Fund strives to ensure that all problems, if not preventable, become curable.

As the charity has only one full-time and one part-time member of staff, volunteers play a vital role, organising fundraising events and filling in where necessary in the office. The Fund would not be able to function as efficiently, maintaining administrative expenses of less than 10 per cent, without this loyal support.

Médecins Sans Frontières (MSF) UK

124–132 Clerkenwell Road, London EC1R 5DL
Tel: 0171-713 5600 *Fax:* 0171-713 5004
Charity Reg. No: 1026588
Contact: Anne-Marie Huby, Executive Director
Date established: 1971
Annual income: £2m (95) – UK only
Area covered: **International**

The world's largest independent humanitarian organisation for emergency medical relief, Médecins Sans Frontières provides assistance to victims of natural and man-made disasters and armed conflicts worldwide, irrespective of race, religion, creed or political affiliation. The organisation sends approximately 3,000 volunteers to the field every year, most of them from the medical professions, to 64 countries worldwide. The UK office sends approximately 140 volunteers on emergency assignments every year. MSF has an annual budget of 306 million US dollars, 50 per cent of which comes from private donations, with the remainder coming from international institutions such as the European Union, the United Nations and national governments.

Médecins Sans Frontières is an international organisation, of which the UK office is a part. It has offices and emergency centres in 19 countries worldwide, pooling financial and human resources in emergency. Founded in 1971, Médecins Sans Frontières as a whole is celebrating its 25th anniversary in 1996.

Médecins Sans Frontières recruits volunteers, mainly from the health profession, for work in crisis areas worldwide: doctors, surgeons, anaesthetists and nurses who have completed a tropical nursing course. MSF also recruits volunteers for key support functions, such as logisticians with broad-based technical and organisational skills and specialists such as water and sanitation engineers.

Médecins Sans Frontières ensures its independence through raising its own project funds, and it therefore relies on individual donors supporting its work worldwide. Although the young UK office cannot yet provide the logistical support for many fundraising events, it welcomes independent initiatives from individuals and companies.

MUSCULAR DYSTROPHY GROUP OF GREAT BRITAIN AND NORTHERN IRELAND

7–11 Prescott Place, London SW4 6BS
Tel: 0171-720 8055 Fax: 0171-498 0670
Charity Reg. No: 205395
Contact: Alan Duncan, Communications Manager
Date established: 1959
Annual income: £4.7m (94)
Area covered: National

The Muscular Dystrophy Group invests in research to find treatments and cures for people affected by any of the conditions known as muscular dystrophy or by related neuromuscular disorders. These conditions are largely characterised by gradual wasting and weakening of muscle tissue. Sometimes mild symptoms only begin to show in adulthood but children can be so severely affected from birth that they do not have long to live. The charity provides support in the form of expert medical care at eight specialist Muscle Centres based in hospitals throughout the UK; information; a team of Family Care Officers; and financial assistance with essential equipment.

The Muscular Dystrophy Group stages several annual large-scale fundraising initiatives, including the Commit To Get Fit Campaign, in July; sales of lottery tickets; and national Grotty Tie Day, in October. Further information about these and other events is available from Head Office.

The Muscular Dystrophy Group relies entirely upon voluntary donations to continue its work. The Group has over 300 volunteer branches throughout the UK, working on a wide range of fundraising activities which contribute over a quarter of the charity's total annual income. The remainder is generated through income from applications to the corporate sector and grant-making trusts; legacies; investments; direct mail; trading merchandise; and Head Office fundraising. Anyone wishing to volunteer for the Muscular Dystrophy Group should contact the charity's Head Office, who will place them in touch with their nearest voluntary Branch or provide assistance to help establish a Branch in their own area.

MEDICINE AND MEDICAL RESEARCH

THE MULTIPLE SCLEROSIS SOCIETY

25 Effie Road, London SW6 1EE
Tel: 0171-610 7171 *Fax:* 0171-736 9861
Charity Reg. No: 207495
Contact: **Anne Martin, Head of Donor Development**
Date established: 1953
Annual income: £13.8m (94)
Area covered: **National – 368 Branches**

The Multiple Sclerosis Society is the only nationwide organisation dedicated to supporting people with multiple sclerosis, providing the care they need in their everyday lives and the research that is urgently required to find a cure for this distressing disease. In every way, the Society works for and with people who have MS, and their carers, to help them improve the quality of their lives.

The MS Society requires volunteers for all aspects of its work. The Society's network of 368 branches is run entirely by volunteers, who provide essential support to local people affected by MS. Services range from social outings, support groups for newly diagnosed people; counselling and welfare grants to individuals. Grants are available to help with the purchase of wheelchairs and scooters; home adaptations and domestic appliances; computers; education; therapy and respite care.

Fundraising activity takes place in all MS Society Branches. Volunteers are always needed, either to organise events or help out on Flag Days, or to take responsibility for the Branch's fundraising programme. The MS Society has a membership scheme for people with MS, their families and carers, as well as for health-care professionals. Please call the above telephone number for details. The Helpline provides a listening and information service. (Monday–Friday 10am–4pm, 0171-371 8000)

ST. JOHN AMBULANCE

1 Grosvenor Crescent, London SW1X 7EF
Tel: 0171-235 5231 *Fax:* 0171-235 0796
Charity Reg. No: 235979
Contact: **John Mills, Communications Director**
Date established: 1877
Annual income: £30m (94/95)
Area covered: **National/International**

St. John Ambulance is the country's leading First Aid organisation, passing on lifesaving skills to nearly half a million people each year in schools, companies, factories and to members of the public. The St. John Ambulance volunteer members, in their familiar black and white uniforms, are a familiar and reassuring sight at so many sporting and public events. St. John Ambulance provides care for those who are vulnerable or in need, particularly children, the elderly and the disabled. It is international, with a presence throughout the Commonwealth. As part of the Order of St. John, it can trace its history back nearly 900 years to Jerusalem prior to the Crusades.

Volunteers give their service for the benefit of the community. St. John Ambulance needs volunteers across the age range from

6 to 65. The 82,000 members in the UK include volunteer professional doctors and nurses and members of the public who receive thorough training in first aid and other caring skills. Volunteers are also needed in fundraising and finance, to help keep on the road over 1,100 ambulances and other vehicles; as youth leaders of the 'Badgers' (6–10 years) and 'Cadets' (11–18 years) and as carers to help with the Care in the Community and hospital welfare work.

St. John Ambulance has to raise funds and sponsorship to continue its work in the community. A fully equipped ambulance costs up to £40,000, and a defibrillator £5,000, and even the members' duty first aid kits cost £30 each. It can cost £4,000 to recruit, train and develop youth leaders. On average, each day, the volunteers give over 10,000 hours, treat 550 members of the public and drive over 5,000 miles. To find out how to give time or financial support to help The Order of St. John (St. John Ambulance and the St. John Ophthalmic Hospital in Jerusalem), contact them at the address above.

TENOVUS, THE CANCER CHARITY

11 Whitchurch Road, Cardiff, CF4 3JN
Tel: 01222-621 433 *Fax:* 01222-615 966
Charity Reg No: 1054015
Contact: Peter Searle, Appeals Manager
Date established: 1944
Annual income: £2.7m (94)
Area covered: National

One in three people will develop cancer; one in four will die from it. Created in 1944, Tenovus has grown from modest beginnings into an organisation committed to fighting cancer through research, care and counselling. Tenovus scientists are acknowledged amongst the world's experts. Drugs such as Tamoxifen, used worldwide in the treatment of breast cancer, were developed with the help of Tenovus. These scientists are working on new anti-cancer treatments which offer real hope for present and future generations.

The charity remains committed to providing support and counselling for cancer patients and their families through the Freefone Cancer Helpline (0800-526 527). Tenovus receives no Government funding for its vital research programmes. It needs volunteers to help in its charity shops or to organise fundraising events at home or in the workplace.

WELLBEING

27 Sussex Place, London NW1 4SP
Tel: 0171-262 5337 *Fax:* 0171-724 7725
Charity Reg. No: 239281
Contact: **Rosie Barnes, Director**
Date established: **1964**
Annual income: **£1.1m (94)**
Area covered: **National**

WellBeing aims to save the lives of women and their babies, as well as improve the quality of their lives. It aims to educate women about their own health and wellbeing, to enable them to make informed choices. The charity's three main areas of research are: all aspects of pregnancy, birth and the care of newborn babies, especially those with difficulties; the diagnosis, better screening for and treatment of women's cancers, including cervical, ovarian, endometrial and breast cancers; quality of life issues, such as infertility, endometriosis, period problems, the menopause and osteoporosis.

Throughout the country, over 70 branches work very hard on WellBeing's behalf. People support the charity for a variety of reasons: some have suffered some of the problems it addresses, either themselves or within their family; others want to say 'thank you' for their own and their babies' good health; yet others simply enjoy arranging social events and feel that to do so for the benefit of WellBeing gives added depth to the occasion. All the branches welcome extra help and, in some key areas, there is still no branch, so do get in touch if you would like to help.

WellBeing obtains funds solely from the generosity of the public, raising well over £1 million per year from three main sources: individual and corporate donations; WellBeing's branches; and its London Appeals Committee. WellBeing offers a comprehensive health paperback on all aspects of women's health (price, £7.95 plus £2.50 p&p). You can also become a 'Well Wisher' or, through a £10 donation, become a lifetime supporter of WellBeing, receiving regular information on its research and a five-year health check card.

SEE ALSO

Health Unlimited
Malcolm Sargent Cancer Fund for Children
Marie Curie Memorial Foundation
Research into Ageing

MENTAL HEALTH

COMBAT STRESS

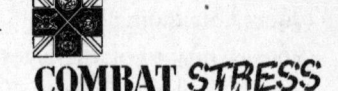

**Broadway House, The Broadway, Wimbledon,
London SW19 1RL**
Tel: 0181-543 6333 *Fax:* 0181-542 7082
Charity Reg. No: 206002
Contact: **Major Colin Crawford, Appeals Direcor**
Date established: **1919**
Annual income: **£3.9m (94)**
Area covered: **National**

For over 75 years Combat Stress has brought peace to troubled minds for ex-servicemen and women who are the mental casualties of war. They are now looking after some 4,500 victims of the Second World War, Korea, Northern Ireland, the Falklands and the Gulf, as well as all other conflicts since 1945. The Society's 12 regional welfare offices provide care and support in the community, helping with applications and appeals for war disablement pensions, as well as arranging short-term care for treatment, rehabilitation and respite.

Despite the welcome feeling that the nation should look to the future, following the 50th anniversary commemorations of VE Day and VJ Day, it is important not to forget the needs of wartime casualties who will never recover. The older they get, the more help they will need. The casualties of more recent conflicts will also need help for many years to come. The wounds that do not show also never heal, and continuing care is vital for their peace of mind.

MENTAL HEALTH

FAMILY WELFARE ASSOCIATION

501–505 Kingsland Road, London E8 4AU
Tel: 0171-254 6251 Fax: 0171-249 5443
Charity Reg. No: 264713
Contact: **Lynne Berry, Chief Executive**
Date established: 1869
Annual income: £4,600 (94/95)
Area covered: National

FWA helps families at times of stress and hardship to plan and secure futures in their communities for all their family members. FWA does this by providing community care and mental health services, family support in drop-in centres, and practical and financial help, including grants for household needs to support families in poverty. Underpinning FWA's work is a set of beliefs and values: helping people control their own lives; dignity and respect for each other; high professional standards; equality of opportunity; collaboration and partnership; reciprocity and interdependence; independence of thought and action; and a belief in creating a caring and secure society.

Volunteers are always needed to take part in structured befriending programmes for isolated and vulnerable people, to act as informal advisers in drop-in centres, to sit on committees, or to bring additional expertise to add to those of the professional staff. Recent volunteers have helped with running shops, developing computer systems, writing newsletters and, of course, fundraising. Some volunteers like to be 'hands on', others use their skills behind the scenes. All are very much needed and appreciated.

FWA relies on donations from individuals, charitable trusts and companies. Individuals can increase their donation's value by taking out a covenant or, if it is over £250, by filling in a gift aid form. FWA is very grateful for donations through legacies and can provide advice for people when writing their wills. FWA operates several charity shops selling second-hand clothes and other goods and would appreciate any donations of stock. For general information and opportunities for volunteering, please contact Lynne Berry, Chief Executive; for information on fundraising please contact Nicky Bellotti, Head of Fundraising. Both are at the above address.

FIRST STEPS TO FREEDOM

22 Randall Road, Kenilworth, Warwickshire CV8 1JY
Tel: 01926-864 473 *Fax:* 01926-864 473
Charity Reg. No: 1006873
Contact: **Lesley Hobbs, Secretary**
Date established: **1991**
Annual income: **£10,000 (93/94)**
Area covered: **National**

First Steps to Freedom offers advice and support to those who suffer from anxiety disorders such as panic attacks, phobias, obsessive compulsive disorder (excessive washing, checking or unwanted thoughts) and tranquilliser withdrawal, together with help and support for their carers. The charity is run by people who have either overcome an anxiety disorder or have been closely associated with someone who has, so everyone fully understands the feelings of fear and isolation sufferers have.

The charity does not receive any Government funding; it relies on donations from charitable trusts, membership fees, leaflets and tapes. The charity has a great deal to offer: a telephone helpline, leaflets, self-help booklets, audio relaxation tapes and OCD video. For members there are telephone self-help groups, a penpal list and a regular newsletter. The charity urgently needs more funds to extend the helpline to a 24 hour service. At present it is open only from 10 am to 10 pm, every day of the year. The number is 01926-851 608.

Volunteers have all been through, or have been associated with someone who has been through, an anxiety disorder. Only those who have been through fear can fully understand how it feels. They give their time free of charge for four hours each week, giving hope and understanding.

MACA (The Mental After Care Association)

25 Bedford Square, London WC1B 3HW
Tel: 0171-436 6194 *Fax:* 0171-617 1980
Charity Reg. No: 211091
Contact: The Fundraiser
Date established: 1879
Annual income: £8.3m (95/96)
Area covered: National

MACA helps people in the community who have long-term health needs. Countrywide, the charity's 60 projects provide: residential and supported accommodation; support for carers and people in their own homes; social clubs; employment training schemes; and work within the criminal justice system.

While there are very few opportunities for volunteering, MACA would like to hear from you if you would like to know more about our work, wants to make a donation, or if you are interested in becoming a member.

Mental Health Matters

mental health matters

34/35 West Sunniside, Sunderland SR1 1BU
Tel: 0191-510 3399 *Fax:* 0191-510 2639
Charity Reg. No: 514829
Contact: **Cedric McCullough, Fundraising Co-ordinator**
Date established: 1984
Annual income: £3.5m (95)
Area covered: National/Transnational

Mental Health Matters is committed to extending and improving the range and quality of services it provides, through research and by developing working partnerships based on mutual respect with all those involved in promoting good mental health, both regionally and transnationally. With over 600 members, 60 volunteers and a staff of over 150, MHM provides a range of innovative services, developed to high standards of quality, to over 2,500 people. These services include: residential day centres; a telephone helpline 01642-231 216 – cheap rate 0345-573 129; carers' counsellor; advice and information centres; out-of-hours services; advocacy; GP counselling; domiciliary care; vocational care; and employment training. All Mental Health Matters activities should promote the health and wellbeing of people with mental health problems and their families/carers. Mental Health Matters is the major non-statutory provider of care in the north of England for those suffering from enduring mental illness.

The charity's present areas of research include: crisis care in the community; the GP counselling service; the homeless mentally ill; and specialist counselling for sufferers hearing voices. For those interested in helping by fundraising, volunteering or simply by making a donation, please contact the charity at the above number.

NATIONAL SCHIZOPHRENIA FELLOWSHIP

28 Castle Street, Kingston-upon-Thames, Surrey KT1 1SS
Tel: 0181-547 3937 *Fax:* 0181-547 3862
Charity Reg. No: 271028
Contact: Nigel Dunbrell, Appeals Manager
Date established: 1972
Annual income: £12.1m (95)
Area covered: National – 8 regional offices

NSF is the UK's largest voluntary organisation providing support, help and advice to over a quarter of a million sufferers of schizophrenia, their families and carers. NSF provides services including advice and advocacy, befriending, housing and accommodation, training and employment, drop-in centres and over 160 self-help groups throughout the country. NSF advice service provides intensive one-to-one advocacy support to over 15,000 enquirers each year, achieving success in improving the lives of sufferers and carers.

NSF has many innovative methods of gaining donations from donors and is keen to promote its services to employers, talking to staff and customers in an effort to dispel the myths and stigma surrounding the illness. If you would like further information about NSF, please telephone the office on the above number.

SEE ALSO

The Care Fund
Hampshire Autistic Society
Turning Point
United Response

OVERSEAS AID

ACTIONAID

**Hamlyn House, MacDonald Road, Archway,
London N19 5PG**
Tel: 0171-281 4101 *Fax:* 0171-263 7605
Charity Reg. No: 274467
Contact: Marion Jackson, Head of Fundraising
Date established: 1972
Annual income: £37.3m (94)
Area covered: International

ACTIONAID is one of the UK's leading overseas charities, working in Africa, Asia and Latin America to improve the quality of life for some of the world's poorest communities. ACTIONAID's long-term projects help over 3 million people. Programmes seek to improve education and adult literacy, to provide clean water and health care, to deliver agricultural training, to enable the poorest to generate an income and find ways to save and credit. ACTIONAID also provides emergency relief at times of disaster. ACTIONAID has no religious or political affiliations, working with people regardless of their race, colour or religion.

ACTIONAID's work is supported by child and community sponsors. They make regular contributions and receive messages from the children, hearing directly how their support is helping the whole community.

ACTIONAID needs volunteers to help with fundraising work around the UK and with essential office-based activities in

London and Chard in Somerset. Several hundred volunteer fundraisers in supporter groups around the UK (and some in Europe) hold events to raise funds and awareness of the charity's work. In the office volunteers take on important roles in areas as diverse as fundraising administration, research, finance, personnel, systems, publicity and press office work. ACTIONAID does not send volunteers overseas.

Each June during ACTIONAID Week, 50,000 volunteers all over the UK raise money through a variety of activities, including house-to-house collections and special events.

ACTIONAID's award-winning educational resources, designed to support the National Curriculum and GCSE requirements, are an excellent way to introduce young people to life in developing countries and the nature and causes of poverty. Schools and youth groups can also take part in ACTIONAID Week and the child sponsorship programme.

CAFOD (CATHOLIC FUND FOR OVERSEAS DEVELOPMENT)

2 Romero Close, Stockwell Road, London SW9 9TY
Tel: 0171-733 7900 *Fax:* 0171-737 6877
Charity Reg. No: 285776
Contact: **Brendan Walsh, Head of Communications**
Date established: **1962**
Annual income: **£22.9m (94)**
Area covered: **International**

CAFOD is on the side of people in need, whatever their race or religion. CAFOD is one of the UK's major relief and development agencies, and the official aid agency of the Catholic Church in England and Wales. CAFOD is making possible over a thousand projects improving the quality of people's lives in over 75 countries. CAFOD is a voice for the world's poor, raising awareness of the root causes of poverty, and campaigning for change.

CAFOD is people like Denis Lucey of Goring-by-Sea, Sussex, whose local CAFOD group has raised over £5,000 for Brazilian street children through fiesta evenings with Latin American food, music and dancing. CAFOD is people like four-year-old Sion Roberts of Cardigan, who collected pennies in his home-made piggy bank for a pig bank in Cambodia that provides local farmers with animals.

CHILDREN'S AID DIRECT

82 Caversham Road, Reading, Berks RG1 8AE
Tel: 0118-958 4000 Fax: 0118-958 8988
Charity Reg. No: 803236
Contact: D. Grubb, Chief Executive
Date established: 1990
Annual income: £18m (95)
Area covered: International

Children's Aid Direct specialises in delivering aid directly through its own in-country teams, to children and their carers, where rapid relief is needed. Formerly known as Feed the Children, the organisation has already made an effective and measurable contribution to the vast field of overseas aid. Reaching over one million children and their carers, it has delivered over £40 million worth of aid directly to hospitals, schools, orphanages and displaced people in Romania, Bulgaria, Albania, former Yugoslavia, Rwanda, Azerbaijan, Armenia, Georgia, Sierra Leone, North Korea and Haiti as well as to the Kurds in Iraq.

Children's Aid Direct work depends on the generosity of its donors, whether individual, corporate or statutory. A real sense of purpose and achievement is created by regular reports from the front-line, demonstrating the impact of aid. Campaigns and public presentations all contribute to the core belief in action and resolution.

Children's Aid Direct focuses on the needs of children, in the belief that they are the most vulnerable and innocent, and that they are the future. The charity's culture is therefore child-centred and embraces the needs of the whole child: physical, mental and social.

Children's Aid Direct believes in 'People to People Aid', encouraging volunteers to give time and skills to help children in desperate need. Hundreds of volunteers collect, sort and pack donated aid. They also undertake essential administrative functions. Within Community Support Groups, or as individuals, they raise money and create awareness. Children's Aid Direct aims to create a rewarding and long-term relationship with volunteers, enabling them to energise and enhance the charity's work. One of the most successful initiatives made possible by volunteers has been the creation of 'Baby Boxes' full of essential supplies for mothers with newborn babies.

OVERSEAS AID

Concern Universal

14 Manor Road, Chatham, Kent ME4 6AG
Tel: 01634-813 942 *Fax:* 01634-402 942
Charity Reg. No: 1278887
Contact: A Donnelly, Executive Director
Date established: 1976
Annual income: £3.5m (95)
Area covered: International

Concern Universal responds to the direct needs of impoverished communities in the developing world by striving to improve levels of health care, education, nutrition, work and social skills and sanitation. By responding to their needs and initiatives it helps whole communities to develop. The charity focuses on long-term development programmes with a special emphasis on the needs of the most disadvantaged: children, women, refugees and displaced persons and disabled people. Where necessary Concern Universal undertakes emergency response programmes.

By working in partnership with British and European funding agencies, the European Union, churches and Government bodies such as the British Overseas Development Agency, Concern Universal can double the value of each pound donated to it. Its Annual Report is available from the above address.

FEED THE MINDS

Robertson House, Leas Road, Guildford, Surrey GU1 4QW
Tel: 01483-577 877 *Fax:* 01483-301 387
Charity Reg. No: 291333
Contact: **Dr Alwyn Marriage, Director**
Date established: **1964**
Annual income: **£400,000 (96)**
Area covered: **International**

Communities in developing countries need literature of their own language and culture – books from the West are not the answer. FTM supports the literacy, literature and communication projects of Christian churches in developing countries and Eastern Europe, through grants for publishing, distribution, training, literacy projects and equipment. The aim is that these churches gain experience in publishing and broadcasting within and for their communities so the gospel can be proclaimed and some of the root causes of poverty addressed, through sustainable education.

Feed the Minds involves all Christian denominations, and Associate Membership is available for individual churches, schools and groups. In Britain volunteers are needed throughout the year to help with second-hand book sales, in the offices or with other fundraising events. A newsletter with details of current projects is sent to all supporters. Please ring for further details.

HEALTH UNLIMITED

Prince Consort House, 27–29 Albert Embankment, London SE1 7JS
Tel: 0171-582 5999 *Fax:* 0171-582 5900
Charity Reg. No: 290535
Contact: **Pam Rumfitt, Fundraising Manager**
Date established: 1984
Annual income: £1.5m (95)
Area covered: **International – 11 countries**

Health Unlimited helps poor, war-torn communities rebuild their lives through practical training and support. Trapped behind the lines, neglected and discriminated against, they are often cut off from life-saving health care for many years. Health Unlimited invests in people – through training – which means that communities can choose for themselves how best to meet their own health needs. Health Unlimited sends skilled medical teams of doctors, nurses, midwives and health educators to work long-term in conflict zones around the world. It is currently working with local partner organisations on 19 projects in Latin America, Africa and Asia, bringing health and hope to over 7 million people worldwide.

Health Unlimited offers opportunities to volunteers who are interested in development. There is a particular need for people who are willing to help organise fundraising events, eg charity concerts, sponsored events, marathons etc. The charity has a number of places in the London Marathon each year for runners willing to raise sponsorship. In the London office, the charity welcomes volunteers who have administrative and computer skills to help with fundraising.

For just £15 a year you can become a Friend of Health Unlimited and in return you receive its quarterly newsletter, *Health Outpost*, Annual Review, project updates and invitations to the Annual meeting and fundraising events. Health Unlimited can provide speakers for schools and groups. Free publications include: *Health Outpost*; a Schools' Pack on the Brazilian Rainforest; and *Health Behind the Lines*, a report on conflict, health and development. For more information call 0171-582 5999 or e-mail Health Unlimited at ael61@dial.Pipex.com.

INTERMEDIATE TECHNOLOGY

Myson House, Railway Terrace, Rugby, Warwickshire CV21 3HT
Tel: 01788-560 631 *Fax:* 01788-540 270
Charity Reg. No: 247257
Contact: **Peter Watts, Fundraising Manager**
Date established: 1966
Annual income: £7.536 (95)
Area covered: **International**

Intermediate Technology (IT) is a British charity working with rural communities in the Third World, helping people to develop practical solutions to the problems of poverty. Training and transferring knowledge is at the heart of IT's approach. Working out solutions with the people themselves, the charity encourages the use of tools, machinery and methods that make the best use of local skills and resources. Communities thus gain more control over their own lives and can contribute to the long-term development of their societies. IT was founded in 1966 by Dr Ernst Friedrich Schumacher, author of *Small is Beautiful*.

Donations of all kinds are welcome. IT receives support from individuals, trusts, companies, churches and a variety of organisations. There are also subscription schemes that provide various levels of involvement: Partners, Friends and Associates.

IT also publishes and distributes a comprehensive range of books and journals, and produces development education materials for schools. IT has set up a network of local support groups in the UK. Their role is to raise awareness of IT's work in their area by, for example, representing IT at exhibitions and responding to requests for talks, and by fundraising. A variety of skills is needed and enquiries from potential new members are welcome. The groups are co-ordinated from IT's headquarters in Rugby. All volunteers and supporters are invited to the annual open weekend, where demonstrations of IT's overseas work are given.

INTERNATIONAL CARE AND RELIEF

16 St John's Hill, Sevenoaks, Kent TN13 3NR
Tel: 01732-450250 *Fax:* 01732-741190
Charity Reg. No: 298316
Contact: Terri Lewis, Assistant to Executive Director
Date established: 1978 as International Christian Relief
Annual income: £3m (December 94)
Area covered: International

The ultimate aim of International Care and Relief is to promote and establish sustainable, long-term development in deprived areas of the Third World. However, ICR also operates in crises, providing emergency care for those suffering from the effects of natural and man-made disasters. The charity is currently working in Africa and Asia. ICR's mainstream programmes include emergency nutrition and medical projects, health education, water and sanitation schemes, child sponsorship and community development.

Supporters (whether singly or in groups) help International Care and Relief in a variety of ways: by responding to appeals and newsletters, by regular giving, through covenants, and by holding fundraising events such as jumble sales and coffee mornings. Bequests are also most welcome.

MISSIONS TO SEAMEN

St Michael, Paternoster Royal, College Hill, London EC4A 2RL
Tel: 0171-248 5202 *Fax:* 0171-248 4761
Charity Reg. No: **212432**
Contact: **Mr Michael Cartright, Deputy Secretary General**
Date established: **1856**
Annual income: **£1.9m (94)**
Area covered: **International**

The Missions to Seamen, a voluntary society of the Anglican Church, cares for the welfare of seafarers of all races and creeds in over 300 ports worldwide. It works through a network of chaplains and staff who visit seafarers on their ships and offer welcome, comfort in times of distress, spiritual support and help for those with problems. In 100 major ports the Missions also run seafarers' centres.

We depend on seafarers to bring us many essential items, but in order to carry the trade so vital to our economy, seafarers have to leave their homes and families for months at a time, and face danger, loneliness and isolation. Please help to ensure there is welcome and help for them when they reach port.

THE MOTIVATION CHARITABLE TRUST

Brockley Academy, Brockley Lane, Backwell, Bristol BS19 3AQ
Tel: 01275 464012 *Fax:* 01275 464019
Charity Reg. No: 1014276
Contact: **David Constantine, Director**
Date established: **1991**
Annual income: **£338,513 (95)**
Area covered: **International**

Having the right wheelchair can literally change the life of a disabled person by giving him or her greater independence, confidence and dignity. Motivation has established self-financing workshops in ten countries including Bangladesh, Poland, Cambodia, Russia, and Nicaragua. Every month it receives new requests from organisations around the world to help provide much-needed, low-cost wheelchairs.

The charity works with local groups to set up self-financing workshops that produce low-cost, appropriately designed wheelchairs which can be made entirely from locally available materials. The emphasis is on training local staff – most of them with a disability – in the skills needed to produce wheelchairs. Motivation establishes a comprehensive distribution system in each country to ensure that each individual is given a wheelchair that suits his or her needs. Motivation encourages disabled people to become as independent as possible through teaching wheelchair skills, and by promoting participation in sports.

Due to the nature of its work, Motivation is rarely able to use the skills of volunteers on its overseas projects, and the small UK staff base means that at any time help from volunteers is limited to a small group of dedicated people who assist with administrative and fundraising work.

Motivation welcomes fundraising help. A donation of £35 can sponsor a wheelchair in Bangladesh; £100 provides the educational materials for a training programme in a region of El Salvador; £2,000 can fund an 'Active Rehabilitation' programme in Albania to teach vital wheelchair skills. For more information on current projects and funding needs, please contact Motivation at the address above.

THE OCKENDEN VENTURE

Constitution Hill, Woking, Surrey GU22 7UU
Tel: 01483-772 012 *Fax:* 01483-750 774
Charity Reg. No: 1053720
Contact: **Nick Davis, Development Officer**
Date established: **1951**
Annual income: **£1m (95)**
Area covered: **International**

The Ockenden Venture is an international charity serving the needs of refugees and displaced people. Ockenden works mostly overseas but also in the UK with refugees to this country. Ockenden's work is carried out through programmes designed to promote the independence of both communities and individuals. It makes long-term commitments to refugees – for instance the Afghans in Pakistan – and continues to work with the same people when they return home, as with Ockenden's current programme in Afghanistan.

There are over 50 million refugees and displaced people in the world today. Ockenden's long history and expertise in working with such communities results in its being constantly in demand. The limits to its ability to help are set by its financial limits. The public's support as donors or volunteers is therefore vital to Ockenden's efforts.

OXFAM

274 Banbury Road, Oxford, OX2 7DZ
Tel: 01865-311 311 *Fax:* 01865-312 380
Charity Reg. No: 202918
Contact: **Peter Vicary-Smith, Head of Appeals**
Date established: 1942
Annual income: £99.7m (94)
Area covered: International (UK based)

Oxfam exists to relieve poverty, distress and suffering, and works in over 70 countries, giving emergency relief and long-term support to poor people, irrespective of race, colour, gender, politics, or religion. When emergencies occur, Oxfam responds quickly, providing shelter, food, water and sanitation. Oxfam helps vulnerable communities to survive disasters, to prevent disaster, and to restart community life once disaster has passed. Above all, Oxfam helps poor people to help themselves, by offering advice, encouragement, and direct support for people's own initiatives. Oxfam also works to raise awareness about the causes of poverty, through its education, advocacy, and campaigning work.

Oxfam depends on its volunteers. Without the hard work, enthusiasm and expertise of more than 27,000 volunteers throughout the UK and Ireland, Oxfam could not continue to fight against poverty and its causes. Volunteers assume a wide variety of roles in Oxfam – from pricing goods in its 850 shops, to specialist consultancies. Campaign volunteers undertake tasks as diverse as lobbying their local MP to generating local media coverage. Issues of concern to volunteers are discussed at Regional Forums and Oxfam's biannual Assembly.

Oxfam sells crafts and food through its shops in the UK and Ireland, and through Oxfam's mail-order catalogue. Through the Bridge Scheme, Oxfam links producers in developing countries with consumers in the UK and Ireland. Fair prices are paid to producers, who receive practical support and annual dividends.

Money comes from donations from individuals, companies, and trusts, plus that raised by Oxfam's 850 shops. Oxfam benefits from the British Government's Overseas Development Administration, UN agencies, and from the European Union. Eighty-four per cent of Oxfam's income funds overseas programmes, and a further six per cent, information, education and campaigns. Fundraising and administration costs currently account for only 10 per cent.

Sight Savers International

**Grosvenor Hall, Bolnore Road, Haywards Heath,
W. Sussex RH16 4BX**
Tel: 01444-412 424 *Fax:* 01444-415 866
Charity Reg. No: 207544
Contact: **Wilma Van Berkel, Information Officer**
Date established: 1950
Annual income: **£7.7m (95)**
Area covered: **International**

People in developing countries are 10 times more likely to go blind than those living in the UK. With simple treatment or surgery, over three-quarters of this suffering could be avoided. Sight Savers International and its overseas partners are bringing essential eye-care services to communities in city slums and remote rural areas. Since 1950 the charity has helped nearly four million men, women and children to see again, and treated over 35 million for potentially blinding conditions. Sight Savers projects also work with incurably blind people, helping children to attend standard schools and training adults to lead active and fulfilling lives.

Sight Savers acts as a catalyst in developing projects. After just a few years the charity gradually withdraws, as the local partner takes on more responsibility. Regular support from donors during these years – through a covenant or as a Sight Savers Partner – enables the charity to lay firm foundations for permanent programmes. Events ranging from walks to auctions, from picnics to singalongs, play an essential part in raising funds for Sight Savers' work. Volunteers are always needed to organise and take part in these events, which also raise awareness of Sight Savers. Culinary skills are in great demand with volunteers being asked to cook a Feast for the East fundraising. The recipes are kindly provided by Meena Pathak of Patak's Indian Foods. In 1997 a special appeal is being launched to prevent river blindness in Africa and a whole range of activities linked to water and rivers are planned. For details, or a copy of the recipe leaflet, contact Sue Castle.

Young people are invited to support Sight Savers through a joint initiative with the charity 'Christmas Cracker'. Youth groups and schools being asked to produce a 'Cracker' newspaper, raising money through advertising and magazine sales. There will be a special Cracker Award for the best newspaper.

VOLUNTARY SERVICE OVERSEAS

317 Putney Bridge Road, London SW15 2PN
Tel: 0181-780 2266 *Fax:* 0181-780 1326
Charity Reg. No: 313757
Contact: **Paulette Cohen, Head of Publicity**
Date established: 1958
Annual income: £22.7m (95)
Area covered: **International**

VSO (Voluntary Service Overseas) is Europe's largest development charity working through volunteers. VSO enables men and women to work alongside people in poorer countries in order to share skills, build capabilities, and promote international understanding and action in the pursuit of a more equitable world. Since it was founded in 1958, VSO has sent over 20,000 volunteers to developing countries in Africa, Asia, the Pacific, the Caribbean and, since 1990, to 11 countries in Central and Eastern Europe through its new initiative, Eastern European Partnership.

Each year VSO sends around 900 volunteers overseas in a wide variety of posts – teachers, mechanics, midwives, agriculturalists, accountants etc. VSO looks for skilled volunteers with commitment and enthusiasm to work overseas for two years. Volunteers must be aged between 20 and 70 without dependent children and must be qualified (diploma, degree etc) with relevant work experience. Volunteers are also needed in the UK to support VSO's network of 80 local groups and to become involved in Development Education activities which aim to change attitudes towards development issues in this country. Volunteers are also welcome to join in VSO's awareness week – VSO week – in July each year.

It costs over £11,000 to send one volunteer overseas for a year, therefore VSO has a growing need for funds. An annual programme of events is organised for supporters who are also encouraged to help with collections. VSO welcomes the support of clubs, businesses and individuals who could sponsor a volunteer while they are overseas. VSO produces an extensive range of literature to support all fundraising or volunteer enquiries. All calls are welcome and if you have a specific enquiry please let VSO know so that they can send the most appropriate publication.

WOMANKIND WORLDWIDE

6 Albion Place, Galana Road, London W6 0LT
Tel: 0181-563 8607/8/9 *Fax:* 0181-563 8611
Charity Reg. No: 328206
Contact: **Ms Trudi Harris, Fundraising Dept.**
Date established: 1989
Annual income: £500,000 (94/95)
Area covered: **International**

WOMANKIND Worldwide is an international development agency working in the developing world, supporting women in their struggles against poverty and discrimination. WOMANKIND does not set up its own projects, instead offering support only when it is requested. Support may be direct (providing training, land or credit) or indirect (strengthening organisations and facilitating link-ups with similar groups). WOMANKIND works to empower women at local, national and international levels, to ensure that women's voices – in all their diversity – are heard for the benefit of all.

WOMANKIND's needs are great and it is always grateful for any assistance which members of the general public offer. This may be volunteering in the office, setting up a local group or offering professional advice/support in critical areas. Please contact Trudi Harris on the above number if you can support WOMANKIND in any way.

SEE ALSO

British Red Cross
Save The Children Fund
SOS-Children's Villages UK
Youth with a Mission

RELIGIOUS

COUNCIL FOR WORLD MISSION (CWM)

Livingstone House, 11 Carteret Street, London SW1H 9DL
Tel: 0171-222 4214 *Fax:* 0171-233 1747
Charity Reg. No: 232868
Contact: **Mr Adrian N Wylie, Secretary for Finance**
Date established: **1795**
Annual income: **£4.7m (95)**
Area covered: **International – 31 churches**

The Council for World Mission is a community of Churches sustained by a commitment to sharing common resources in partnership. Rich and poor Churches alike take part in decision making. All have equal rights and responsibilities, and contribute financially and through the sharing of experience and people. Hence, CWM is neither an aid agency nor a missionary society but a new way of relating to people and their needs worldwide. The same spirit that calls the Churches to be part of God's mission for the world enables them to cross cultural and national boundaries, to spread knowledge of Christ throughout the world.

The Council for World Mission was restructured from the London Missionary Society, founded in 1795, whose bicentenary was therefore celebrated in 1995. CWM is committed to supporting mission and unity efforts beyond itself and pledges five per cent of annual income towards ecumenical work. CWM believes that each Church's mission is enriched by meeting people from other Churches. Each Member Church offers, recruits and trains people who are able to be useful in other cultural contexts. About 38 per cent of such people currently in service come from the United Kingdom. Opportunities are available for periods of three months and longer.

CWM welcomes contributions to fund its missions. It also welcomes support for youth opportunity programmes, relief in emergencies (droughts, floods and cyclones) and action on the global priorities of breaking down structures which perpetuate injustice. A 'Second Mile Giving' Scheme supports specific and current concerns whilst Mission Priority Application directs resources to special projects.

YOUTH WITH A MISSION

13 Highfield Oval, Ambrose Lane, Harpenden, Herts AL5 4BX
Tel: 01582-463 300 *Fax:* 01582-463 305
Charity Reg. No: 264078
Contact: **Lucinda Ashby, PR Assistant**
Date established: **1970**
Annual income: **£2m (94)**
Area covered: **International**

Youth With a Mission (YWAM) is a Christian organisation that operates in 130 nations, from rural Cambodia to England's inner cities. YWAM is committed to caring for those in need, through short-term relief and long-term community development projects. The charity trains and sends people to bring hope, and is especially concerned with motivating young people into Christian service. Nearly 500 YWAM volunteers serve local communities across the UK, in youth work, AIDS counselling, rehabilitation of drugs users, and community development projects.

YWAM's dedicated helpers work with the needy from Edinburgh to London. Funds go directly to where they are most crucially needed: to pay for the cost of transport to safe houses for ex-prostitutes; intensive rehabilitation programmes; and computers for inner city literacy projects. YWAM's Urban Fund is designed to meet these needs. Can you help? If so, contact YWAM at the address above.

SEE ALSO

Feed the Minds

SERVICES AND ARMED FORCES

ARMY BENEVOLENT FUND

The Army Benevolent Fund

41 Queens Gate, South Kensington, London SW7 5HR
Tel: 0171-581 8684 *Fax:* 0171-584 0889
Charity Reg. No: 211645
Contact: Major Gen. GMG Swindells, Controller
Date established: 1944
Annual income: £5.7m (94/95)
Area covered: National

Founded in August 1944, the Army Benevolent Fund is the Army's central charity, working in support of, and in co-operation with, the Regimental and Corps Associations of the British Army. The Fund provides help to serving soldiers and ex-soldiers and their families when they are in real need. Financial help is given to individuals through their Regimental or Corps Associations. Practical help is provided through the financial support given by the Fund, on behalf of the whole Army, to those national charitable organisations which provide for the special needs of soldiers and their families.

Deciding to whom to give and how much is no easy matter. Excellent working relationships with the Associations, who forward individual cases, means a quick response time. An experienced committee considers bids from other charities, many of which are regular beneficiaries who rely on the Fund for their core funding.

The Army Benevolent Fund's success in fundraising is dependent on a large band of dedicated and loyal unpaid volunteers, who work tirelessly to achieve their aims. There are some 60 Appeal Committees operating in the counties of England and Wales, in Scotland, Ulster, the Channel Islands, Isle of Man and Cyprus. Close links exist between the Regular Army, the Territorial Army and the Army Cadet Force and these Committees. A common interest in the Army and a caring feel for comrades in need unites those in and out of uniform to work together for the Fund.

The small executive staff includes a Director of Appeals, who co-ordinates the work of the voluntary fundraising committees through 12 part-time Regional Organisers, and manages the Fund's advertising campaign. The Director of National Enterprises organises major fundraising events with a national interest.

KING GEORGE'S FUND FOR SAILORS

8 Hatherley Street, London SW1P 2YY
Tel: 0171-932 0000 *Fax:* 0171-932 0095
Charity Reg. No: 226446
Contact: **Col Richard Preston, Deputy Director General**
Date established: 1917
Annual income: £3.59m (94)
Area covered: National

King George's Fund for Sailors is the Fund for all charities which assist seafarers or their dependants in need. It exists to give financial aid and advice to maritime benevolent organisations and institutions. Each year around 85 such bodies receive help from KGFS which, in 1995, totalled £2.6 million, categorised as follows:

1. For the disabled. For hospitals, homes and sheltered housing;

2. For children's homes, training ships, schools and scholarships;

3. To support seafarers and their dependants;

4. For missions, societies and associations caring for seafarers and their families.

KFGS is the only Fund which supports all who have made their living on the sea and their dependants.

KGFS needs volunteers to help in all aspects of its fundraising. The Fund has over 60 volunteer committees throughout the United Kingdom, all of which would welcome help either to run events or to support them. Events range from coffee mornings, street and house-to-house collections, manning a stall selling KGFS branded goods at Navy Days and other large events, to over 20 Royal Marines Band concerts every year. Administrative and accounting skills would also be welcomed, both in the volunteer committees and in Head Office.

In 1996 The Fund has been granted the privilege of a Charity Race Day at Ascot on July 26. This is a major addition to the standard range of events throughout the country. Sponsorship opportunities exist at all levels; from the Race Day to one or more of the Royal Marines Band concerts planned for the year.

Anyone wishing to receive further information on the Fund should contact Richard Preston at Head Office and can be placed on the mailing list.

ROYAL AIR FORCE BENEVOLENT FUND

67 Portland Place, London W1N 4AR
Tel: 0171-580 8343 *Fax:* 0171-636 7005
Charity Reg. No: 207327
Contact: **Air Commodore C H Reineck, OBE
Director of Appeals**
Date established: 1919
Annual income: £15m
Area covered: **National**

The Royal Air Force Benevolent Fund was founded in 1919 by Lord Trenchard, 'Father of the Royal Air Force', for the relief and assistance of all ranks who are serving, or have served, with the Royal Air Force or its associated air forces, and their dependants who may need such assistance by reason of poverty, disability, infirmity or other disadvantage. Currently the Fund spends more than £10 million a year to meet these criteria and, as many thousands of Second World War veterans reach old age, annual expenditure on welfare will rise.

Relief of distress takes many forms, with voluntary help restricted mainly to fundraising and case work. Assistance provided ranges from provision of central heating and a wheelchair for an arthritic Lancaster bomber rear gunner to providing an RAF Benevolent Fund Housing Trust home for a present-day Junior Technician crippled in a motorcycle accident. Beneficiaries may also obtain residential care, respite or convalescence in either of the Fund's homes or, according to circumstances, receive free or assisted education at the Fund's Duke of Kent School in Surrey.

Much of the Fund's income is provided by serving men and women subscribing half a day's pay a year. Considerable sums are also raised at Station and other Service events. However, income from these sources is diminishing steadily as the number of serving RAF personnel decreases from 90,000 to 52,000. Fundraising is thus being energetically developed, not least through RAF Benevolent Fund Enterprises, which organises the annual International Air Tattoo, band concert tours and other commercial ventures. The Fund welcomes revenue from donations, legacies and a variety of other sources. Fortunately, a generous public continues to heed the postwar message broadcast to the Nation by Winston Churchill. 'To support the Royal Air Force Benevolent Fund,' he said, 'is to repay "the debt we owe" to the Royal Air Force.'

CHARITIES MENTIONED IN THE EDITORIAL

Acorn Children's Hospice
103 Oak Tree Lane
Selly Oak
Birmingham
B29 6HZ	0121-628 0212

Action on Elder Abuse
Astral House
1268 London Road
London
SW16 4ER	0181-679 2648

BACUP (British Association of
Cancer United Patients and their
Families and Friends)
3 Bath Place
Rivington Street
London
EC2A 3JR	0171-696 9003

BBC Children in Need	0181-280 8057
PO Box 7
London
W5 2GQ

British Dyslexia Association
98 London Road
Reading
Berks.
RG1 5AU   01734-662 677

BIBIC (British Institute for Brain Injured Children)
Knowle Hall
Knowle
Bridgewater
Somerset TA7 8PJ   01278-684 060

British Kidney Patients' Association
Bordon
Hampshire
GU35 9SZ   01420-472 021

Bryson House
28 Bedford Street
Belfast
Northern Ireland
BT2 7FE   01232-439 156

Camden Housebound Link
13 Troyes House
Lawn Road
Hampstead
London
NW3 2XT   0171-722 3982

Chaucer Heritage Trust
St Peter's Street
Canterbury
Kent
CT1 2BZ   01227-470 379

CHARITIES MENTIONED IN THE EDITORIAL

Chelsea Physic Garden
66 Royal Hospital Road
London
SW3 4HS					0171-352 5646

Children's Country Holidays Fund
42–43 Lower Marsh
Transwell Street
London
SE1 7RG					0171-928 6522

Children's Hospice for the Eastern Region
Church Lane
Milton
Cambridge
CB4 6AB					01223-860 306

Children's Society
Edward Rudolf House
Margery Street
London
WC1X 0JL					0171-837 4299

Comic Relief		General information: 01891-405 060

Community Network
50 Studd Street
London
N1 0QP					0171-359 4594

Contact a Family
170 Tottenham Court Road
London
W1P 0HA					0171-383 3555

Evergreen Trust
51 Weston Street
Upper Norwood
London
SE19 3RW   0181-771 7114

Farnham Maltings
Bridge Square
Farnham
GU9 7QR   01252-726 234

Foundation for Conductive Education
Calthorpe House
30 Hagley Road
Edgbaston
Birmingham
B16 8QY   0121-456 5533

Friends of Covent Garden
Royal Opera House
45 Floral Street
Covent Garden
London
WC2E 9DD   0171-240 1200

Green Light Trust
Lawshall Green
Bury St Edmunds
Suffolk
IP29 4QJ   01284-828 754

Help the Hospices
34–44 Britannia Street
London
WC1X 9JG   0171-278 5668

CHARITIES MENTIONED IN THE EDITORIAL

Kensington Tabernacle
Powis Square
London
W11 2AY   0171-243 8621

L'Arche Ltd
10 Briggate
Silsden
Keighley
W. Yorks.
BD20 9JT   01535-656 186

Leprosy Mission
Goldhay Way
Orton Goldhay
Peterborough
PE2 5GZ   01733 239 252

Look London
Royal London Society for the Blind
105–109 Salusbury Road
London
NW6 6RH   0171-625 1570

Methodist Homes for the Aged
Epworth House
Stuart Street
Derby
DE1 2EQ   01332-296 200

Metropolitan Society for the Blind
Duke House
6–12 Tabard Street
London
SE1 4JT   0171-403 6184

National Trust
35 Queen Anne's Gate
London
SW1H 9AS   0171-222 9251

PHAB Ltd
12–14 London Road
Croydon
Surrey
CR0 2TA   0181-681 1399

Riding for the Disabled Association
Avenue R
National Agricultural Centre
Kenilworth
Warks.
CV8 2LY   01203-696 510

Royal British Legion
48 Pall Mall
London
SW1 5JY   0171-973 7200

SANE (Schizophrenia: A National Emergency)
2nd Floor
199–205 Old Marylebone Road
London
NW1 5QP   0171-724 6520

Salvation Army
101 Queen Victoria Street
London
EC4P 4EP   0171-236 7020

CHARITIES MENTIONED IN THE EDITORIAL

See-ability
56–66 Highland Road
Leatherhead
Surrey
KT22 8NR   01372-373 086

SENSE
11–13 Clifton Terrace
London
N4 3SR   0171-272 7774

Shaftesbury Society
16 Kingston Road
London
SW19 1JZ   0181-542 5550

SHAPE London
356 Holloway Road
London
N7 6PA   0171-700 8139

St Dunstans
PO Box 4XB
12–14 Harcourt Street
London
W1A 4XB   0171-723 5021

Tools for Self Reliance
Netley Marsh
Southampton
SO40 7GY   01703-869 697

Whiteley Homes Trust
Whiteley Village
Walton-on-Thames
Surrey
KT12 4EH   01932-848 414

INDEX OF CHARITIES

Abbeyfield Society (The) 43, 279–80
Acorn Children's Hospice 9, 21, 53–4
Action for Blind People 43, 55–6, 59–60, 98, 242
Action on Elder Abuse 21
ACTIONAID 321–2
Age Concern 23, 34, 42, 280–1
Age Exchange Theatre Trust 281
Alexandra Rose Day 29, 42, 66–7, 288
Animal Health Trust 146–7
apa Community Drug and Alcohol Initiatives 171
Army Benevolent Fund 342–3
Artsline 164–5
ASBAH 123–4, 243
ASH 293–4

Barnardos 115–16, 191–2
BIBIC 68–9
Bird Life International 147–8
Blue Cross 148–9
Boys' and Girls' Welfare Society 192–3
Bridge House Estates 4
British Diabetic Association 116–18, 294–5
British Heart Foundation 296–7
British Kidney Patients' Association 31, 72, 91–2
British Liver Trust 297–8
British Lung Foundation 298–9

INDEX OF CHARITIES

British Museum 165–6
British Red Cross 40, 47, 171–2
British Sports Association for the Disabled – BSAD 244–5
British Union for the Abolition of Vivisection 149–50
British Wireless for the Blind Fund 245
Bryson House 67

CAFOD 322–3
Camden Housebound Link 25, 30, 94–5
Camphill Village Trust 246–7
Cancer Relief Macmillan Fund 173–4
Cancer Research Campaign 299–300
Cancerlink 301
Care Fund (The) 247–8
Carers National Association 174–5
Cats Protection League (The) 150–1
Changing Faces 92–3, 176
Chaucer Heritage Trust 97–8
Chelsea Physic Garden 104–6
Children in Need 16
Children Nationwide Medical Research Fund 301–2
Child Poverty Action Group 193–4
Children's Aid Direct 323–4
Children's Country Holiday Fund 63
Children's Hospice for the Eastern Region 62, 69, 86–7
Children's Society (The) 32, 41, 60, 70
Children's Trust (The) 194–5
Christian Aid 34
Combat Stress 314
Comic Relief 22
Community Network 63
Compassion in World Farming Trust 151–2
Concern Universal 81, 88, 118, 325
Contact a Family 19, 63–4
Contact the Elderly 282–3

Council for the Protection of Rural England 232–3
Council for World Mission (CWM) 124–5, 339–40
Country Trust 273
Crisis 131–3, 218–19
Crossroads (Caring for Carers) 177
Crusaders 195–7
Cruse Bereavement Care 178–9
CSV (Community Service Volunteers) 39, 43, 217
Cystic Fibrosis Research Trust 302–3

Disability Network UK 179–80
Disabled Housing Trust 289–90
Dogs Home Battersea (The) 152–3
Donkey Sanctuary (The) 153–4
Down's Syndrome Association (DSA) 15, 248–9
Dyslexia Institute 274

Enham Trust (The) 250–1
Evergreen Trust 41

Fairbridge 23, 70–1, 219-20
Families Need Fathers 197
Family Service Units 221
Family Welfare Association 315–16
Farms for City Children 198
Farnham Maltings 88–9
Feed the Minds 326
First Steps to Freedom 316–17
Foundation for Conductive Education 101–2
Foundation for the Study of Infant Deaths 304–5
Friends of the Royal Academy 167

Game Conservancy Trust (The) 233–4
General Welfare of the Blind (The) 251–2
Great Ormond Street Children's Hospital Fund 198–9

INDEX OF CHARITIES

Green Light Trust 99–101
Guide Dogs for the Blind Association 252–3

Hampshire Autistic Society 71, 254
Health Unlimited 327–8
Hearing Dogs for the Deaf 255–6
Help the Aged 283–4
Help the Hospices 40
Hill Homes 284–5
Home Farm Trust 256–7
Home-Start UK 126–7, 222–3
HYPED 10, 290–1

I CAN 199–200
Inter-Action Trust 19–20, 275–6
Intermediate Technology 328–9
International Care and Relief 329–30
International League for the Protection of Horses 155
Iris Fund for Prevention of Blindness 305

John Grooms Association for Disabled People 257–9
Joseph Rowntree Foundation 14
Jubilee Sailing Trust 259–60

Kensington Tabernacle 33
Kids' Club Network 201–2
KIDS 202
King George's Fund for Sailors 16, 343–5

L'Arche 112
Leonard Cheshire Foundation (The) 260–1
Leprosy Mission 125
Leukaemia Care Society (The) 180–1
Life Education Centres 83–4, 203–4
London Zoo 17, 23–4, 32, 156

Look 19, 64

MACA 317–18
Malcolm Sargent Cancer Fund for Children (The) 204–5
Marie Curie Memorial Foundation 118–20, 181-3
Médicins Sans Frontieres (MSF) UK 47–8, 306–7
MENCAP 261–2
Mental Health Matters 318–19
Mental Health Volunteers Scheme 37
Methodist Homes 36, 40
Metropolitan Society for the Blind 42
Missions to Seamen 330–1
Motivation Charitable Trust (The) 331–2
Multiple Sclerosis Research Trust 263
Multiple Sclerosis Society (The) 309–10
Muscular Dystrophy Group of Great Britain and Northern Ireland 307–8

National Association for Voluntary Hostels 61, 223–4
National Autistic Society (The) 25, 34, 264
National Canine Defence League 156–7
National Deaf Children's Society 40–1, 120–2, 205–6
National Foster Care Association 183–4
National History Museum Development Trust 168–9
National Lottery Charities Board 14
National Playing Fields Association (NPFA) 207
National Schizophrenia Fellowship 319–20
National Star Centre 276–7
National Stepfamily Association 208
National Trust 17
National Trust for Scotland (The) 234–5
NCH Action for Children 209–10
New Bridge (The) 224

Ockendon Venture (The) 78, 332–3

INDEX OF CHARITIES

Order of St John (see St John's Ambulance)
Oxfam 11, 22, 38, 43, 44, 46, 54, 62, 86, 89, 102-3, 333-4

PARENTLINE 184-5
PHAB 30
Prison Reform Trust 113, 225-6

Research into Ageing 285-7
Riding for the Disabled 6, 26
Royal Air Force Benevolent Fund 106, 345-6
Royal British Legion 43
Royal National Institute for the Blind 131-4, 265-6
Royal National Institute for Deaf People 266-7
Royal National Lifeboat Institution 17, 108-10, 226-7
Royal Society for the Protection of Birds 17, 236-7
Rural Housing Trust 291-2

Salvation Army 9-10, 34, 69
Samaritans (The) 43, 55, 76-7, 186-7
SANE 129-30
Save the Children Fund 12, 43, 60, 69, 70, 87-8, 114-15, 210-11
Scottish Council on Alcohol (The) 227-8
Scottish Wildlife Trust 237-8
Seeability 22-3, 61
Sense 44-6
Shaftesbury Society 15
Shape 42
Shelter – National Campaign for Homeless people 228-9
Sight Savers International 335-6
SOS – Children's Villages UK 212
Southern Marine Life Rescue 159-60
Spinal Injuries Association 267-8
St Christopher's Fellowship 213-14
St John's Ambulance 107-8, 310-11
St Dunstan's 7

St Tiggywinkles – The Wildlife Hospital Trust 157–9
Sustrans National Network 85–6, 238–9

Talking Newspapers Association 268
Tenovus 30–1, 78–9, 311–2
Terrence Higgins Trust Ltd 230–1
Tidy Britain Group 239–40
Tods for Self Reliance 7, 68
Treloar Trust 277-8
Turning Point 187–8

UFAW 160–1
United Response 269–70

Victoria and Albert Museum 169–70
Voluntary Service Overseas 12, 79-81, 336-7

WellBeing 17, 25, 312–13
Westminster Society 270–1
Whiteley House 32
Whizz-Kidz 81–3, 214–15
Wildfowl & Wetlands Trust 161–2
Winged Fellowship 95–6, 271
Womankind Worldwide 65, 338
Women's Royal Voluntary Service 188–9
Wood Green Animal Shelters 162–3
Woodland Trust (The) 240–1

Youth with a Mission 340-1